The Discerning Traveller

Let every new day
broaden your horizons

Craig Briggs

By the same author

The Journey series

Journey To A Dream

Beyond Imagination

Endless Possibilities

Opportunities Ahead

Driving Ambition

The Discerning Traveller

A Season To Remember

Short story

Roast Pig and Romance

Copyright © 2020 Craig Briggs

The moral right of the author has been asserted. This is a work
of non-fiction that recounts real events and experiences. Some
names, places, conversations, and identifying characteristics have
been changed to preserve anonymity of those concerned.

Copy editing/proofreading by Louise Lubke Cuss at
wordblink.com
Cover design and Photography by Craig Briggs
Portrait photo by Melanie Briggs
All rights reserved.

ISBN-13: 979-8641688497

In Memory

Kathleen Delbridge
(13 Feb 1913 – 9 Nov 2008)

CONTENTS

Introduction

If life deals you a bad hand, don't fold, take a chance; a good player will always come out on top.

I entered this world on the 12th of July 1962, in St. Luke's Hospital, Huddersfield. The second child, and only son, of Donald and Glenys Briggs. Donald, a humble lathe operator, worked for one of the town's largest employers, David Brown Tractors of Meltham.

The birth of their first child, Julie, had been a joy. The arrival of a son would make the family complete. Donald couldn't wait to groom his boy for sporting success. Notification of my arrival came via a phone call to his work, a call that dashed his parental hopes. Young Craig was not a 'normal' lad: he'd been born with congenital feet deformities. I cannot imagine a crueller message.

Unaware of my disability, I got on with life as any infant would. My first birthday brought a gift that would change my life forever. Not a cuddly toy from Mum and Dad, nor a silver-plated trinket from friends or relatives. My life-changing gift was a marvel of modern engineering, manufactured by J. E. Hanger and Co. of London for and on behalf of the National Health Service. Bespoke footwear gave me what the Vespa had given the youth of the fifties: freedom and independence. They weren't quite as stylish as an Italian built scooter but I didn't care. From now on, Master Briggs was on the move and no one would hold me back.

Over the next five years a series of surgical procedures changed the way I moved. Recollections are few but these infant experiences would influence the rest of my life. In the 1960s bedside visits were restricted to one person for one hour per day. The anguish of a young mother listening to the tortured screams of her infant son begging her to stay must have been horrific; it wasn't much fun for me either.

When the time came, Mum walked me to school like other proud mothers. For his part, Dad gave me his first and only piece of worldly advice. 'If anyone hits you, hit 'em back.'

With one exception, my mind proved sharper than my boxing prowess. Kids can be cruel, particularly to those who stand out, but only once did I break down in tears and ask, 'Why? Why me?' It's a question I sometimes ask myself today, but for very different reasons. Academia was not my thing. I found it difficult to concentrate on anything that didn't interest me.

I left secondary education with a mediocre haul of four 'O' levels and drifted aimlessly into an 'A' level course. It seemed preferable to starting work. If my 'O' level tally was disappointing, my 'A' level results were pitiful. I blamed a perforated appendix, two months before my finals, but if truth be known I'd had my fill of education.

In May 1980 I left college and entered the employment market. Margaret Thatcher was busy dismantling British industry and unemployment was running at a post-war high. I signed on to receive unemployment benefit and spent the summer lounging around the house watching the

Wimbledon Tennis Championship on telly. As the tournament drew to a close, parental pressure to find work intensified. In September, during one of my many visits to the Job Centre, a job card caught my eye: 'Wanted: trainee retail managers'. The idea of becoming a manager appealed, so I applied.

Five hundred and sixty applicants chased six positions. I pleaded my case at an interview and ended up being selected. After a two-week training course in the seaside town of Southport, I passed with honours, achieving the rank of assistant manager. When asked where I'd like to ply my newfound retail skills, I chose London, a city paved with gold.

In October 1980, I left Huddersfield a naïve child and returned three and a half years later a wiser and more mature young man. A brief period of letting my hair down followed, catching up on lost time and lost youth. During these wild and hedonistic months, I met the love of my life and future wife, Melanie.

My career in retail spanned six and a half years with five different companies. Each one expanded my experience and knowledge but to realise my dream I would have to go it alone. Not long after my twenty-sixth birthday, I handed in my notice. My future lay in leather jackets. Unfortunately, no one shared this vision and my aspirations fell at the first hurdle.

The prospect of returning to the retail trade pushed me into pursuing a different path. I reached a compromise and worked as a self-employed agent for one of the nation's largest insurance companies. The job title, Financial Consultant, exaggerated the role. In reality I was nothing more than a desperate insurance salesman. Life was hard and the insurance industry ruthless. Trying to sell a product that nobody wants, and which by its nature will never benefit the payee, is not easy. Unlike most recruits, I managed to survive and learnt some difficult but valuable lessons.

My 'Big Break' came when two of my clients asked me to invest in their fledgling printing business. The first year's accounts showed greater losses than actual sales. Against all professional advice I jumped at the chance, remortgaged the house and bought an equal stake.

By accident rather than design, I'd finally found my true vocation. The company was losing money hand over fist. The bank had taken a second charge on the partners' homes and my investment was swallowed up in a black hole of debt. Just when things couldn't get any worse, the bank called in the overdraft. While others worried, I applied myself to the problem. Through hard work and determination, we weathered the storm, but casualties were high.

After thirteen years of blood, sweat, and holding back the tears, I ended up owning a modestly successful little business. The time was right to begin my journey to a dream.

In May 2002 my wife Melanie and I decided to sell up and chase our dream. We packed all our worldly belongings, including our dog Jazz, into my ageing executive saloon, and headed off to Spain.

Not for us the tourist-packed Costas of the Mediterranean or the whitewashed villages of Andalucía. Our destination was Galicia: a little-known region in the northwest corner of Spain.

The contrast in lifestyles from England's industrial north to Spain's rural interior proved far more traumatic than either of us had imagined. Three and a half years at night school studying the Spanish language was little help. Galicia has its own language, galego. A proudly spoken tongue that has more in common with Portuguese than Spanish.

Dubious estate agents and questionable property descriptions turned our search for a new home into a lottery. Clear objectives became blurred and after several failed attempts to buy a property, we were forced to reassess our goals.

Eventually, we found our dream house, a tiny bungalow on the outskirts of the sleepy village of Canabal. Coping with Spain's laid-back approach while managing a building project tested our resolve. What could go wrong did and by Christmas we were ready to throw in the towel and head back to Blighty. But Yorkshiremen are made of sterner stuff.

A timely visit from my dad re-energised our ambitions. Twelve months and ten days after arriving in Galicia, we moved into our new home and completed the first part of our *Journey To A Dream*.

Choosing a name for our renovated property proved difficult; eventually we settled on El Sueño (The Dream). After the challenges of the first twelve months, we settled into a more relaxed lifestyle. Drinks at sunset, or Teatime Tasters, became an integral part of our daily lives and the warmth and generosity of our village neighbours made us feel at home.

With Melanie's help, I set about transforming our barren plot into a garden paradise. It wasn't all plain sailing and dealing with Spanish bureaucracy proved difficult. As time drifted by we started to enjoy a life *Beyond Imagination*.

For the first time in a long time, I had the freedom to take up some hobbies. Little did I know that writing and viniculture would become my pastimes of choice. With help from our neighbour, Meli, I took my first tentative steps on the road to winemaking. The success of my fledgling hobby was left in the hands of Mother Nature. Initial results were encouraging. My love of winemaking had begun.

As with viniculture, my efforts at writing took time to develop. Under the tutorage of Peter Hinchliffe, former editor in chief of Huddersfield's daily newspaper and founder of an online magazine, my writing slowly improved.

Hobbies are one thing but the financial requirements of day to day living were never far from our thoughts. After successfully buying, renovating, and selling a second property, we decided to look for another. Eventually, we found the ideal project, a romantic ruined farmhouse with *Endless Possibilities*.

Events have a way of keeping our lives in perspective, and this was particularly so when Melanie's dad was diagnosed with terminal cancer. A surprise fortieth birthday party turned into an emotional, but happy, final family reunion.

Later that year we offered to help our friends, Bob and Janet, convert their unloved house into a luxury holiday rental. Weeks before the first guests were due to arrive, the builder had a serious on-site accident. We had no alternative but to roll up our sleeves and finish the job. A season that could have turned into a disaster ended in success and satisfied customers. The question was, could we duplicate that success and build our own holiday rental property?

Finding the perfect place was challenging; buying it proved far more difficult. The lack of official paperwork led to lengthy delays. Thirteen months after agreeing the purchase, we finally took possession. That's when the problems really began. The wisdom of buying a house without water or electricity was put to the test. By the time we resolved those issues another twelve months had passed. The time had come to put the frustrations of the past behind us and concentrate on the *Opportunities Ahead*.

Throughout the wait we'd kept ourselves busy. There can't be many people who can add moonshine distillation to their curriculum vitae. Our second year in property management presented an unexpected opportunity, a house swap to the far side of the world. All we had to do was make the arrangements. After all, how difficult could it be to organise the trip of a lifetime?

We soon discovered that restoring a Spanish ruin requires a unique skill set. The two most important are a vivid imagination and a great sense of humour. Above all, be prepared to sacrifice your sanity: if you're not crazy when you start, you will be by the time it's finished.

Keeping the costs down came at a price. The work was hard and the hours long. Suppliers and subcontractors tested our patience but throughout it all we manged to maintain a healthy work-life balance.

During our house swap holiday to Australia I realised a *Driving Ambition*. The trip of a lifetime took us from rural Galicia to Wollongong in Australia via Shanghai in China. A forty-nine-day tour to six countries on three continents, flying 27,000 miles and driving over 13,000 kilometres. On our return the house restoration had moved on apace but there was plenty still to do before we could welcome paying guests to our holiday rental home.

1

Indemnity Assured

Travel broadens the mind. Unfortunately, it has the same effect on my waistline. Gingerly I stepped onto the bathroom scales, exhaled, and peered down at the digital display. The chant "Who ate all the pies?" sprang to mind. I blamed the pie shop in Kangaroo Valley and their self-proclaimed World's Best Pies, but I needn't have worried. Within a month of returning from Australia, Melanie and I were back to our fighting weights. Renovating a Spanish farmhouse tends to have that effect.

'What's for dinner?' I asked, as we watched the setting sun dip behind the woody knoll.

'I thought we'd have a barbecue,' replied Melanie.

That's exactly what Spanish summers are designed for and a rumbling stomach demands.

'I've been thinking.'

'Really.'

Melanie rolled her eyes. What harebrained scheme had I come up with now?

'Yes.'

'And what exactly have you been thinking about?' she asked.

'Christmas.'

'Christmas!'

Her response was understandable.

'I know it's only June but if we're going to go away, we need to start making plans. What do you think?'

'What do I think to what?'

'Going away for Christmas.'

'Sounds like a great idea.'

'How does a month sound?'

'A month!'

'Why not?'

On our recent trip to Australia we'd been away from home for seven weeks. In all that time nothing untoward had happened to the house. I figured we could easily go off for a month without any problems. Besides which, I liked the idea of a longer holiday.

'Can we afford to go away for a month?'

'That depends on what sort of deal I can negotiate.'

'And where were you thinking of going?'

Winters in Galicia can be harsh and my joints aren't getting any younger. Four weeks in the sun would do both of us the world of good. We'd spent the last two Christmases on the Mediterranean coast. The weather had been warm and sunny and it's a destination we can drive to which is a major consideration when travelling with a dog.

'I thought we might go to Mijas again.'

The municipality of Mijas, on the Costa del Sol, sits between Fuengirola to the east and Marbella to the west.

'I like the sound of that,' replied Melanie.

'OK, I'll email Maria tomorrow morning and see what she has to offer.'

Maria is the owner-operator of Just Mijas, a boutique property rental company based in the village of Pueblo Aida. This modern holiday resort is situated in the hills overlooking the coastal town of Fuengirola and has been built in the style of a traditional Andalucian village.

The setting sun had painted the evening sky subtle shades of pastel pink. Time for dinner. While Melanie prepared a seasonal salad, I grilled some sausages on the barbie.

'What have you got planned for tomorrow?' asked Melanie as we tucked in to our alfresco feast.

'I thought we could get the entrance lobby and the staircase ready for painting.'

'Will you need me?'

'Yes please, unless you have something better to do.'

Since returning from Australia all our energy had been focused on finishing our property project. We'd christened the house *Campo Verde*. It suited its rural location and rolls off the tongue regardless of nationality. Manolo, the main contractor, had finished his work at the end of May and we were delighted with the results. Our task was to convert this brand-new restoration into a warm and inviting home. We were too late to take advantage of this year's letting season but were determined to start marketing the house as soon as possible.

'What is there to do?' asked Melanie.

'We need to mask off everything that doesn't need painting.'

Using a roller gives a professional finish to new plaster but makes a hell of a mess.

'I want to get the lobby painted before José Manuel starts fitting the false ceiling,' I added.

We'd decided to have a false wooden ceiling in the downstairs entrance lobby to match the look of the upstairs living accommodation. José Manuel is a skilled carpenter. He'd done a great job crafting the external doors so we'd asked him to do the work.

The sound of magpies tap dancing on the roof tiles eased us gently into a new day. I flung open the window shutters to reveal a bright summer's morning. Before setting off to work I emailed Maria with our Christmas holiday dates.

'Are you ready?' I asked, as I stepped into the kitchen.

'Ready when you are.'

The summer sunshine made the twenty-minute drive to the village of Vilatán a joy. The route took us through the low lying plain of the Val de Lemos and up into the surrounding hills. A landscape of pine forests, grassy meadows, and natural woodlands are stitched together with drystone walls and sprinkled with tiny hamlets and isolated farmhouses. Before long we were trundling through the narrow lanes of the village and into the driveway.

Masking off the entrance lobby was quite straightforward; the staircase proved far more challenging. At its highest point it measures six metres from floor to ceiling. To reach the top of the stairwell I cobbled together a working platform using two ladders. The first I leant against the wall at the foot of the stairs. The second bridged the gap from the first-floor landing across to the other ladder.

'Do be careful,' said Melanie, as I made my way cautiously along the makeshift platform.

In situations like this I convince myself there are no other options.

As I edged towards the centre of the ladder my trembling knees caused it to shake. One false move and I'd end up in intensive care. I inched forward, determined to overcome my fear. Melanie looked as terrified as I felt.

Eventually I made it to the far end and paused for breath. After regaining my composure, I began. First one side and then the other. Within the hour I'd masked off the ceiling and successfully made my way back to the safety of the landing. By the end of the day the lobby and staircase were ready for painting. First thing tomorrow I would make a start.

Lengthening summer days gave us plenty of time to relax after a hard day's work. Before smothering myself in suntan lotion I checked to see if Maria had replied to my email. She had but the news was mixed.

'There's a problem,' I announced, as I stepped outside.

Melanie was lying on a sunlounger reading Jodi Picoult's latest novel.

'What problem?'

'We've had an email from Maria.'

'What did she say?'

'The apartment we stayed in last year is already booked over Christmas.'

Melanie looked disappointed.

'She's given us a couple of options,' I added.

The first was a ground floor apartment that was available for the whole month. Alternatively, we could spend the first ten days in a one-bedroom penthouse and the remainder of the holiday in the two-bedroom apartment we'd had last year. I explained the options to Melanie.

'Penthouse, is that the same as a top floor flat?' she asked.

We both smiled. Pretentiousness is not a Yorkshire trait.

'That's right,' I replied.

On closer scrutiny the ground floor apartment had an east facing aspect which is ideal during the hot summer months but less appealing in winter. The penthouse was directly above the two-bedroom apartment, both of which were south facing. To offset the inconvenience of moving from one apartment to the other, Maria had offered us a generous discount. For a couple of thrifty Yorkshire folk, that proved the clincher.

The very next morning I confirmed the booking. Christmas was sorted.

Two days and two coats of paint later the entrance lobby and staircase looked clean and fresh. The morning after that, José Manuel turned up with two of his employees. While they made a start on the ceiling I kept out of the way. I had plenty to do upstairs.

'*Hasta luego* (See you later),' called José Manuel.

I looked at my watch. The time had ticked around to 1:00 pm, lunchtime.

'*Hasta la tarde* (See you this afternoon),' I replied.

For the first time since they'd arrived the house fell silent. For most of the morning it had sounded as if they'd been knocking lumps out of the place. I locked the back door and made my way downstairs. When I reached the bottom, I could hardly believe my eyes. The newly tiled floor was littered with building rubble and my freshly painted walls had a series of holes chiselled out of them.

In my ignorance I'd thought the new ceiling would be fixed to the existing one. It seemed José Manuel had other ideas. By the look of it he intended to reverse engineer the entire ceiling which would be a much better if somewhat more difficult job. Given the mess, all the walls would need repainting. Not for the first time I'd have to clean up someone else's mess.

By the time I'd driven home, eaten lunch, and listened to an hour of Jeremy Vine on BBC radio it was time to head back to *Campo Verde*. At the end of their first day, José Manuel and his team had chiselled out all the holes for the new joists and made a start on fitting them. I'd masked up the twin bedroom which was now ready to paint.

The following morning disaster struck. The internet has become an essential part of our daily life, so much so that the briefest interruption becomes a major inconvenience.

'Did you use the computer yesterday?' I asked Melanie.

'No.'

Computers aren't really her thing. 'They never do what I want them to do,' she would say. Isn't that the truth, but therein lies the challenge.

13

'Well it won't boot up.'

'Don't blame me. I haven't touched it.'

'Don't get your knickers in a twist. I was only asking.'

'And I'm only answering. I haven't been anywhere near it.'

That told me.

'I'll take it to Jesús on my way to work.'

Jesús owns a small computer shop in Monforte de Lemos. A few years ago, he'd correctly diagnosed and repaired the laptop when all seemed lost. If anyone could fix it, he could.

'I'll ring you this afternoon when I've had a look at it,' he said.

When I arrived at *Campo Verde* José Manuel and his lads were hard at it. While they measured, sawed, glued, and hammered I donned my overalls and made a start on painting the bedroom. At exactly 1:00 pm the house fell silent. Unlike José Manuel, I wasn't bound by traditional Spanish working practices and continued to a finish. By the time I left, José Manuel was returning from lunch.

Melanie had become quite used to my irregular timekeeping. Sometimes it's easier to finish a job than break for lunch and start again later.

'Busy day?' she asked.

'I wanted to get the first coat of paint on the bedroom walls,' I replied.

'What did Jesús say about the computer?'

'He was going to have a look at it this morning and ring me later.'

Melanie was putting the finishing touches to a tasty-looking salad. Dining in the sunshine is a real privilege. For most of my working life, lunch had been an inconvenient interruption. I would sit in a windowless office catching up on essential paperwork. Nowadays, we share our lunch breaks with a host of feathered friends. Wagtails are my favourite. They're bold and fearless and have lightning reflexes. Often a pair of storks circle overhead, riding the thermals like giant paper planes.

After a long, lazy lunch I had a few domestic chores to catch up with before chilling out.

'I'm just taking these to the bin,' I said, standing in the kitchen doorway holding two empty five-litre water bottles.

I'd been keeping them just in case but it was time to get rid; they were taking up too much space.

'Will you take the rubbish as well?' asked Melanie.

Communal refuse collection is a feature of Spanish life. Down in the village we have a green dumpster for general waste, a blue one for paper and cardboard, and a yellow one for plastic. There's also a bell-shaped bin on the village green for glass recycling.

I picked up the two bulky bottles and pulled the rubbish bag out of the kitchen bin. Jazz came running inside. She recognised the rustle of a bin bag and knew exactly what it meant.

'Are you coming, lass?'

She didn't need asking twice and sprinted to the French doors.

'Come on then.'

I opened the door and she ran to the gates.

'Just you be careful,' I said, pulling one open.

Jazz wandered slowly into the lane.

'*Buenos tardes* (Good afternoon).'

Teresa's greeting caught me by surprise.

'*Hola, buenos tardes*,' I replied.

Teresa and her husband Chuchi are village neighbours. They're both in their mid-eighties, not that you'd guess; the pair never stop.

'I'm going to the cemetery,' she said.

I'd guessed as much. In common with many of the villagers, hardly a week goes by when we don't see her walking to the cemetery with a posy of flowers from her garden.

'What are you doing with them?' she asked, pointing at the empty water bottles.

Jazz had taken an interest in the conversation and wandered over to Teresa hoping for some attention.

'I'm taking them to the bin.'

'Can I have them?'

Galicians are nothing if not direct. Personally, I like it; they remind me of Yorkshire folk.

'Of course,' I replied.

'Leave them there and I'll collect them on my way back.'

Recycling assumes many guises and I'd rather a neighbour made use of them than they end up in landfill.

When Jazz and I returned, Melanie was on the phone.

'OK, *hasta luego.*'

'Who was that?' I asked.

'Jesús, he wants us to call into the shop this afternoon.'

'What did he say about the computer?'

'He said it would be easier to explain in person.'

'Let's go now,' I said.

I was anxious for a diagnosis. We jumped into the car and drove into town. My laptop was sitting on his desk. After the customary greetings he got straight down to business.

'Have you dropped it?' he asked.

'Not that I know of.'

I turned to Melanie.

'Don't look at me, I haven't been anywhere near it.'

'Unfortunately there's nothing I can do about the computer but I have managed to download everything off the hard drive,' he said.

My heart sank. The laptop was dead.

'Well that's good news,' said Melanie.

'Good?'

'That he's managed to save everything,' she added quickly.

I'm sure she was right but all I could feel was a profound sense of loss. My digital world had just collapsed.

'Do you have insurance?' asked Jesús.

'Only household insurance,' I replied.

'That should cover it against accidental damage.'

My expression prompted an explanation.

'I'm just saying, if anyone asked me, I'd have no hesitation in saying the damage was caused by a fall,' he added.

Melanie and I glanced at each other. Was Jesús suggesting what we thought he was? He handed me the laptop and I slipped it into my computer bag. We thanked him and left.

'What are we going to do?' asked Melanie, as we walked back to the car.

'I don't know. What do you think we should do?'

Making a fraudulent insurance claim didn't sit well with either of us but Jesús was convinced the laptop's demise was linked to a mysterious trauma. Should our ignorance of an accident deter us from investigating the possibility of making a claim?

'Perhaps we should call into the insurance office while we're in town and have a word with Eva,' suggested Melanie.

Eva was our insurance agent and the office was less than two minutes away.

'She's bound to ask us what happened. What are we going to say?'

'I don't know, perhaps we could blame Jazz,' said Melanie.

'We couldn't do that, could we?'

Melanie said nothing. A few minutes later we were sitting at Eva's desk trying to explain.

'Jesús said the damage was caused by a fall. Is it covered against accidental damage?'

'What exactly happened?' asked Eva.

I could feel Melanie staring at me. When push came to shove, I just couldn't bring myself to blame Jazz.

'We're not sure,' I replied, 'but Jesús was certain it had hit something hard.'

Eva looked unconvinced.

'It's just that some people drop things down the stairs accidentally on purpose. I'm not suggesting that you did but some people do,' she said.

Despite our innocence, Eva's insinuation had us shuffling uncomfortably in our seats.

'We wouldn't do that, would we?' I turned to face Melanie.

'No, we wouldn't do that.'

'Besides which, we live in a bungalow.'

My attempt at humour fell on deaf ears.

'Leave it with me and I'll ask head office. As soon as I know anything, I'll ring you.'

She couldn't say fairer than that. Whatever the outcome, one thing was certain, I was going to need a new computer.

As soon as we got home, I dug out the insurance policy and checked the small print.

'Look,' I said, waving the paperwork in the air.

Melanie was sitting in the sunshine with her nose in a book.

'What?'

'I'm sure this passage covers accidental damage.'

I thrust the policy under her nose. Melanie studied it carefully.

'Yes, *daño accidental* means accidental damage.'

Our explanation of events surrounding the laptop's demise had been vague to say the least but the policy details were unequivocal. My resolve stiffened. Household insurance premiums are part and parcel of owning a home. We'd been paying them for the past twenty-three years. Admittedly, our current insurer hadn't been the beneficiary of all those premiums but the industry as a whole had. In all that time we'd only ever made one claim and that was for a burglary at an uninsured high street jeweller's where Melanie was having a bracelet repaired. Surely, by the laws of probability we were due a claim. My feeling of entitlement, however illogical, became overwhelming.

Later that afternoon Eva rang.

'I'm sorry but the computer isn't covered under the policy,' she said.

Reluctantly I accepted the verdict and thanked her for her efforts.

'That was Eva,' I said, stepping out into the back garden.

'What did she say?'

'She said it's not covered.'

'Oh dear.'

Oh dear indeed.

The more I thought about it the greater my feeling of injustice. Disappointment turned to annoyance. The policy document was clear. Accidental damage was included. After reflecting on the matter for an hour or so I felt less inclined to acquiesce without a fight.

'I'm not having it,' I announced.

'You're not having what, darling?'

'I'm not giving in that easily. They're quick to take your money; they should be a bit more flexible when it comes to paying out.'

'What are you going to do?'

'Will they be open tomorrow?'

'It's Saturday so they should be open in the morning.'

'In that case we'll go to the office and find out why they won't cough up.'

Within the space of a few hours my mood had inexplicably changed from resignation to rebellion.

I woke the following morning with a steely determination to right the wrongs of corporate injustice. Armed with the policy document we headed into town to do battle with a global titan. The office was all but abandoned when we arrived. Eva was nowhere to be seen but her colleague Ricardo was sitting behind his desk.

'Is Eva working today?' I asked.

'She won't be in until later. Is there anything I can help you with?'

I was in no mood to wait. I explained about the computer and the response Eva had received from head office.

'Look,' I said, showing him the policy document, 'it states here that computer equipment is covered against accidental damage.'

While Ricardo studied the paperwork, I continued.

'We pay our premiums every year without fail and the first time we make a claim it's turned down.'

'Let me take a look,' he replied calmly.

Ricardo entered our details into his computer. Melanie and I waited in silence.

'Is this your current address?' he asked, pointing at the insurance policy.

'That's correct, Calle San Pedro.'

'And the policy is in your name?'

'Yes, my name, Craig Briggs.'

Ricardo stared at the screen.

'Do you have another policy with us?' he asked.

'We used to have our car insured with you but we cancelled that about five years ago.'

I looked at Melanie for confirmation. She nodded.

'Five years ago, you say?'

'That's right, five years ago.'

'That explains it.'

Melanie and I exchanged glances.

'That explains what?' I asked.

'This policy was cancelled at the same time.'

'Cancelled!'

20

Melanie and I were gobsmacked. Talk about eating humble pie. I could feel blood racing through my cheeks and filtering out across my entire face. The silence seemed endless. The consequences of being uninsured for the past five years were unthinkable.

'Oh,' I blurted.

Ricardo smiled.

'We'd better take out a new policy then,' I added.

I'd entered the office determined to be compensated for the untimely demise of my cherished laptop and ended up handing over another annual insurance premium.

On reflection, the savings we'd made over the past five years would more than compensate for a new laptop. At least now the house and its contents are fully insured against future calamities, accidental or otherwise.

2

Border Crossing

Drawing the curtains on a six-year relationship was never going to be easy. Sure, we'd had our ups and downs. I'd often thought of throwing in the towel and walking away. Building a strong and stable partnership takes time and effort. Rome wasn't built in a day. Eventually we overcame our differences and, despite its untimely demise, Windows XP will forever hold a special place in my heart.

The search for a replacement began in earnest. Microsoft's latest edition to its half-baked operating systems was Windows Vista. Its title had a familiar, almost Spanish ring to it; or was that an alarm bell? It hadn't crossed my mind that language would be a problem. Asking a neighbour for a lettuce is one thing; deciphering the jargon of computer-speak is quite another.

These linguistic shortcomings created another problem. If I bought a laptop in Spain, I'd be lumbered with the additional cost of purchasing an English version of Windows Vista. The solution was obvious: buy a laptop online and get it delivered. The mechanics of doing that were slightly more problematic. How could I order something online without a computer? Melanie suggested phoning a friend.

'I have an old laptop you can borrow,' said Penelope.

Penelope moved to the area a few years after us and we've been friends ever since. She's an intelligent and independent woman with a passion for nature and an environmental conscience.

'You'll have to update the operating system and download an antivirus programme,' she added.

Without delay I drove over and picked it up.

When Penelope said it was old, she wasn't kidding. I thought mine was bulky; this one weighed a tonne.

Somewhat surprisingly the lump of antiquated technology booted up at the first time of asking and connected to the internet without complaint. Things were looking up, but not for long. A lifetime of computing had taken its toll on the RAM (random-access memory). Its artificial intelligence had become far more random and much less accessible. Downloading an antivirus programme proved tortuously slow. Six hours after clicking the download button the software was ready to install.

With technology that ponderous I'm amazed home computing ever caught on.

'Dinner's ready,' called Melanie.

I wandered through into the kitchen.

'Have you found a laptop?' she asked.

'Found a laptop? I've only just managed to install the antivirus. Heaven only knows how long it'll take to update the operating system.'

'Oh dear.'

The following morning, I set about updating something called Windows 95. I wasn't sure if that referred to the year it was released or the number of attempts it had taken Microsoft to get it to work. Whatever the reason, there was no way I was wasting another day staring at a blank screen.

'Would you like to go out for lunch?' I asked.

'What about the computer?'

'If yesterday is anything to go by it'll take forever. I'll start the update and hope for the best.'

'Are you sure?'

'Certain. I've watched paint dry quicker than that machine works.'

'OK, lunch sounds great.'

'I thought we might go to Bragança.'

'Where?'

'Bragança, it's in Portugal.'

'What's there?'

'I'm not sure. That's why I thought we could take a look.'

'OK.'

It took an hour to reach the Portuguese border and a further two to drive to Bragança. The route took us high into the mountains of northern Portugal. As we neared our destination the road followed the boundary of the Parque Natural de Montesinho. It's a wilderness famed for its wolves, wild boar, and roe deer, none of which were on show that day. It's a sparsely populated area blanketed in moorland scrub and interspersed with patches of natural deciduous woodland and managed coniferous forests, the perfect hiding place for wolves, wild boar, and roe deer. In places it reminded me of the North Yorkshire Moors: bleak and uninviting.

'What about there?' I asked, as we entered the city.

The signpost read Castelo de Bragança (Bragança Castle).

'Why not?'

Bragança is typical of many Portuguese cities. In the old quarter the streets are narrow and cobbled, each granite sett no bigger than fifteen centimetres cubed. We followed the signposts until we reached the outer wall of the castle.

'Breathe in,' I said, as we drove through an impressive arched gateway.

Medieval castles weren't designed for modern motor vehicles but we made it through with inches to spare. A second entrance, fifteen metres from the first, looked even narrower. It led into a lane fronted by whitewashed houses. A hundred metres further along the area opened out into a large bailey (another word for a fortified area within a medieval castle).

If the first defensive walls were breached the fallback position was an imposing *torre* (castle keep) surrounded by another wall. A series of semicircular flanking towers gave the *torre's* defenders a clear line of sight to repel invaders.

'Wow! That's impressive,' I remarked.

'It looks like a toy.'

'A toy?'

'Not a toy exactly, but toylike. I'm sure Charles had something similar.'

Charles is Melanie's brother.

'Lucky Charles. I had to make do with an empty cornflakes box and a lot of imagination.'

'Poor you.'

Melanie was teasing.

'Anyway, talking about cornflakes, what are we going to have for lunch?'

As the rationale for driving all that way I thought I'd better mention it.

The area around the castle was quiet which was hardly surprising given how isolated the city is. I parked the car and we stretched our legs.

'What's that over there?' I said, pointing towards one end of the bailey.

A few parasols had caught my eye. We strolled across for a closer look. The sign outside a bar read "Tasca do Zé Tuga". A number of diners were sitting outside enjoying lunch in the warm sunshine.

'What about here?'

'Why not,' said Melanie.

We took a seat and before long a waiter came to attend us. He took our drinks order and left a menu.

'What do you fancy?' asked Melanie.

'I'm going to have the goat.'

Goat is one of my favourite Portuguese dishes.

'What about you?'

'I think I'll try the pork chop.'

Lunch was everything we'd expected. Nothing fancy, just wholesome home-cooked fare at a reasonable price.

'Right then, let's have a look inside this castle,' I suggested.

A notice outside read, "Entry two euros".

'What do you think?' I asked.

Melanie smiled.

'It sounds a bit expensive.'

The paltry fee included access to the military museum which was housed within the enormous keep. Of particular interest to me was the role the castle had played in Wellington's success during the Peninsular War. After retreating from Spain in 1812 his army entered Portugal to regroup. Porto provided the perfect staging post to re-equip his men. When they were ready, Wellington split his forces in two. He sent sixty thousand men to Bragança in readiness for another push to defeat the Napoleonic forces. Wellington's tactic proved successful and in 1813 the French were routed from Spain.

Having wandered through the museum and clambered over the ramparts we set off home. The route to Bragança had been quite arduous with many twists and turns and little of interest along the way, so we decided to take a different route home.

A signpost on the outskirts of the city pointed the way to Spain along the N15. The road took us directly through the Parque Natural de Montesinho. It was easy to imagine the inspiration behind Bernard Cornwell's *Sharpe* stories as we meandered our way through the wilderness. His main character was the heroic Richard Sharpe who led his Chosen Men into battle. I couldn't help wondering if he'd encountered any wolves, wild boar, or roe deer; we certainly hadn't.

The end of the National Park marks the boundary between Portugal and Spain. The road became the ZA-925 but the scenery remained the same. Desolate moorland as far as the eye could see, which given the undulating topography wasn't that far. We were starting to think it would never change when we crested a hill and quite unexpectedly caught sight of a fairytale village clinging to the side of a wedge-shaped hill and topped with a church and medieval castle.

'Look at that.'

'Where is it?' asked Melanie.

'There's a signpost coming up, see what it says.'

'Puebla de Sanabria.'

'Let's stop and take a look around.'

As we entered the village I turned left and headed towards the castle. The road rose sharply and narrowed to a single cobbled track. Stone-built houses lined the steep incline. It reminded me of Haworth, a village in Yorkshire which was home to the Brontë sisters. Unlike Haworth, Puebla de Sanabria hadn't succumbed to the commercialism of mass tourism.

At the top of the hill the area opened out into the Plaza Mayor. I parked the car and we went for a stroll.

Dominating the square is the 13th century church of Nuestra Señora del Azogue. Its single spire houses the village clock and an impressive array of bells. To the right of that is the town hall, a 16th century, twin towered, two-storey building with two rows of arches: three on the ground floor and four above. To the left of the church is the castle, built in the 15th century by the Counts of Benavente.

'Let's see what's down there,' I said, pointing towards a narrow alley leading off the plaza.

The alleyway took us to the edge of the fortifications. The view over the surrounding countryside was stunning. Hundreds of feet below us the Río Tera snaked through the valley. Downstream the river is joined by the Río Castro. This confluence has created the wedge-shaped hill we were standing on. A wide floodplain stretches out across the valley with patches of pine forests and deciduous woodland sitting comfortably between cultivated fields. In the distance, weathered hills form an enclosed backdrop which fades into the distant horizon.

We stood in silence, soaking up the panorama. Melanie was first to speak.

'That's beautiful.'

To our left was an imposing *torre* towering over the castle ramparts.

'No wonder it looks brand new. Can you imagine laying siege to that?' I tipped my head towards the *torre*.

'They wouldn't stand a chance,' replied Melanie.

Within the castle grounds was an information board detailing the castle's history. Despite its appearance the defences had been the scene of a number of great battles. Its strategic location, close to the Portuguese border, had seen to that.

'Let's walk a bit further,' suggested Melanie.

This delightful little village was seducing us with its charm and character. Wandering through the narrow streets was like stepping back in time. Unlike many isolated *pueblos*, the houses here were immaculately maintained with architectural wonders around every corner. Granite stonework, slate roofs, and hardwood windows were complemented with potted plants that climbed exterior walls and cascaded over iron-railed Juliet balconies. Intricately carved coats of arms were proudly displayed on façades of ancestral manor houses.

'I wish we could stay overnight,' said Melanie, as we made our way back to the car.

'I know what you mean. It's beautiful.'

Within ten minutes of leaving we were speeding along the A-52 highway heading towards Ourense. Two hours later we were home. Jazz ran to the gates to greet us. As usual she was delighted we were back. Whether it's seven minutes or seven hours, her excited tail wagging is always a welcome sight.

'What's that?'

Someone had left a carrier bag hanging over the gate.

'I bet it's a lettuce,' replied Melanie.

She hopped out of the car to unlock the gates.

'Yep, lettuce.'

A Galician lettuce is much more than a tasty salad leaf. People share them as an expression of their feelings. They're used to complement a greeting or as a symbol of friendship. On that occasion, I suspected they were a gesture of gratitude.

Melanie open the gates and I pulled into the driveway.

'I wonder who's left them,' said Melanie.

'How many are there?'

Melanie peered into the bag.

'At least three.'

The neighbours don't do things by half.

'I bet it's Teresa,' I replied.

'Teresa?'

'Yes, to say thank you for the empty water bottles.'

'No.'

'I bet it is.'

'Come on then, let's take Jazz for a walk and see if she's out in the garden.'

'If she isn't, Chuchi will be,' I replied, and off we trotted down into the village.

On such a beautiful day I was certain at least one of them would be out in the garden.

True to form they were both outside. Chuchi was chopping wood in readiness for winter and Teresa was weeding their *huerta* or vegetable plot. I spotted the water bottles straightaway. She'd cut off the bottoms and made cloches to protect her fledgling blooms.

'*Hola*,' I called, as we reached their garden gate.

They both stopped and looked up.

'*Buenas tardes*,' replied Chuchi.

'Did you get the lettuce I left you?' asked Teresa.

'Told you,' I whispered to Melanie. 'Yes, thank you.'

'If you get any more bottles will you save them for me?' she asked.

'We have another. I'll drop it off tomorrow,' replied Melanie.

'Just leave it outside your gate. I'll pick it up on my way to the cemetery.'

'OK.'

It wasn't until we turned around to head home that I suddenly remembered the computer was still running.

'I forgot to check the update,' I said.

'Will a few more minutes make a difference?'

'I don't suppose so.'

In our absence the laptop had gone to sleep. I pushed the mouse across the mat and waited. A whirring fan confirmed proof of life. Minutes later the screen lit up. Almost eight hours had passed since I had initiated the software update and it was still downloading. At that rate it might take forever. I wandered back into the lounge.

'How's it going?'

'It's still downloading,' I replied.

'Still?'

Before turning in I checked the progress. Little had changed. I was left with two options, cancel the update and start afresh in the morning or leave it running throughout the night. No way was I going to start again tomorrow. I crossed my fingers, wished it goodnight, and went to bed.

A long and demanding drive resulted in a great night's sleep. We woke feeling refreshed and ready to face a new day. While Melanie went to make a cuppa, I flung open the bedroom window shutters. Bright sunlight angled across the driveway. The creaking shutters startled a tiny wren into flight. It paused for a moment on top of the gatepost before flying off down the lane. The grapevines surrounding the house resembled a floating carpet woven in vivid shades of green. Some of the vines had already flowered, creating tiny bunches of grapes. Others were in bloom. Their delicate, white-stemmed flowers resembled fragile fronds of coral.

'What have you seen?' asked Melanie, as she nudged open the bedroom door carrying two mugs of coffee.

Her question jolted me out of my daydream.

'Nothing special.'

How quickly the wonders of Mother Nature become the norm. We slipped back under the duvet and sipped our morning brew.

'You haven't forgotten that Roy is coming this morning, have you?' asked Melanie.

Roy and his wife Maria live about ten minutes from us in the hills above the village of Sober. Before moving to the area, Roy had worked in the construction industry. When I'd asked if he'd like to give me a hand building the new terrace at *Campo Verde*, he'd jumped at the chance. There were plenty of jobs still to do at the house but only one we couldn't do ourselves: the driveway. After much deliberation, and numerous quotations, we'd decided to contract Alfonso the stonemason to build it. His workmanship on the boundary walls was outstanding and his prices were keen. He'd quoted for pouring a reinforced concrete base and paving it with granite slabs. To keep costs down, I'd agreed to prepare the shuttering but was relying on Roy's expertise to complete the job.

I glanced at the alarm clock. Roy would be here in twenty minutes. I downed my coffee, washed, and dressed. As soon as I was ready, I checked the computer.

It seemed to take forever for the screen to light up. When it did, I was greeted by a new message, "Welcome to Windows update installer". I followed the on-screen instructions and the installation commenced. Things were looking up.

'The update has downloaded,' I announced.

'Did you leave it running all night?'

I'd thought it wise not to mention it at the time. I didn't want her worrying.

'It hadn't finished when we came to bed,' I confessed.

'But it is now?'

'Not quite. I need to install the update. I've set it running so whatever you do, don't touch anything.'

'Don't worry, I'm not going anywhere near it.'

'While I'm out, will you ring Alfonso and find out when he can start work on the driveway?'

'Shouldn't we wait until you've finished?'

'We'll have it done today, and you know what Alfonso is like for timekeeping.'

'OK, will do.'

Roy's timekeeping was impeccable. As soon as he pulled up outside, I left. Our first port of call was the timber merchant on the outskirts of Monforte. We bought eight two-metre lengths of four by four centimetre batons and fifteen planks, two metres long by forty centimetres wide. Twenty minutes later we arrived at *Campo Verde*.

'These need sawing into five equal pieces,' said Roy, as we unloaded the batons.

I made a start.

'Do you have an axe?' he asked.

'There's one in the *bodega*.'

'We need to make stakes out of these,' he said.

My previous attempts at fashioning stakes hadn't gone too well. In fact it's a miracle I've still got all my fingers.

'You wouldn't mind doing that, would you?' I asked.

Roy smiled. I suspect he knew exactly why I was asking.

It was clear from his handling of the axe that he'd done it many times before. A full complement of digits was a testament to his skill.

The next job involved a roll of string, a spirit level, and the newly crafted stakes. One by one we hammered them into the ground, ensuring the top of each one was level with the rest, and equally spaced at two-metre intervals. Within an hour we'd mapped out the outline of the new driveway and nailed shuttering to the stakes.

When pouring concrete, it's essential to ensure all the prep work is done beforehand. Ramón the plumber had already laid a water pipe for the sprinkler system that would straddle the new driveway and Félix the electrician had laid the conduit for the doorbell and the driveway lighting. All Roy and I had to do was connect the fall pipe for the gutter to the soakaway.

By the time we headed home for lunch, all the pipework was in position and the shuttering was ready for the concrete to be poured. All we needed now was Alfonso.

'Hello honey, I'm home,' I called, in a cheesy American accent, the origins of which I've long since forgotten.

'How did it go?'

'Very well, we're all finished and ready for Alfonso. Speaking of which, did you manage to get hold of him?'

'Yes, he hopes to make a start in a couple of weeks. He said he'd ring beforehand.'

Not exactly what I was hoping for.

'I also rang to enquire about the Vino Bus (Wine Bus),' she added.

A few weeks ago, we'd followed a bus through the streets of Monforte sporting a colourful advertisement. The words "Vino Bus" had caught our attention so Melanie scribbled down the telephone number.

'What did they say?'

'The woman I spoke to said it was a tour to promote winemaking in the Ribeira Sacra. It's due to start at the beginning of August.'

August is the height of the tourist season, such as it is. The tour would depart from Monforte in the morning and visit a number of historic churches including the monastery in Ferreira de Pantón. It would also visit the village of Vilachá which is famed for its small *bodegas* and traditional winemaking methods.

'The only problem was the price,' added Melanie.

I sensed she was teasing.

'Don't tell me, it's free.'

'Not quite, the tickets are three euros each.'

From Melanie's description, there didn't seem to be much wine involved but at that price we'd be fools not to give it a go.

'I think we can stretch to that,' I quipped.

'I thought I might have a phone around and see if anyone else is interested in joining us.'

'That's a good idea. Perhaps we can get a group discount.'

Melanie smiled.

'How's the installation going?' I asked.

'How should I know? I haven't been anywhere near it.'

'Not even to take a look?'

'I haven't even opened the office door.'

I walked through into the office and nudged the mouse. The screen lit up. "Restart the computer to complete the installation." Not before time.

Straight after lunch I began my search for a new digital companion. The options were mind-boggling. My lack of knowledge was slightly disconcerting but one thing was clear. During the last six years, performance had increased and prices had fallen. As the Americans would say, I'd be getting a lot more bang for the buck. In the end I opted for a Toshiba with an AMD dual-core processor. Perhaps its most appealing feature was the ability to downgrade the operating system from Vista to XP: if all else failed, better the devil you know. I broke the news to Melanie whose eyes glazed over as I listed the specification.

'The only drawback is the delivery. They've quoted twenty days,' I said.

'You'd better get it ordered then,' she replied.

I hovered the cursor over the "buy now" button. Was I making the right decision? My next action would have repercussions for years to come. Nothing ventured nothing gained: click!

3

Finishing Touches

Ordering a new laptop drew a line under an unwanted
distraction. We could once again concentrate our efforts
on finishing the decorating at *Campo Verde*. As the painting
neared an end our attention turned to the interior design.

We'd been hoarding what auctioneers refer to as
decorators' pieces for the best part of twelve months.
What started with a few opportune purchases snowballed
into a compulsive obsession. To date we'd amassed an
eclectic assortment of furnishings which were gathering
dust in the guest bedroom. There were mirrors, paintings,
clocks, vases, ornaments: anything and everything to
transform a blank canvas into a work of art. Due to a lack
of storage space and a limited budget, we'd avoided buying
bulkier items but the time had come to start filling our
empty house.

'I thought we might take a look at some furniture
today,' I said over breakfast.

'Do you have somewhere in mind?'

'Let's see what Ourense has to offer and then drive on to Chaves.'

Ourense is the nearest city to us. We'd bought furniture there in the past. There were a couple of stores I was keen to revisit. Both stocked the style of furniture we had in mind. Chaves on the other hand is across the border in Portugal but lower prices might justify the 280-kilometre round trip.

'Do you think they'll deliver to Vilatán from Chaves?' asked Melanie.

'I'm sure they will but I've no idea how much it'll cost. We can ask for nothing.'

The road to Ourense climbs steadily out of the Val de Lemos before plunging down the valley of the river Miño. Once at the river's edge, it follows its course into the city. It's a beautiful drive at any time of year but during the summer, when the vineyards are in full leaf, the scenery is stunning.

As luck would have it, the first shop we'd earmarked for browsing was in the throes of a sale. If we wanted to take advantage of this biannual event, there was no time to lose.

'What do you think of that?' I asked, pointing at a large reproduction hall mirror.

It had been stained to resemble ebony and featured a wide frame with intricately carved vine leaves and bunches of grapes.

'It's lovely,' said Melanie.

'Right then, we'll have it.'

I picked it up and carried it to the checkout.

'Can I leave this here while we carry on shopping?' I asked the sales assistant.

'No problem.'

The next pieces to catch our eye were two chairs.

'What about these?' asked Melanie.

'They're nice, but what are we going to do with them?'

'We could put one in each bedroom.'

That was a great idea.

'We'll 'ave 'em. You take that one and I'll bring this.'

We added them to the mirror and continued rummaging.

'Do you like that?' I asked.

I'd spotted a dark-stained, three-drawer console table with a slatted shelf at ankle level.

'Where are we going to put it?'

'It could go in the hallway with the mirror above it.'

'That would work really well.'

'OK then, I'll take this end and you grab that.'

Our stock of furniture was building up nicely.

The next thing we saw was a tall wooden display cabinet with three shelves, glass side panels, and a lockable, glass-paned door.

'That would be ideal for displaying all the bits and pieces we've got,' suggested Melanie.

I couldn't have agreed more but it was a bit cumbersome to carry to the checkout. Melanie called a sales assistant over and asked her to mark it as sold. While she sorted that out, I'd spotted a selection of headboards.

'I like those,' I said, squeezing through an array of bedside tables to give them the once-over.

Melanie followed.

'What do you think?'

'There's no two alike,' she replied.

The single bed headboards were crafted in wood and stained to give them a rustic appearance.

'That's all the rage nowadays. Don't you remember the mismatch of tables and chairs at the Hare and Hounds?'

The Hare and Hounds was a trendy, out of town pub and eatery on the moors above Huddersfield.

'When you put it like that, I don't suppose it matters.'

They were leant against a wall. I flicked through them as if thumbing through LPs in a music shop and lifted one out.

'Crikey! It weighs a tonne.'

They might have been cheap reproductions from India but the manufacturer hadn't compromised on materials.

'That one's nice, and what about that one?' asked Melanie, pointing at another.

I lifted it out and we hauled them to the checkout. We were on a roll.

'What about that nest of tables?' asked Melanie.

She'd seen a nest of three occasional tables.

'They've got woodworm.'

I examined them more closely.

'It's fake,' I added.

'Fake?'

'Fake woodworm.'

This was exactly the design we wanted: reproduction furniture with an authentic style. I picked them up and carried them to the checkout. While I was away, Melanie had seen something quite exceptional.

'This is gorgeous,' she said, stroking the wooden panels of an integrated bench and coat rack.

The bench was about six feet tall with a mirror at eye level divided into four panes. Below that was a row of three evenly spaced coat hooks. Underneath the seat were two wicker baskets for storing shoes or sundry items.

'That would be fabulous in the entrance lobby,' I replied. 'How much is it?'

Melanie flipped over the sales ticket which was hanging from one of the coat hooks. It wasn't cheap but such a piece would set the standard for the rest of the house. Everyone who visited would see this before anything else. What price a first impression?

'Let's have it,' I said.

'Are you sure?'

'Certain.'

We scoured the rest of the store, searching for the last remaining items on our shopping list. Alas, all were too expensive for our meagre budget. We settled the bill and arranged to have everything delivered to *Campo Verde* later in the week.

Our next stop was a shop called Eco Muebles which roughly translates to economically priced furniture. The suites and sofas were great value for money but nothing caught our eye. The beds on the other hand were exactly what we'd had in mind, with prices to match. We ordered one double and two singles and found a metal-framed headboard to go with the double.

'What do you think to this?' asked Melanie.

She was standing next to a TV stand with a cupboard below. The pine timber had been distressed and stained to give it an aged oak appearance. The range was limited to the TV stand, a Welsh dresser, and a large, farmhouse-style kitchen table and chairs.

'That's ideal,' I said, referring to the TV stand. 'It's just a pity the dining table is so big.'

We hadn't quite shopped 'til we'd dropped but leaving Eco Muebles brought an end to our shopping in Ourense. The only items we'd still to find were a suite, a dining table and chairs, and wardrobes and bedside tables for both bedrooms.

'Where next?' asked Melanie, as we made our way back to the car.

'Chaves.'

The clock had ticked around to noon but the one-hour time difference between Portugal and Spain meant we'd arrive in plenty of time to search for furniture before grabbing lunch at our favourite Chinese restaurant, Jing Huà.

When it comes to interior design, Melanie and I have very similar tastes. The items we'd purchased so far had almost picked themselves. My choice of suite would divide opinion. We'd had in mind a three-piece cottage suite with tapestry cushions. What called out to me couldn't have been more different.

We'd stopped on the outskirts of Chaves at one of a number of furniture retailers.

'What do you think to that?' I asked.

Taking pride of place on the sales floor was a two-piece suite, comprising of a two-seater and a three-seater sofa in a contemporary design with flecked grey cushions and faux leather arms.

'It's gorgeous but I'm not sure it's for *Campo Verde*.'

I knew exactly what she meant but felt confident that the contrast between new and old would work perfectly. Melanie wasn't convinced.

'I think it'll look great.'

As luck would have it the two sofas were on offer. This was an opportunity not to be missed.

'But what about delivery?' asked Melanie.

'If you like it, I'll ask.'

'I love it. I'm just struggling to visualise it in the house.'

'Trust me, it'll work perfectly.'

'OK, let's ask.'

The sales assistant was very helpful.

'We can deliver to Spain, no problem,' he said.

'It's fifteen kilometres from Monforte de Lemos.'

I thought I'd better clarify.

'That's fine.'

'And how much will it cost?' I asked.

'Delivery is free.'

We were stunned. Everything in Spain has a delivery charge. I glanced at Melanie for confirmation.

'Go on then, but on your head be it.'

We handed over the cash and the sales assistant noted our address.

'We can deliver in three or four days but we'll ring you beforehand,' he said.

We thanked him for his time and left.

By then the clock had ticked around to 12:30 pm local time. Lunch at the Jing Huà was calling. We ordered spring rolls, roast duck hotpot, chicken with cashew nuts, and egg fried rice, a real treat. After eating, our search continued.

In the final shop of the day we found that elusive dining table. It wasn't exactly what we'd hoped for but it was close enough. In common with many European nations, dining in Spain is often a family activity. Finding a table to seat four had been quite a struggle.

'This is just the right size,' said Melanie, pulling out a dining chair and taking the weight off.

I joined her. The size was ideal and the chairs were comfortable. My only concern was the silence; it just wasn't speaking to me. Melanie could sense I wasn't convinced.

'What do you think?' she asked.

'It's OK ...'

'But?'

'I'm not sure. What do you think?'

'I know what you mean but it's not bad, and it is the right size.'

'Yes, it is the right size.'

Melanie and I sat at the table, stroking the wooden top and contemplating our decision.

'Let's go for it,' I said, eventually.

'Are you sure?'

'Not really but we could end up searching forever.'

All in all, we'd had a terrific day. With the exception of wardrobes and bedside tables, we'd furnished the entire house.

When we moved to Spain, I'd hoped the days of working on my birthday were behind me, but not this year. People were arriving at the rental property we manage for our friends Bob and Janet. Making sure it was spick and span was our responsibility. I had just enough time to open my cards and presents before we headed off to work. Unlike Brits, Spaniards don't really do greetings cards. The one Melanie gave me had more in common with my shoe size than my age.

'Sorry about the card. It was all I could find.'

'It's the thought that counts,' I replied.

A bottle of ruby port and bar of Nestlé chocolate more than compensated.

After a busy morning we spent the afternoon relaxing at home, soaking up the sun's rays and chilling in the pool. That evening I lit the barbecue and we ended the day sipping port and munching chocolate. I even managed to win a few games of backgammon.

'When do Richard and Yvonne get here?' I asked.

Richard, Yvonne, and their two kids Mason and Erren are regular summer visitors to *El Sueño*. Melanie is Erren's godmother and I'm Uncle Craig. It's a title I feel privileged to hold and despite their tender years, Mason and Erren have introduced me to the merits of the chaos theory. I'm now of the opinion that everyone should experience at least one week of chaos every year. Where trepidation once reigned, anticipation now resides.

'Friday,' replied Melanie.

'This Friday?'

'That's right.'

'Crikey! That's come around quick.'

We paused for a moment, contemplating the speedy passage of time.

'I've been thinking,' I said.

'Oh yes.'

'Yes.'

'What about?'

Melanie knew it could be anything from the meaning of life to a suggestion for tomorrow's dinner.

'Bedroom furniture.'

Melanie's bewildered expression said it all.

'Bedroom furniture?'

'For *Campo Verde*.'

'And what have you been thinking?'

'I've been wondering if José Kitchen's wife might have something.'

José Kitchen is an address book designation rather than his actual name. Here in Spain, most people are named after a Catholic saint. This results in a limited name pool and a high instance of repetition. To compensate for this confusion, Melanie has devised a system based on people's trade rather than their surname. José Kitchen works from premises in Monforte de Lemos above a homeware shop run by his wife, Maite.

'She might have,' replied Melanie.

'If she doesn't have anything, the painters and decorators might have.'

Pinturas Trigo e Hijos is the main decorator's merchant in Monforte de Lemos. As well as decorating supplies they also stock a wide range of unfinished pine furniture.

'I thought all their stuff was plain.'

'It is but how difficult can it be to stain a few sticks of furniture and add some handles?'

Melanie looked sceptical. I on the other hand felt confident.

First thing on Monday morning we drove into town. Maite greeted us warmly and left us to wander around the shop. The main sales floor was stocked with household items and gift ideas; furniture was in the back.

'I like that,' I said.

Standing in one corner of the room was a quirky, cello-shaped wine rack. A statement piece if ever I saw one.

'We're searching for bedroom furniture,' replied Melanie.

'I know, but what do you think?'

'I think it's a wine rack Craig, and we want bedroom furniture.'

It's never a good sign when Melanie uses my name. I continued regardless.

'But don't you just love it.'

Melanie paused for a moment.

'It's certainly unusual.'

'Don't you think it would look great in the dining room?'

'It might do.'

Melanie seemed to be warming to the idea.

'Let's get it.'

'How much is it?'

At under one hundred euros, it seemed like a bargain.

'OK. Why not?'

'That's lovely as well,' said Melanie, pointing at a small table with two drawers.

Due to a technical oversight, the twin-bedded room was slightly narrower than we'd anticipated. To make the most of the available space we'd decided to have one central bedside table with the beds on either side. This piece fitted the brief perfectly.

'That's ideal. Let's get it,' I replied.

All we needed now were two wardrobes and the bedside tables for the master bedroom, neither of which we were going to find here.

'We'll buy these and then see what the decorator's has to offer,' I said.

A few minutes later we were climbing the stairs to the first floor in Pinturas Trigo e Hijos. The first thing to strike me was the size of the wardrobes. Without exception, the ones we'd seen so far were enormous. These were much closer to the size we'd had in mind.

'This would be ideal for the twin bedroom.'

I'd spotted a double wardrobe with three built-in drawers.

'What about that one for the master bedroom,' said Melanie, pointing at a standard double.

Standing next to the wardrobe was a six-drawer tallboy. Even in its unvarnished condition it emanated style.

'That would be a real statement piece in the master bedroom,' I said.

'It would but are you sure you can stain and wax all this furniture?'

She had a point. If I messed up it would be a very expensive mistake.

'Let's have a chat with the shop owner.'

His description of the process seemed straightforward. I suspected it wouldn't be quite as easy as he was making out but confidence was high and besides which, we were running out of options.

'We'll take them,' I said. 'Can you deliver?'

The answer was a resounding no. It seemed ironic that the furniture shop in Portugal was more than happy to make a 280-kilometre round trip but the decorator's merchant in Monforte refused to travel thirty.

The next day, I hitched the trailer to the back of the car and we drove into town. Try as I did, I couldn't get everything to fit. A straightforward pay and collect turned into a 120-kilometre marathon.

Over the next three days, the furniture we'd ordered in Ourense and Chaves was delivered. Slowly but surely our blank canvas was being transformed into the masterpiece we'd dreamt of. In between deliveries, I worked on the bedroom furniture.

'Hola!'

I was concentrating so much on the job in hand that the caller had taken me by surprise. I turned to see Alfonso standing in the doorway.

'Oh, hello.'

'You're painting,' he said.

"It's oak-coloured varnish,' I replied.

'Very nice.'

Alfonso's reply was accompanied by a cheeky smile. Did he like it or not?

'I'll be starting the driveway tomorrow,' he added.

That was great news, although there was a certain inevitability to his timing. Richard, Yvonne and the kids would also be arriving tomorrow.

'What time will you start?' I asked.

'About 9:00 am.'

'OK, I'll see you then.'

'*Hasta mañana* (See you in the morning),' he replied, and left.

By the end of the day I'd given each piece of furniture its first coat of varnish. One more and a polish with beeswax should complete the job. Perhaps it wasn't going to be as difficult as I'd thought.

'How did it go?' asked Melanie, when I got home.

'I've finished the first coat. They're going to look really nice by the time I've done.'

'That's good.'

'Alfonso called while I was there.'

'Oh yes. What did he want?'

'He's going to make a start on the driveway tomorrow.'

'Tomorrow!'

'I know. Wouldn't you just know it. What time do Richard and Yvonne expect to arrive?'

'Yvonne said she'd ring as soon as she knows.'

'I told Alfonso I'd see him in the morning so I'll have to show my face.'

'You won't be there all day, will you?'

'I wouldn't think so. The last thing he'll want is me hanging around. As soon as I know everything is alright, I'll come home.'

That night I set the alarm for an early start.

4

Chaves Not Chavs?

We were jump-started into a new day by the piercing tone of the alarm clock. What was once a routine awakening has become an infrequent intrusion. It's an unwelcome reminder of less sedate times. Within an hour I was ready for off.

'See you later,' I said, as I picked up the car key.

'Try not to be late back,' pleaded Melanie.

When I arrived at *Campo Verde* Alfonso and his mate were already there. They were busy dragging reinforcing steel mesh into position down the length of the driveway.

'*Buenos días* (Good morning),' I called.

'*Hola*,' replied Alfonso.

His mate looked up, smiled, and tipped his head.

'Is the shuttering OK?' I asked.

'Everything's fine,' replied Alfonso.

Beep! Beep! Beep! Beep!

The unmistakable sound of a reversing alarm echoed down the lane. Alfonso looked up.

'It's here,' he said to his companion.

The two of them stopped what they were doing and walked to the end of the driveway. I waited in the garden and peered over the wall. Through the trees the rotating drum of a cement mixer edged slowly down the lane. With great skill the driver reversed into the driveway.

A key element of any restoration project is keeping costs under control. In that respect *Campo Verde* had fought us all the way. On reflection, buying a house without water or mains electricity wasn't the smartest move. Those issues aside, it was the property's location that had put the greatest strain on our finances. Vehicle access had been an ongoing issue. This morning's delivery was no exception.

Concrete is priced by the cubic metre. As a rule, the larger the quantity the more competitive the unit price. Limited access meant that only a small-scale concrete mixer could be used. That resulted in smaller loads, more deliveries, and a higher unit price. Creating a driveway would be our final financial hoorah.

I waited to see the first load poured before heading home.

'Have you heard from Yvonne?' I asked on my return.

'They're expecting to get here at about four o'clock. How did things go this morning?'

'Not too bad. It was a tight squeeze but they managed to get the mixer into the driveway.'

Melanie had spent the last few days preparing for the arrival of our friends. All we had to do now was wait.

Clang, clang, clang, clang!

The sound of the brass doorbell woke Jazz from her sleep. She leapt to her feet and ran around the side of the house, barking with excitement. I glanced at my watch and set off after her. Eight-year-old Mason was holding the gates open for his dad to drive through.

'I'll get them,' I said to him, as he struggled to close them.

Within five minutes both kids had changed into their swimwear and were splashing about in the pool. Some things never change, which is more than could be said for their modesty. Gone were the days of disrobing in the garden: eight-year-olds require more privacy.

Clang, clang, clang, clang!

Melanie and I looked at each other. Who on earth could that be?

'I'll go,' I said.

I walked through the kitchen and looked out of the French doors. A delivery van had stopped in the lane and one of its rear doors was open. I walked outside and a driver jumped down from the back holding a box.

'Señor Bricks?' he asked.

'That's me.'

'*Firma aqui* (Sign here).'

I signed his form and he handed me the box. The word Toshiba set my heart racing. I knew exactly what this was.

'*Gracias,*' I said, as he jumped back into his cab.

Wouldn't you know it, the first time we'd had guests in ages and my new computer had arrived.

'Look what I've got,' I said, as I stepped out onto the terrace.

The temptation to sneak a peek proved too strong but booting it up would have to wait for another day.

At 5:30 pm I excused myself and drove back to *Campo Verde* to check on progress. I parked in the lane and walked down to the house. When I reached the end of the driveway I was surprised and delighted in equal measure. The concreting was almost complete. Alfonso and his mate were waiting for the final load.

'What do you think?' he asked, looking very pleased with himself.

'It's …' I paused, not really knowing what to say, 'long.'

It looked more like the runway at Heathrow than a driveway.

'How soon will it dry?' I asked.

'You'll be able to walk on it tomorrow but give it three or four days before you drive the car over it.'

'What about watering?'

Manolo had taught me the importance of keeping concrete moist during the curing or hardening process.

'Don't worry about that, I'll keep popping back to douse it,' he replied.

Alfonso lived in the next village. Keeping an eye on it wouldn't be a problem.

'And when will you be able to start the paving?' I asked.

Alfonso smiled; he knew I was fishing for a start date.

'I'll ring you.'

In a little over a week everything and everyone would stop for the August holiday. It didn't take a genius to work out that we wouldn't see him again until September at the earliest.

Over the next few days, I managed to steal enough time to get my new toy up and running. The operating system seemed to take forever to boot up but I got there in the end. Only time would tell if Windows Vista could live up to the performance of its predecessors.

Time seemed to fly by in a mêlée of swimming pool activity and boisterous family lunches. Only chicken nuggets and baked bean dinners gave the adults a brief interlude. Once refuelled, our tiny human dynamos continued until bedtime. Pleas for extra time fell on deaf ears and lights-out signalled a period of calm.

This joyous chaos continued unabated for three days until Mummy intervened. The time had come to add a little culture to the mix. Melanie and I were prepared.

'We thought you might like to visit Chaves,' said Melanie.

'Where's that?' asked Mason.

'It's in Portugal.'

'Is that where the castle is?' he asked.

I was surprised he'd remembered his previous visit to Portugal; he was only five at the time.

'There is a castle in Chaves but not the one we went to last time. This is a different town,' explained Melanie.

'Do we have to?' pleaded Mason, who would have happily spent his entire holiday jumping in and out of the pool.

'Yer, do we have to?' echoed Erren, mimicking her older brother.

'Yes, we have to,' insisted mum.

'You'll love it,' I said. 'There's a tourist train to go on.'

'Like last year?' asked an excited Mason.

Last year's day of culture had been a trip to the natural hot springs in Ourense. To get there we'd taken the road-going train from the Plaza Mayor.

'That's right. Just like last year.'

'Yeah!' they sang in unison.

My intervention seemed to have done the trick.

A cloudless blue sky set the mercury soaring. As we crossed the border into Portugal the temperature hit 40°C. By the time we reached Chaves it had topped 44°C. On arrival we checked the timetable. The first train after lunch departed at 3:00 pm.

'Who'd like Chinese for lunch?' I asked.

'Yeah!' cried Mason and Erren.

The Jing Huà Chinese restaurant was less than a hundred metres from the train's departure point.

After a delicious lunch we strolled along the cobbled pavement towards the waiting train. The kids posed for photos in front of the bright yellow and blue engine which proudly displayed the flags of Portugal and Chaves.

'Oh look,' said Yvonne, 'chavs.'

'What does that mean, Mummy?' asked Mason.

'That's what you and Erren are,' she joked.

'Why?'

'Yes Mummy, why?' echoed Erren.

Yvonne was teasing but the mantra of youth required a response.

'Yes Mummy, why?' I joined the chorus.

Yvonne gave me one of those "Don't encourage them" looks.

'Because you're wearing sunglasses and look like chavs.'

As if to emphasise the point, Erren lifted the wilted flag and pointed at the word Chaves.

'Hold that pose,' said Yvonne, as she whipped out her camera.

Mason and Erren were naturals. Another one for the holiday album.

By the time Yvonne had finished her photo shoot the train driver had returned from lunch. We paid the fare and hopped aboard.

There's nothing more indicative of the passage of time than the actions of children. Last year they'd insisted on sitting next to Melanie and me. This year they sat together at the back of the carriage. What hadn't changed was their affection for one another. At their age, my sister and I didn't have a civil word for each other, never mind sitting together.

The train departed ten minutes behind schedule from the corner of Rúa Dr. João Morais. At the end of the road it turned right and headed up a limited access street towards the castle. At the Praça de Camões it stopped, giving passengers the opportunity to wander around the square and visit the ruined castle. The kids were becoming restless. Medieval ruins and weathered statues aren't exactly exciting at their age.

'When are we going home?' asked Mason.

'Soon,' I replied, as the train continued its journey.

The children made the best of it but given a choice, I knew where they'd rather be.

Their seven-day stay at *El Sueño* passed far too quickly. On their final day Mason asked for a lunchtime paella and Uncle Craig was happy to oblige.

The house felt eerily quiet without our raucous guests. We kept ourselves busy transforming *Campo Verde* into a home worthy of the accolade, quality accommodation for the discerning traveller. The results were stunning and exactly what we'd hoped for. A pristine palace with a homely feel. Everything was brand new but looked as though it belonged. Farmhouse living with all mod cons.

Having put all but the finishing touches to the interior we turned our attention to the gardens. Low maintenance was key. We decided to have a gravelled area directly in front of the house. A steel-framed gazebo would provide the perfect place to enjoy a good book or Teatime Taster. Lawns would flank both sides of the driveway.

Preparing the ground for seeding wouldn't be easy. The first job was to convert these patches of sun-baked earth and building rubble into smooth, flat, stone-free soil, four inches deep. A difficult job at the best of times but doing it in the height of summer made it even more challenging. Melanie helped out whenever I asked but the bulk of the work was down to me.

'Ian rang while you were out,' said Melanie, when I returned home one evening.

Ian and his wife Kathy have a holiday home in the area. They'd been introduced to us by Roy and Maria and we'd hit it off straightaway.

'What did he want?'

'He asked if we'd like to go with them to the football tomorrow.'

Like me, Ian is an avid fan of the beautiful game.

'What football?'

'Apparently Tottenham Hotspur's academy side are playing in a competition in Monforte.'

'Tottenham Hotspur! Are you sure?'

'That's what he said.'

The likelihood of a Premier League club, albeit their academy team, playing in Monforte de Lemos sounded too outrageous to be true.

'What time?' I asked.

'The first match kicks off at 6:30 pm.'

'The first match? How many are there?'

'He didn't say. Apparently, the tournament is being played over two days but we won't be able to go the following day because we're on the Wine Bus tour.'

'Is Kathy going?'

'Yes.'

'Do you want to go?'

'Why not.'

'OK, let's go.'

'He said they'd meet us outside the stadium at 6:00 pm if we were interested.'

If the word stadium conjures up images of Wembley or the Coliseum in Rome, forget it. The Campo Municipal de A Pinguela in Monforte de Lemos is an enclosed pitch with a covered stand running down one side.

'How many of us are going on the Wine Bus?' I asked.

'Nine.'

'Nine?'

'Yes, there's Ian and Kathy, Bill and Di, Peter and Veronica, Penelope, and you and me.'

'What time does it set off?'

'The bus leaves Monforte at 10:00 am.'

Not for the first time, we had a full weekend ahead of us. Tottenham Hotspur indeed.

The following evening, we drove the eight kilometres into Monforte. The area outside the stadium was a hive of activity. Perhaps Spurs were in town.

'There they are,' said Melanie, as I drove cautiously through the crowds.

I parked the car and we went to say hello.

'Hiya, Melanie said something about Spurs playing,' I said to Ian.

'That's right. Can you believe it?'

His expression gave nothing away.

'You are talking about Tottenham Hotspur, the Premier League side?'

'Not just Spurs but Benfica from the Portuguese Primeira Liga and La Coruña of La Liga.'

'You are joking?'

'No joke. When I saw the poster in town, I had to look twice.'

I was speechless.

'It's a four team, academy side tournament,' he added.

'Who's the fourth team?'

'Get this, Club Lemos.'

Club Lemos is the name of the local team from Monforte. To put this into perspective, the other three sides play at the highest level in their respective national leagues; Club Lemos ply their trade in Primeira Autonómica – Group 3, the sixth tier of Spanish football. How on earth they managed to entice such titans of European football to this neck of the woods was anyone's guess.

The cost of admission was a very reasonable six euros and included a list of each team's players. Seating was on a first come first served basis. Our early arrival afforded us a central position close to the halfway line.

Out of all the names on the team sheet only one stood out, Danny Rose of Spurs. He'd been bought a few months earlier from Leeds United for the princely sum of one million pounds. Had I known then that he'd go on to play for England I might have asked for his autograph.

Tonight's fixtures pitted Spurs against La Coruña followed by Club Lemos against the mighty Benfica. Winners and losers would play each other tomorrow to determine the overall champion.

From a footballing perspective, the matches were fascinating. In the first game the players of Tottenham looked like mature young men compared to the boys from La Coruña. Despite this physical disadvantage their distinctive brand of football, referred to as tippy-tappy by the British press, saw La Coruña take the lead. For most of the first half the young men of Spurs were left chasing shadows. As the match progressed, the boys from La Coruña tired and the physicality of the Spurs players took control. In the end, Spurs ran out 3–1 winners. Did they deserve it? On the balance of play they probably did but I couldn't help wondering exactly how far this high energy, low skill style of play would take these lads. When the boys from La Coruña matured into athletic young men their silky-smooth skills would undoubtedly give them the advantage.

The game against Benfica and Club Lemos ended in a thumping defeat for the home side which was hardly surprising given the gulf in their respective leagues. Tomorrow, the two giants of European football would face each other in the final. My loyalty was split. On the one hand I wanted Spurs to triumph but for the sake of the beautiful game, I hoped the silky skills of Benfica would overcome the power and athleticism of their English counterparts.

An early start meant another unwanted alarm call. The Wine Bus wouldn't wait. People were relying on us to get there in time but even the best-laid plans can go awry. When we finally got to Monforte, an anxious group of friends were waiting impatiently to board the minibus.

'Morning,' called Melanie as we hurried towards them.

Bill exaggerated a glance at his wristwatch.

'It's in the name of Melanie.'

The tour guide checked his list.

'*Si*, Melani, *para nueve* (For nine).'

'That's correct.'

'OK,' he said, gesturing us to board.

One by one we climbed the steps. Eight other passengers were already seated. Melanie and I followed Ian and Kathy to the back of the bus. No sooner had we taken our seats than we departed.

'My name is Miguel,' shouted the tour guide from the front of the bus. 'Our first stop is the 12th century Romanesque church of San Miguel in the village of Eiré.'

I controlled my urge to ask if he was related. The subtleties of British satire are often lost on our Spanish hosts.

Within fifteen minutes we were pulling up outside the small church in Eiré.

'Wait here a minute,' said Miguel, before wandering off up the lane.

'I bet he's gone to get the keys,' I joked.

Searching for a key holder is a common occurrence when house-hunting in Galicia. It's quite usual for a dodgy estate agent to abandon his clients in the middle of nowhere and go off in search of the keys. I should have known better. A few minutes later Miguel returned with said key holder.

'If you'd like to follow me,' he said.

One by one we disembarked and regrouped outside the church. Miguel did his best to put an interesting spin on the building's unremarkable exterior. One of the more unusual aspects of early Roman Catholic churches is their use of pagan imagery. A stone archway over the entrance featured intricate carvings of horned monsters with hoofed feet and other creatures with human heads and the torso of a beast. I'm sure academics would have found his narrative fascinating but for a group of Spanish and English tourists it was rather highbrow. Miguel sensed his audience was growing restless and suggested we move inside.

The interior was slightly more interesting. The star of the show was the remnants of a medieval fresco recently unearthed during restoration work. I managed to take a few shots before my camera battery died.

'Bugger,' I whispered.

Hardly appropriate given our surroundings. Thankfully, only Melanie heard.

'What's matter?'

'The battery has gone flat.'

'I'm sure Penelope will email you a few photos if you ask her nicely.'

I thought *I* was a happy snapper but Penelope seemed intent on photographing anything that didn't move and everything that did.

'Does anyone have any questions?' asked Miguel.

Having satisfied everyone's curiosity we returned to the minibus.

'Our next stop is the monastery of Santa María in Ferreira de Pantón,' announced Miguel.

Both Melanie and I were looking forward to this part of the tour. We'd spent the first year of our life-changing move renting a property in Ferreira de Pantón and often thought of visiting the monastery. For whatever reason, we hadn't got around to it. Miguel explained that as a working monastery we should be respectful of its current incumbents: no blaspheming here.

The monastery has the distinction of being the only one in Galicia to have been in continuous use since its formation in the 12th century. Firstly, with nuns of the Benedictine order, and latterly with those of the Cistercian.

The bus pulled off the road and we followed Miguel to an impressive gated entrance. The solid wooden gates were locked. Miguel yanked a bell-chain and we waited patiently. After a few minutes a small hatch opened. Miguel explained who we were and why we were here. It was clear from the respondent that we weren't expected. Miguel pleaded our case.

'Officially, the monastery is closed today,' he explained.

A murmur of disappointment rippled through the group.

'But we can visit the chapel,' he added.

Over the years we'd become accustomed to the right hand not knowing what the left was doing. As usual, a compromise had been reached which allowed everyone to save face. We listened as a key turned in the lock and three bolts were yanked open.

'No talking inside,' said Miguel as one by one we tiptoed through the gate.

As we stepped over the threshold a resident nun commandeered Miguel's tour guide duties. Her canter around the chapel was so brisk I thought she might be hiding roller-skates under her habit. One of the institution's most prized artefacts was an ancient wooden sculpture depicting Mary cradling the baby Jesús. What struck me about it was its primitive form: it wouldn't have looked out of place atop a totem pole. Despite our unannounced intrusion, when it came to manning the gift shop there seemed to be plenty of volunteers. One can only admire the enterprise of the Catholic faith.

Back on the bus we settled in for a relaxed drive along the N-120 heading east. We'd travelled this exact same route many times but the elevated seating position gave us a whole new perspective on this stunningly beautiful stretch of road. Forty minutes after leaving Ferreira, we crossed the bridge over the river Sil and drove into the village of San Clodio.

'This is the Iglesia de San Clodio,' said Miguel, as the bus came to a halt.

'Remind me again, why is this tour called the Wine Bus?' whispered Ian.

I was beginning to wonder myself. One 12th century church is interesting, two less so, but three in under three hours was becoming a little obsessive.

'I think the next stop is the wine part of the tour,' I replied.

At least I hoped so.

Out of the three churches this was by far the most interesting. It had a cosy feel like a warm duvet in winter. The villagers took great pride in their prized possession.

Before long we were back on the road heading to our final destination, the village of Vilachá. As the crow flies it's less than eight kilometres from San Clodio. But as the bus drives, it's over thirty. Having retraced our route along the N-120 we turned left at the village of A Estación and headed into the wilderness. The road twisted and turned through dense forests. At times the uneven surface made it feel more like a rollercoaster than a minibus.

The village of Vilachá is famous for its centuries-old *bodegas*. The fifty or so stone-built, slate-roofed wineries have survived the passage of time. The tour coincided with the annual village Feria del Vino (Wine Fiesta). We would finally get the chance to taste the region's wines.

We were quite taken aback by the number of people milling around. The narrow village lanes were bustling with partygoers.

'Please be back at the bus by two o'clock,' said Miguel, as the doors opened.

We eased our way through the crowds and into the first *bodega*. The place was packed with small groups of people sipping wine and chatting. Melanie and I made our way to a makeshift counter where two young people were pouring wine into white plastic cups. I smiled and picked up two.

'Here you go,' I said, handing one to Melanie.

Ian and Kathy had followed us in.

'Take this one,' I said, handing the second to Kathy.

I turned and grabbed two more. Drinks aloft, we shuffled our way through the crowd to stand by the doorway.

'That's nice,' remarked Kathy, having taken a sip.

Standing opposite were a group of Spaniards. They'd brought with them a round of cheese and a *rosca* (sweet cake). Noticing us watching, they immediately offered us some.

'*Gracias,*' we replied, accepting their generous gift.

These dark, dusty *bodegas* are as far removed from modern, clinically clean wineries as you can imagine but the wine and the atmosphere were irresistible. After finishing our first taster we headed next door. Other members of our group were enjoying the fruits of someone else's labours. We joined in. Our forty-minute stay passed quicker than any other point throughout the day.

'We'd better make our way back to the bus,' I said.

Reluctantly everyone agreed.

Despite an overemphasis on religious architecture, the day had been a great success and we'd seen and experienced some wonderful things. When Miguel handed each of us a hessian bag containing a bottle of regional wine, three euros per head seemed a small price to pay for such an interesting tour. Now that's what I call a bargain.

5

Strategic Planning

The weather in Galicia has a reputation for being unpredictable. During August, temperatures along the coast are tempered by the Atlantic Ocean. Further inland, heat and humidity rise hand in hand, often culminating in spectacular electrical storms. So far this month we'd enjoyed fabulously sunny days without the stifling humidity. A small but welcome mercy as we toiled in the garden at *Campo Verde*. By the middle of the month the end was in sight and the barometer was on the rise.

'We're not going to have enough soil,' I said, as Melanie wheeled another barrowful from one side of the garden to the other.

'How much more are we going to need?'

'A few trailer loads should do the trick.'

'Where can we get it from?'

'I've no idea.'

'Perhaps Pablo might know somewhere,' suggested Melanie.

Pablo lives in the village with his wife Ana, daughter Sara, and Ana's parents. He was our go-to guy for village related issues. If anyone knew where we could get some soil, he would.

'El Monte,' he said.

'Where?'

El Monte was an area of common land on the outskirts of the village. Reading between the lines it sounded like a communal dump for recyclable waste: rocks, boulders, garden rubbish and the like. It didn't sound very promising but it was worth a look.

'Come with me. I'll show you.'

We hopped into the car and Pablo directed us through the village.

'Take the next right.'

A gap between two drystone walls led into an area of rough ground.

'There,' he said, pointing at some grassy mounds.

We took a closer look. The mounds consisted of the same mix of materials we'd spent the last few weeks digging out of the garden. There was no way we were starting all over again.

'We can't use this, Pablo, it's full of rocks,' I said, trying not to sound ungrateful.

Pablo paused for thought.

'There is the track,' he said.

'What track?'

'I'll show you.'

The three of us jumped into the car and drove back through the village.

'Turn right here.'

We'd joined the LU-617, the old road linking the village of Escairón with the town of Chantada. Five hundred metres along we turned left into a dirt track.

'Keep going,' he said.

The rough track gave agricultural vehicles access to the surrounding fields. It certainly wasn't designed for a two-door coupé.

'It's coming to an end,' I said.

I'd been dodging potholes for well over half a kilometre but I drew the line at rallying across a ploughed field.

'You can turn around over there,' said Pablo, pointing towards an ungated entrance.

I reversed into the field and pulled forward.

'Stop here.'

I switched off the engine and we followed Pablo back along the track.

'You can take this soil.'

Pablo kicked a pile of dusty earth at the side of the track. It didn't look like much but it was weed-free and would be easy to dig up.

'OK, that should work,' I replied.

I could tell from Melanie's expression that she thought I'd lost my marbles.

'But you mustn't take any from the fields.'

'Don't worry, we won't go anywhere near them. We'll make a start this afternoon, and thank you.'

We dropped Pablo back in the village and headed home for lunch.

'How are we going to get that dust from the lane to *Campo Verde*?' asked Melanie.

'In the trailer.'

'But there's nowhere to turn around.'

She had a point.

'We'll have to drive down the track, uncouple the empty trailer and wheel it into the field. That way I'll be able to turn the car around and then hook the trailer back up.'

It sounded like an awful lot of work for a bit of soil but what choice did we have?

While Melanie prepared lunch, I checked the emails and connected to the BBC Radio Two website. Lunch without Jeremy Vine was unthinkable.

'It's ready,' called Melanie.

While Jeremy quizzed his guests on the pros and cons of supermarkets charging customers for carrier bags, Melanie and I sat in the sunshine and ate our lunch. The news at 2:00 pm signalled a return to work.

'Are you ready?' I asked.

'I'll just nip to the loo.'

I should have known.

Half an hour later we were trundling down the uneven track with the empty trailer bouncing in and out of the ruts. Turning the car and trailer around proved as awkward and time-consuming as I'd expected. Shovelling the earth into the trailer was a hot, dusty job.

'That should be enough,' I said.

Pulling a heavy load over rough terrain was challenging. Eventually we made it back to the main road. As we gained speed, clouds of dust billowed out of the trailer. It wasn't until we tipped it in the garden that we realised exactly what we'd let ourselves in for.

'Is that it?' asked Melanie, shocked by how little there was.

'This is going to take a bit longer than I thought.'

An understatement if ever I'd heard one.

By the end of the day we'd fetched another three trailer loads. The pair of us were covered in dust and absolutely knackered. It wasn't so much the amount of earth we'd shifted as all the pushing and pulling of the trailer.

'Come on, let's call it a day,' I said.

Melanie looked relieved.

That evening we retired to the back of the garden with a bottle of inexpensive Chardonnay and nursed our aches and pains.

Ring, ring … Ring, ring!

'I'll go,' said Melanie.

She disappeared inside and returned a few minutes later.

'That was Ian on the phone.'

He'd rung to tell us the result of last night's clash between Tottenham Hotspur and Benfica in the final of the football tournament. The match had ended in a 3–3 draw with Benfica coming out on top after a penalty shootout. Despite my national loyalties I was pleased that the real winner was the beautiful game.

Benfica's victory coincided with the start of the Football League season in England. My beloved Huddersfield Town had started their League One campaign with an unconvincing 1–1 draw at home to Stockport County.

Following your team on the news is one thing but there's no substitute for standing on the terraces and cheering them on. If I could find some cheap airfares, I was confident I could persuade Melanie to go back to the UK for a long weekend. Her granny had been in poor health for some time and since our last visit in March her condition had deteriorated. The sands of time were slipping ever more quickly through life's hourglass. If we didn't go back soon, she might never see her again.

It took us two and a half days to excavate enough soil to level the garden. The next job on our list was the area in front of the house. Mindful that the new septic tank was buried just below the surface, we used the hardcore from the garden to roughly level the area and ordered six tonnes of sand to finish the job. This would be topped with a weed-proof membrane and then covered with gravel. In short, we were about to create one of the biggest privately owned soakaways in Spain. The hope was that the addition of a steel-framed gazebo would also make it one of the prettiest.

Before ordering the sand I needed to build two manholes above the twin-chambered septic tank. If used correctly a modern tank shouldn't need emptying. Micro-organisms break down the solids and the filtration chamber cleans the resultant liquid. That said, it couldn't do any harm to ensure we had access if or when it was needed. All that could wait until tomorrow. We'd done quite enough for one day. The clock had ticked around to midday and the weather was calling for an afternoon of sunbathing and swimming.

That evening I lit the barbecue and we wilted in the humid conditions.

'It feels like a storm is brewing,' I said.

Within hours of turning in, we were rudely awoken by a deafening explosion. My first thought was an earthquake. I opened my eyes and caught a flash of blinding light illuminating every chink around the wooden window shutters. A second almighty clap confirmed my earlier prediction. An electrical storm of biblical proportions had descended on *El Sueño*.

Melanie leapt from under the covers and chased around the house unplugging all the electrical items. We'd learnt from experience that storms like that can have devastating effects on appliances.

'What time is it?' asked Melanie as she flopped back into bed.

I rolled over and squinted at the digital display.

'Three twenty-seven.'

'Night, night.'

'Goodnight,' I replied.

As the thunder rolled away the rain began to fall. Lightly at first and then the heavens opened. Torrents of rainwater collided with the terracotta roof tiles with such ferocity it sounded like a shower of marbles on a bass drum. Slowly the storm moved off, leaving behind the gentle pitter patter of raindrops.

By the time we woke, the only evidence of this summer storm were damp surfaces and damaged grapevines.

'Have you seen the vines?' asked Melanie.

She'd taken Jazz out for her morning constitutional and returned with two mugs of coffee.

'Yes, I'll take a closer look before I go to Vilatán.'

This year's harvest was less than eight weeks away. The last thing we needed was storm damage or too much water. Overwatering at this stage can cause the grapes to swell and split, allowing harmful bacteria to develop. Fingers crossed.

'Are you going to work this morning?' asked Melanie.

Weekends are the playtime of nine to fivers, something I hadn't been for a very long time.

'I'll be back at lunchtime.'

'Will you need me?'

'Not if you've got something better to do.'

'There's the bedding to iron for *Bon Vista*,' she replied.

Casa Bon Vista is the holiday rental property we manage for our friends Bob and Janet. We're responsible for marketing, handling the reservations, and the day to day running. This year had been the most successful to date but a six-week summer booking had actually meant less work for us. A weekly linen change is much easier than cleaning the entire property.

'No problem, I'll see you at lunchtime.'

Before leaving I inspected the grapevines. The damage looked worse than it was. Despite a number of broken canes, the leafy foliage had protected the fruit. Only time would tell if they'd drunk too much.

On route to Vilatán I stopped off at Ramón Otero builder's merchant to buy two wrought iron manhole covers.

What a difference it made having a driveway to park on at *Campo Verde*. Tiptoeing through a sea of mud had never been much fun. The rainfall had transformed the patches of dusty earth into rich dark soil. I couldn't wait to see them carpeted with lush green lawns.

My arrival hadn't gone unnoticed.

'Buenos días.'

I recognised the voice as that of our neighbour, Luis.

'*Hola Luis. ¿Qué tal* (How are you)?' I asked.

'There's a problem,' he replied.

Before I had chance to ask what, he continued.

'Water is pouring into my *bodega*.'

By inference, he seemed to be laying the blame at my door. I didn't know what to say.

'Look,' he added, pointing at the fall pipe from the gutter.

I hadn't given water much thought until we moved to Spain. Back in the UK I would turn on a tap and hey presto, out it flowed. When I pulled out a plug it drained away; and when I flushed a toilet the waste disappeared, never to be seen again. It wasn't until there was a hosepipe ban or leak that I gave it a second thought.

Here in Spain things are very different. To start with it's much more colourful. We have grey water and black water, spring water and well water. There's water from a borehole or village water, which shouldn't be confused with town water or council water. When it comes to drainage, there are black holes and septic tanks, mains sewerage, and soakaways. From the tone of Luis' protestations, it seemed I'd unintentionally diverted my rainwater into his *bodega*.

'What can I do?' I asked.

'The water from your roof is seeping into my *bodega*,' he replied.

Identifying a problem isn't the same as suggesting a solution.

The offending drainpipe discharged rainwater from the roof into my soakaway which is bordered on one side by Luis' house. What I hadn't taken into account was the porosity of Luis' foundations.

'What if I connect another pipe to the outlet and divert the water into the far corner?' I said, illustrating my proposal with a sweeping arm movement.

Luis seemed almost disappointed that I'd suggested a solution. Spaniards much prefer a bit of argy-bargy in their negotiations.

'I'll sort it out first thing on Monday,' I added.

Proposing a timetable really took the wind out of his sails.

'OK,' he replied, before trudging off home.

The rest of the morning was mine. I mixed some cement and built two manholes roughly forty centimetres deep and topped with the wrought iron covers. When I got home, Melanie had finished her ironing and prepared lunch.

'How did it go?' she asked.

'Building the manholes was a doddle.'

'But?'

I told her about Luis' visit.

Lunch in the sunshine is one of the many things I love about living in Spain. I can't ever remember salads tasting that good in England.

After lunch I retired to the office on the pretext of checking my emails. Melanie relaxed in the afternoon sunshine with her nose in a book. My search for a cheap route to England began in earnest. I started by checking the fixture list. It's important to get the priorities right. One match caught my eye: Huddersfield Town against Leicester City on the 4th of October.

Leicester City were odds on favourite to win the league. Their recent and rapid demise from the Premier League meant there'd be a good crowd and an electric atmosphere. This match would be one of the highlights of the season. All I had to do now was find some flights.

Cheap air tickets meant one thing, Ryanair. It's the discount airline everyone loves to hate. Without too much effort I found a flight departing on Thursday the 2nd and returning on Tuesday the 7th. The price of the outbound flight was a ridiculously low £9.99. Don't ask me how they do it but the return flight was free. The challenge was to match these low-cost airfares with cheap transfers.

On previous trips to the UK our biggest expense had been the car hire. I checked the daily rates from all the main hire companies but for a five-day rental there was nothing for less than £100. That's when I stumbled across a Friday to Monday, weekend special from Enterprise Rent-A-Car for just £29. The price was tempting but left us with one problem: how to get to and from the airport. The outbound flight time didn't help.

The plane was scheduled to depart from Santiago de Compostela at 21:22. Taking into account the one-hour time difference between Spain and the UK and the two hours and twenty minutes' flying time, the aircraft would touch down in Liverpool at 22:42. The challenge was to get from Liverpool to Huddersfield at that time of night.

My first thought was the railway but the last train from Liverpool departed at 22:35. The good news was that it took over an hour to reach Manchester, calling at every station en route before continuing on to Huddersfield and arriving at 00:15. If I could find a cheap way to get from Liverpool John Lennon Airport to Manchester Piccadilly station in under an hour, we were in business.

Hailing a taxi was out of the question as that would cost far too much. The only other option was a bus. I checked online and found a company called Terravision. They operate airport bus services worldwide and their fares were incredibly low. For just £2.60 per person we could catch the 22:55 from Liverpool Airport and arrive in Manchester bus station thirty-four minutes later. According to Google Maps, the walk from the bus station to the railway station would take seven minutes. That would give us four minutes to find the platform and board the train to Huddersfield. Talk about cutting it fine.

Excluding the airport run to Santiago and the five-day car parking fee, the total cost for both of us was under eighty pounds. It was time to don my salesman's cap and pitch my proposal to Melanie.

'I've been thinking,' I said, as I strolled outside.

'Oh yes.'

'Yes.'

'And what have you been thinking?'

'How would you like to go back to the UK for a few days to see your granny?'

'When?'

'I've found some cheap flights from the 2nd until the 7th of October. What do you think?'

'What days are those?'

'Thursday until Tuesday.'

'I see. Who's playing?'

'What do you mean?'

'Who are Town playing?'

She knew me too well.

'Leicester City. They're favourites to win the league.'

'So, besides the football, why Thursday to Tuesday?'

I unveiled my cunning plan for a cut price getaway.

'Liverpool to Manchester sounds to be cutting it fine,' she commented.

'I know, but look on the bright side, Ryanair flights always land early.'

I'd suspected for some time that Ryanair overstate their flight times in order to boast about their good timekeeping.

'So exactly how much is this cheap getaway going to cost?'

'Including the flights and car hire, just under eighty pounds.'

'Each?'

'No, for both of us.'

Any doubts quickly fizzled out.

'And who's going to look after Jazz?'

'I thought we could ask Roy and Maria.'

Roy and Maria love looking after her. Whenever we meet them the first thing they ask is, 'When are you going away again?'

'But what about *vendimia* (the grape harvest)?' asked Melanie.

'The grapes will have to wait until we get back.'

This was too cheap an opportunity to miss.

'You'd better get it booked then.'

I didn't need telling twice.

That afternoon we relaxed in the garden. Melanie read while I gave the battered grapevines my undivided attention. The humidity had dipped but the summer temperatures were blistering. By early evening my body was crying out for a dip in the pool. The warmer the body the more refreshing the water. It took a while to get used to it but after a few minutes I felt fantastic.

'Are you coming in?' I called to Melanie.

'Is it warm?'

Last night's rainfall had made a noticeable difference to the temperature.

'It's not bad.'

Melanie looked unconvinced.

'Come on,' I encouraged her.

In an effort to show willing she marked the page in her book and wandered over to the shallow end. She steadied herself and dipped her toe into the water.

'It's freezing,' she moaned, whipping it out.

'It's not that bad once you're in.'

'I think I'll give it a miss,' she replied.

It took me a little over half an hour to complete my daily challenge of 160 lengths.

'Is it time for a Teatime Taster?' I asked, having dried myself and dressed.

'I don't see why not.'

That evening we sat on the front terrace watching the sun set behind the woody knoll. Only then did we retire to the back garden.

'I'm just going to give Mark a ring and see if he can get me a ticket for the match,' I said, before disappearing inside.

Mark is a good friend and Huddersfield Town season ticket holder.

'What did he say?' asked Melanie when I returned.

'No problem. He'll get it the week before.'

Sorted.

August was drawing to a close and workers throughout Spain would soon be returning from their month-long break. There were a number of jobs still to do at *Campo Verde* but the only ones we couldn't do ourselves were pave the driveway, set up the garden sprinkler system, and install the driveway lighting and doorbell.

'Will you ring Alfonso, Ramón, and Félix this morning?' I asked, as I readied to leave.

'What for?'

'To find out when they can start work.'

Alfonso had the driveway to pave, Ramón the sprinklers to set up, and Félix the lighting and the doorbell to install.

'OK.'

When I returned home at lunchtime Melanie had spoken to them all.

'Alfonso said the paving for the driveway should be delivered later this week and he'll make a start next Monday.'

That was great news. Tying Alfonso down was no mean feat. It didn't guarantee he'd show up but it was a good starting point.

'What about Ramón?'

'He's busy at the moment but he'll ring us next Monday with a start date.'

Not exactly what I'd hoped for but at least he knew we wanted him.

'And Félix?'

'He's working away but should be back this weekend. He said he'd ring.'

Over the years we'd learnt to manage our expectations. Getting things done at the first time of asking is the exception not the rule. Patience is key.

As a stonemason Alfonso is one of the best but when it comes to timekeeping he's like a broken wristwatch: unreliable. On Monday morning I arrived early at *Campo Verde*. Time drifted by so I gave him a ring.

'The stone has been delivered,' he said. 'It's on a patch of waste ground just outside the village.'

'I didn't see it on my way in.'

'Not your village, mine.'

'Yours?'

'There's too much of it.'

Alfonso's answer didn't make any sense. Perhaps I'd misunderstood him. Questioning his reasoning served no purpose. We'd trusted his judgement so far and there was no reason to doubt him now. He'd already saved us a small fortune by recommending we buy the paving material from a supplier in Portugal.

'What time do you expect to get here?' I asked.

The line fell silent.

'Hello,' I called.

'I can't move it until Thursday or possibly Friday.'

Alfonso's admission was disappointing but not altogether unexpected.

'Are you sure you can start this Thursday?'

'Or Friday.'

I knew which day my money was on.

When I arrived home for lunch, I gave Melanie the news. She had some of her own.

'Ramón rang.'

'Oh yes, what did he say?'

'He's got flu and won't be able to start work for two weeks.'

'Two weeks?'

'That's what he said.'

I know from experience it takes time to get over a bout of flu but stating an exact recovery time sounded rather suspicious.

'Félix rang as well.'

I'd just about had enough disappointment for one day.

'What did he have to say?'

'He's back home and he'll meet us at the house tomorrow evening at 8:30 pm.'

At last, a piece of good news.

6

That Rings a Bell

It's uncanny how straightforward tasks have a tendency to be the most troublesome.

We'd arranged to meet Félix at *Campo Verde* at 8:30 pm. The late hour was a result of his work commitments. Félix is an employee and as such has to schedule the work he does for us around his day job. We were happy to wait. He'd done a great job wiring the house, at a fantastic price.

'*Hola*,' he chimed.

Félix has a cheeky smile and a glass-half-full approach to life.

'*Buenas tardes*,' I replied.

Unlike the English, Spaniards don't really do evenings. It's either *buenas tardes* or *buenas noches* (good night), with the latter beginning after dark. During the summer months that's well after 10:00 pm.

To help speed things up, Félix had brought his friend Carlos. Without delay they got down to business. Their job tonight was to install a doorbell. If time allowed, they would make a start on connecting the power supply to the three lights running down the driveway. The conduit for both installations had been laid prior to the drive being concreted.

To feed cables through conduit, electricians use a nifty tool called a fish tape. It's made from a long length of spring steel that's as rigid as it is pliable. Think of a bodkin with a length of wire attached to it. The fish tape is fed into one end of an electrical conduit and pushed through, usually from one wall socket to the next. Once the fish tape appears at the other end, an electrical wire is secured to it and it's pulled back through the conduit. Simple but efficient. Félix delegated that job to Carlos while he mounted the doorbell inside the house.

'Where do you want it?' he asked.

'Upstairs in the dining room, if that's OK?'

'No problem.'

The three of us marched upstairs.

'What about there?' he said, pointing at the wall outside the kitchen.

'Perfect.'

Melanie and I kept busy while Félix and Carlos cracked on. Within half an hour Félix had mounted the bell on the wall and run a cable into the fuse box in the downstairs lobby. From there he fed another cable outside. In contrast, Carlos was struggling.

'What's the matter?' I asked.

Félix and Carlos were deep in conversation.

'The fish tape keeps getting stuck,' replied Carlos.

'Why?'

As soon as I'd asked I realised how stupid it sounded. The conduit was sitting below six inches of reinforced concrete. How on earth were they supposed to know why it kept getting stuck!

'I'm not sure. Forty metres is a long way to feed a fish tape. There could be a blockage or it might have been crushed when the concrete was poured,' replied Félix.

Nightmare visions of digging up the driveway flashed through my mind.

'What can we do?' I asked.

'We'll have to keep trying and see what happens.'

After a fruitless hour of pushing and pulling, twisting and turning, they called it a day.

'What's the problem?' I asked.

'This fish tape is not strong enough. I have a better one at home. We'll come back tomorrow and try again.'

Our disappointment was clear to see.

'Don't worry,' he added, doing his best to reassure us.

On the drive home, Melanie asked what I'd been unwilling to consider.

'What are we going to do if they can't get it through?'

'I don't know but we're not digging up the driveway.'

Abandoning the installation would require a major rethink. The system we were using at *Casa Bon Vista* required guests to collect the house keys from a secret location on the day of their arrival and let themselves in. The following morning, Melanie and I would nip up to the house, welcome them properly, and answer any questions they might have. We'd hoped to continue this practice when we started letting *Campo Verde*. Yelling at guests from the end of the driveway was hardly the image we were trying to portray.

The following evening Félix and Carlos arrived as promised.

'This is much stronger,' said Félix, waving his heavy-duty fish tape in the air.

To my untrained eye it looked exactly the same but I smiled and nodded my acknowledgement.

Félix handed the tape to Carlos who dropped to his knees and began pushing it into the conduit. The contrast to yesterday's efforts was amazing. I turned to Melanie and smiled. As time passed progress slowed. The further the fish tape advanced, the less leverage Carlos could apply.

All of a sudden, the forward motion stopped.

'Félix,' called Carlos.

He was feeding another fish tape through the lighting conduit on the opposite side of the driveway.

'¿*Qué* (What)?'

'It's stuck.'

Félix left what he was doing and came to investigate.

'Let me have a go,' he replied.

Melanie and I looked on, helpless. Hope now rested with Félix succeeding where Carlos had failed.

Using a combination of gentle persuasion and brute force he finally managed to push it past the offending obstacle. We breathed a sigh of relief. He handed it back to Carlos and inch by strenuous inch it disappeared down the conduit. The time had ticked around to 10:10 pm and the light was fading fast.

On the opposite side of the driveway, Félix was having problems of his own.

'How long is this conduit?' he asked.

The three lights were equally spaced along the length of the driveway.

'About ten metres each section,' I replied.

'There's definitely a blockage on this one,' he said.

'*Joder por fin*!' called Carlos.

The three of us turned and stared at him.

Roughly translated, Carlos was expressing his delight at forcing the fish tape forty metres through the three-centimetre diameter conduit. I'll leave the literal translation to your imagination.

Félix dropped what he was doing, picked up a spool of electrical cable and skipped down the driveway. Within minutes he'd secured the cable to the end of the fish tape.

'OK,' he called to Carlos, 'but be careful.'

Carlos pulled gently on the fish tape while Félix fed the cable into the conduit. Melanie and I held our breath. If the wire became detached, they'd have to start all over again. What had taken Carlos two days to push one way took less than five minutes to pull the other. I looked at the time: 10:34 pm. We'd all had enough for one day.

'We'll finish off at the weekend,' said Félix.

He wouldn't hear any complaints from us.

'What time?' I asked.

'After lunch on Saturday. Let's say 3:30 pm.'

We agreed and all went our separate ways.

As expected, Thursday came and went without so much as a phone call from Alfonso. On Friday morning we drove to *Campo Verde*, more in hope than expectation. Imagine our surprise when, within half an hour of our arrival, Alfonso turned up. He arrived in style, towing a trailer-load of granite behind his white Lamborghini. That's the four-wheel drive tractor version as opposed to a thoroughbred supercar.

'*Buenos días*,' he beamed.

'*Hola*,' we replied.

With great skill he reversed this heavy load down the narrow lane and into the driveway in one seamless manoeuvre.

'Where can I tip it?' he asked.

'Anywhere except over there,' I replied, pointing at the soakaway.

'What about here?'

'That's fine.'

Alfonso had chosen a spot adjacent to the driveway. This was the first time we'd seen the granite paving and the size of the pieces took us by surprise. Some of the slabs were as big as a snooker table. Not as regular but enormous nonetheless. The pieces we'd ordered were a by-product of the mining process.

Granite quarries often resemble amphitheatres with giant steps carved into the hillside. Large, regular-shaped blocks are extracted using a method of drilling and leverage. It's not uncommon for excavated blocks to be the size of a double garage. Once removed they're transported to the sawmill where the rough edges are removed. These uneven edges were what we'd bought. Placed rough side down, the result was a perfectly smooth surface for a fraction of the cost of regular paving slabs.

Alfonso's flatbed trailer had been retrofitted with a hydraulic ram, enabling him to tip the contents. Watching snooker-table-sized slabs of granite, some of which weighed more than a tonne, sliding off the back of a trailer was quite a sight. Breakages were inevitable, indeed desirable.

Three more loads filled the bottom end of the garden.

'We'll make a start on Monday,' said Alfonso.

'Is that all of it?' I asked.

Alfonso smiled.

'No. There'll be between ten and twelve loads altogether but we'll have to use this before we bring any more.'

Alfonso had made it clear that he'd finished for the day but at least he'd made a start. I for one was confident he'd be back on Monday morning.

'OK, *hasta lunes* (See you Monday),' I replied.

'*Hasta lunes*,' he repeated.

On Saturday afternoon Félix and Carlos arrived at *Campo Verde* as promised. Within minutes of their arrival the sound of *ding dong, ding dong*, echoed through the house. One job done and one to go. Félix tried again to feed the fish tape through the lighting conduit but without success.

'We're going to have to dig it up and find out what the problem is,' he said.

As luck would have it, the lighting conduit had been something of an afterthought and ran adjacent to the garden wall rather than under the driveway. Digging it up wasn't my preferred choice as it had taken us weeks to prepare the ground for seeding, but there was no alternative. We had to find the blockage. Reluctantly I agreed.

'OK, go ahead.'

Carlos started hacking at the ground with a mattock. Melanie and I looked on. Within minutes he'd found the culprit.

'There,' said Carlos, pointing at a break in the black plastic conduit.

No wonder they were having problems. A large rock had fallen onto the fragile tube and sliced through it. By the time they'd repaired it, the pair were ready for off.

'We'll come back on Monday evening and finish off,' said Félix.

We thanked them for their efforts and arranged to meet again on Monday evening at 8:30 pm.

By mid-September the stifling humidity of summer had waned. Mornings were cooler but temperatures rose quickly to create hot, sunny days and comfortably warm evenings that were perfect for al fresco dining. Autumn was just around the corner but we were determined to enjoy the fine weather for as long as possible.

Conscious of having a long day ahead but confident Alfonso would turn up for work as promised, we eased ourselves into the day. By the time we arrived at *Campo Verde* the clock had ticked around to 10:00 am. Alfonso had solicited the help of two others. The three men were mapping out the level of the new paving using a long aluminium straight-edge and some small pieces of granite. They reminded me of Inuksuit, the piles of stones balanced one on top of another built by the Inuit people.

'*Hola*,' I said, as we walked past them and into the house.

They all reciprocated in their individual way.

By the time we headed home for lunch, they'd finished the prep. On their return, the paving could begin.

Melanie and I spent the afternoon relaxing at home in the sunshine. Lazy days had been few and far between over the last few months. By 6:30 pm we were back at *Campo Verde* to check on progress.

It hadn't crossed my mind how they would move the heavy granite slabs into position. The last thing I expected them to use was a baling spike. Under normal circumstance these medieval looking metal spikes are mounted onto a tractor and used to lance round hay bales. Alfonso had slipped heavy-duty polyester straps around the slabs of granite, hooked them over the baling spike and used the hydraulics on his Lamborghini to lift them. This ingenious system seemed to be working fine although I couldn't help wondering what a health and safety official might make of it. Once the slabs had been lowered into position, Alfonso coaxed them in place using a heavy metal rod and brute force.

'What do you think?' he asked.

'It looks great.'

At 7:00 pm Alfonso and his team packed up and headed home. Félix and Carlos wouldn't be here for another hour and a half.

'Would you like to go for a drink and tapas?' I asked.

'That sounds like a great idea.'

The town of Escairón is exactly four kilometres from the house. We headed for one of our favourite bars, Sala Avenida. They serve the most delicious *patatas bravas* and their portion sizes would put an English chippy to shame.

'One white wine, one red, and two *patatas bravas*,' was my order.

Refraining from the use of please and thank you takes discipline. Mother's mantra of "What do you say?" echoes to this day but many locals find the habitual use of such pleasantries unnecessary and insincere. Instead of *gracias* (thank you), I've taken to responding with *muy bien* (very good). It's a compromise that satisfies everyone, although I'm not sure Mother would agree.

By the time we'd taken a seat the waiter had filled our order.

'*Salud* (Cheers),' I said, raising my glass.

Melanie reciprocated and we chinked them together. Five minutes later the barman returned with two small plates piled high with deep fried, cubed potatoes lavished with mayonnaise and *salsa brava*, a spicy version of thousand island dressing. We managed to stretch our refreshment to half an hour but I defy anyone to make a plate of *patatas bravas* last longer than a few minutes.

'Let's have another drink,' suggested Melanie.

'And tapas?'

'Why not?'

'What would you like?'

'Erm … I think I'll have a plate of *patatas bravas*,' she replied with a grin.

'I think I'll join you.'

By the time we'd finished our second wine the clock had ticked around to 8:15 pm.

'We'd better make a move,' suggested Melanie.

I settled the bill and off we went.

We hadn't been waiting long when Félix and Carlos pulled into the driveway. An hour and a half later, Félix flicked the switch and the driveway lights burst into life.

'I'll drop the bill off when I get a minute,' said Félix, as he and Carlos prepared to leave.

Their departure brought the curtain down on two jobs we were delighted to see the back of. Work that should have taken an evening had ended up taking four.

On nights like these the gas barbecue comes into its own. Within fifteen minutes of getting home, we were tucking in to chargrilled chicken breasts and a tasty salad.

'Let's take the day off tomorrow and do some shopping,' I suggested over dinner.

'That sounds like a good idea.'

We'd had a long day and deserved a break. Besides which, working in the gardens while Alfonso was there was nigh on impossible. We could have continued on the interior but finding somewhere to park was proving difficult. The narrow lanes of Vilatán weren't designed for motor vehicles, let alone parking.

Our shopping list of household essentials was dwindling but we had plenty of items still to buy. Before turning in, I took Jazz out for her evening constitutional.

'Come on lass,' I said.

She leapt to her feet, dashed to the French doors, and pressed her nose against the glass. As soon as I opened it, she stepped outside and stopped. Something had spooked her.

'What's matter, lass?'

I squinted into the darkness, searching for signs of life. The glint of two eyes stared back at me from the bottom of the garden. A cat had dared to enter.

When it comes to furry felines, Jazz is as happy in their company as she is with dogs. If only the sentiment was shared. What excites her the most is not the subject of her attention but the speed with which it moves. Whether it's a dog or cat, her reaction is the same. If it runs, she chases. As soon as the cat made a dash for safety, Jazz sprinted after it. With lightning reflexes the cat leapt onto the wall and slipped through the railings before Jazz had got within five metres.

'Good girl, come on now,' I called.

Jazz was in no state to listen to me. She paced back and forth along the boundary wall, tail in the air and nose to the ground, consumed with the desire to identify her quarry.

'Come on then lass.'

The creaking gate caught her attention and she abandoned her search in favour of a night-time stroll. Duty performed, we returned home.

'What was all that fuss about?' asked Melanie.

'There was a cat in the garden but Jazz saw it off.'

A leisurely start to the day was a pleasant change. We made full use of the bright, sunny morning and enjoyed breakfast on the back terrace.

'I thought we could go to Eroski in Lalín,' I suggested.

The town of Lalín is about an hour from home. A large *centro comercial* (shopping centre) had recently opened. The centrepiece of this retail emporium was a huge supermarket. We had a much better chance of sourcing household electricals there than in Monforte. The trip proved worthwhile. We bought two free-standing electric fans, a portable radio and CD player, a hairdryer, lemon zester, serving tray, corkscrew, and a dinner service.

On the way home we dropped everything off at *Campo Verde*. Alfonso and his lads were busy when we arrived. Progress had been slow but they'd completed enough to give us a true impression of how it would look. We couldn't have been happier. Finishing the exterior to such a high standard could only help attract rental customers.

By the time we got home there was ample time for a dip in the pool before a Teatime Taster. The water temperature had been dropping since the electrical storm in August. Every day it took that bit longer to sink my frame into the cool blue water. Melanie hadn't been in since before the storm and it wouldn't be long before I conceded defeat.

Before dinner I decided to take Jazz for a short walk. As soon as I mentioned the w-word her ears pricked up and she dashed to the door. For the second consecutive evening, she stepped outside and froze. Sitting under the fir tree in the far corner of the garden was the same black cat we'd seen yesterday. It wasn't a kitten but it was young.

'Catssssss,' I hissed.

Jazz needed little encouragement and set off in pursuit. The cat turned and clambered up the wall. In its haste to escape it had turned directly into a section topped with wire fencing. By now, Jazz was closing in and my anxiety level rose. Not for the safety of the tiny cat but for Jazz. Cornered cats and sharp claws can do all manner of mischief.

'Jazz, come here,' I shouted, but my command fell on deaf ears.

Thankfully the cat was more resourceful than I'd given it credit for. Before Jazz had time to introduce herself, it had bounced down off the fence and recoiled at right angles through the railings it had escaped through last night.

There's quite a number of cats in the village but they rarely stray far from their home and seldom return after a race with Jazz. I couldn't help thinking this little creature had been abandoned.

'That cat was in the garden again,' I said on our return.

Melanie hadn't heard the kerfuffle.

'That's unusual.'

'I know. It's a lovely little thing, quite young though.'

'Well we're not having a cat.'

I couldn't have agreed more. I don't particularly like cats although they seem to take a shine to me. Owning a dog is more than enough responsibility and besides which, cats don't travel as well as dogs.

'Don't worry,' I replied, 'Jazz saw it off.'

7

As Black as Snow

Melanie and I can turn our hands to most jobs but sewing is not one of them. When it comes to needlecraft our combined talents can best be described as hopeless. Melanie blames her mother; she's left-handed and Melanie isn't. My only excuse is to say I'm a bloke of a certain age who was schooled in woodwork not needlework. It's perhaps not surprising then that the only things missing from finishing off our homely interior were curtains.

With renewed urgency, we headed for the city of Ourense, determined to acquire our missing furnishings. To put this challenge into perspective, finding ready-made curtains in Galicia is akin to tracking down a snow leopard in the Altai mountains of southern Siberia.

'What do you think to this?' I asked.

'It's a teapot,' replied Melanie.

'I know it's a teapot but what do you think?'

I held it out at arm's length.

'I thought we were looking for curtains.'

'We are.'

'Well that's a teapot.'

'I know but do you like it?'

'It's OK, for a teapot.'

'I like it.'

'Why do we want a teapot?'

'I thought we might have a cup of tea for our Teatime Taster.'

'Tea!'

From time to time I have some off-the-wall ideas but this was out there with the fairies. Teatime Tasters are reserved for sipping the fruits of the vine, not tea.

'I thought we could try that Chinese breakfast tea.'

The tea in question was a souvenir from our trip to Shanghai.

'At teatime?'

'Why not?'

'There's a reason it's called breakfast tea.'

'I don't think it really matters. Anyway, what do you think to the pot?'

'Actually, it's quite pretty. OK, let's get it, the change will do us good. You do know you'll need a strainer with that, don't you?'

'Of course.'

The thought hadn't crossed my mind but I wasn't going to admit it. While I searched for a tea strainer Melanie stumbled across some curtains.

'What do you think to these?' she asked.

'They're curtains.'

'Ha, ha, very funny. That is why we're here.'

'Let's have a look.'

Melanie handed me the package.

'They're OK, I suppose.'

'I know what you mean but they are the right length.'

'In that case, they're perfect.'

Beggars can't be choosers.

Jazz greeted our return with her usual excitement, wagging her tail as if her life depended on it.

'Right then, I think it's tea time, don't you?' I asked.

'That would be lovely darling, thank you.'

The implication was that I should make it.

'I don't know anything about making tea,' I replied.

'Well don't look at me. This was your idea.'

My brilliant plan hadn't stretched to the mechanics of brewing up. I'm a coffee man; always have been. As a nipper, water was my beverage of choice. I must have been fifteen before I had my first cup of tea. That experience made a lasting impression.

At the time I was working as a Saturday lad for the Co-operative Retail Society. We'd had to stay late for stocktaking. Halfway through the count we stopped for a break. The drink on offer was tea. To refuse would have marked me out as a child amongst men or, in this particular instance, women. The pale brown liquid resembled the colour of dishwater and didn't taste much better. Since then, the only tea I've made has involved pouring hot water over a teabag and scooping it out with a spoon. That said, how difficult could it be?

'There you go,' said Melanie, handing me the teapot.

'What am I supposed to do with this?'

'It might be a good idea to wash it out.'

'But it's brand new.'

'Exactly, and we don't know where it's been before we picked it up.'

She had a point. While I rinsed out the teapot Melanie searched in the cupboard for the tea leaves.

'Here you go.'

'What do I do now?'

'I don't know, aren't there any instructions?'

The tea was packaged in a presentation caddy made from rigid cardboard. I slit the seal and opened the box. As I lifted the lid a tightly folded leaflet fell onto the worktop.

'Aha, instructions.'

Carefully I unfolded the paper. Chinese on one side, English on the other. The instructions were clear. Boil water, tip some into the teapot, and rinse. Allow the remaining water to cool for two minutes. Add one teaspoon of tea leaves per person per cup to the pot. Pour the settled water over the tea leaves and brew for three minutes.

'Take a seat outside and I'll bring it out,' I said.

I followed the instructions to the letter, placed two cups and saucers on a serving tray, and carried everything outside.

Melanie was relaxing in a garden chair facing the setting sun.

'Here we go,' I said, placing the tray on the table.

We sat quietly, staring towards the setting sun. I checked my watch and, after three minutes, poured. The flavour of the tea invoked wonderful memories of our days in Shanghai and the tea tasting ceremony we'd participated in at the Jade Buddha Temple.

'We must do this again.'

My off-the-wall idea had gained Melanie's seal of approval.

'Drink tea or visit China?' I quipped.

'Both.'

The setting sun signalled a move from the far end of the garden to the back porch.

'I'll take Jazz out before dinner,' I said.

Melanie followed me into the kitchen to make a start.

'Come on lass.'

Jazz ran into the kitchen and dashed to the French doors. For the third evening in a row she stepped outside and stopped. The cat was back.

'Catsssssssss,' I hissed.

Jazz set off after her quarry like a racing greyhound but our fearless feline had had enough. She stood her ground, arched her back, and pointed her tail skyward. Her claws extended and her coat looked like an electric current had passed through it. Striking a gladiatorial pose, she signalled her intent by raising a paw and hissing her disapproval. Jazz was no match for this heavily armed beast. She skidded to a halt, turned tail, and ran.

'Well you're not much of a guard dog, are you?' I joked.

Jazz looked disappointed. It seemed her playmate hadn't read the script.

On our return I told Melanie of the encounter.

'So where is it now?' she asked.

'At the bottom of the garden.'

'Well that's not very good, is it Jazz?'

Poor Jazz, she was getting it from all sides. She tilted her head, widened her big brown eyes, and dropped her ears.

'Aw Jazz, it's not your fault is it lass? All you wanted to do was play,' I said in her defence.

Melanie put the finishing touches to a salad and I fired up the barbecue. As usual, dinner was a great success.

'I don't believe it.'

'What?' asked Melanie.

'Look.'

I pointed towards the corner of the house. Our furry friend had poked its head around the corner and was staring straight at us.

'Shoo!' called Melanie.

If a charging hound hadn't scared it away, Melanie's half-hearted cry was unlikely to intimidate it.

'Shoo! Shoo!'

Her repeated rebuffs had the opposite effect. Undeterred, the young cat crept closer. Jazz looked on, watching its every move. She'd learnt her lesson.

'Just ignore it and it might go away,' I suggested.

Within minutes it was weaving in and out of my feet, leaning its cheeks into my ankles and wrapping its tail around my legs.

'Aw, look at it,' I said.

'Do you think we should feed her?' asked Melanie.

In the space of five minutes Melanie had gone from shooing it away to suggesting we feed it. As cute as it was, if we weren't careful we'd end up adopting it.

'We are not having a cat,' I replied.

'I know but she looks hungry.'

'If we feed it, we'll never get rid of it.'

Not that we'd had much success to date.

'But she looks hungry.'

'Cats can look after themselves.'

As if to prove me wrong, it leapt onto my lap and I felt compelled to stroke it.

'Look who's talking,' said Melanie.

'We are not feeding it.'

'Well what are we going to do with her?'

The bundle of fluff had curled into a ball and was purring relentlessly.

'I don't know.'

'If we take her down into the village she'll only come back.'

'Perhaps we ought to relocate it on our way to the airport,' I suggested.

In a couple of days we'd be driving to Santiago de Compostela for our trip to England.

'We can't do that.'

I was joking but couldn't resist teasing.

'Why not?'

'That would be cruel. I know what we can do.'

'What?'

'Let's ask Roy and Maria if they want her.'

After Roy and Maria's dogs passed away they had decided not to get another but it was clear from their affection for Jazz that they missed not having one around. Perhaps this little kitty could fill the gap.

'That's a great idea. Let's give it a name,' I said.

'A name, why?'

'It's psychological.'

'Psychological?'

'Yes. It's like in a hostage negotiation.'

'What are you rabbiting on about?'

'During hostage negotiations you should always refer to the captive by their name. It makes them seem like a real person rather than an object.'

'We're trying to rehome her not ransom her,' replied Melanie.

'It's the same principle. I know what we can call it.'

'What?'

'Seefor.'

'Seesaw?'

'No Seefor. C for cat.'

'Tsk! We are not calling her that.'

'OK then, what about Arthur?'

'If you hadn't noticed, she's a girl.'

'So?'

'So she needs a girl's name.'

'But it's black.'

'So?'

'It's as black as coal.'

Melanie looked dumbfounded.

'Coal. NUM.'

'What are you going on about?'

'The National Union of Mineworkers.'

Her expression didn't change.

'Arthur Scargill, leader of the NUM. I think it would be a fitting tribute.'

'We are not calling her Arthur.'

'What then?'

'What about Snowflake?' suggested Melanie.

'Snowflake? It's jet black.'

'Except for that tiny fleck of snow-white fur under her chin,' replied Melanie.

I liked her thinking.

'OK, Snowflake it is.'

'Now can we give her something to eat?'

Jazz looked on as Snowflake tucked into a bowl of dog biscuits soaked in milk.

The following day Melanie phoned Maria under the pretext of asking what time we should bring Jazz on the day we left for England.

'There's something else I wanted to ask you, Maria.'

Melanie paused before continuing.

'Over the last few days we've had a night-time caller to the house. A cute little cat.'

Melanie told the story of our failed attempts to scare it away.

'It's a lovely little thing and if we didn't have Jazz we wouldn't hesitate to give her a home.'

Melanie's equivocation only slightly misrepresented our intentions. She continued.

'We were wondering if you and Roy could give her a home.'

Maria's reply was swift.

'What did she say?' I whispered.

'She said no but she's gone to ask Roy.'

We waited with bated breath.

'Are you sure?' asked Melanie. 'OK, we'll see you on Tuesday just after lunch.'

'What did Roy say?'

'He said no.'

My disappointment was clear to see.

'But Maria told us to bring her anyway, she said she can live outside and catch mice.'

Result!

Alfonso and his crew completed the driveway on the 30th of September, two days before we were due to fly to the UK. Finishing the exterior to such a high standard had stretched our budget to breaking point but it was money well spent. One thing we hadn't considered was the

Craig Briggs

thickness of the paving. The finished driveway was fifteen centimetres higher than the ground around it. Our earlier efforts to level the garden had been in vain.

'We're going to need some more soil,' I said.

'Not again! It'll take us weeks to level that.'

Melanie was right. A dozen trailer loads of dirt wasn't going to resolve this deficit. There had to be another way.

'What about the bloke who delivered our soil?'

'José Digger?'

'That's the man.'

José Digger (not his real name) had been recommended to us by Felipe, the architect who designed *El Sueño*. He'd supplied fourteen tonnes of earth to level our garden.

'I'm sure I've got his number somewhere,' said Melanie, scrolling through her phone contacts. 'Here it is.'

'Give him a call.'

Melanie got through to him at the first attempt. He agreed to come and take a look. The following day he arrived just before lunchtime.

'One lorry-load should do it, possibly two,' he said.

'When can you deliver?'

'*Quince días, mas o menos* (A fortnight, more or less).'

It wouldn't be Spain without the more or less.

'I'll call you beforehand,' he added.

That evening we went through the usual pick and mix packing routine associated with weight-restricted air travel.

'Have you got any room in your case?' asked Melanie as she lugged her carry-on off the bathroom scales for the second time.

'I've got plenty of room but I'm almost up to my weight limit.'

Ten kilogrammes sounds a lot until you discover your empty case weighs almost four.

'Can you put these in yours?' she asked, handing me a pair of winter boots.

I slipped them inside, zipped up the case and lifted it onto the scales: 9.9 kilos. I couldn't help wondering how accurate they were.

'If I get stopped, you're going to have to wear these boots.'

'Don't worry, it'll be fine.'

That was easy for her to say.

The flight from Santiago de Compostela to Liverpool was scheduled to depart at 21:20. At lunchtime we drove to Roy and Maria's to drop off Jazz and Snowflake. The only flaw in our rehoming plan was the proximity of their house to ours. Cats have a reputation for finding their way home. They've been known to trek thousands of miles and Roy and Maria lived less than twelve kilometres away. I couldn't shake the thought of returning home to find Snowflake curled up under the front porch.

'Here she is,' said Melanie, handing her to Maria.

'Aww she's lovely.'

'She's really affectionate and loving.'

'And she's no bother at all,' I added.

Roy grinned. Our sales pitch hadn't gone unnoticed. We said goodbye and headed home for a late lunch before setting off to the airport. As usual, we chose to leave our departure until the last minute.

I'm not a fan of air travel. I find the whole experience most unpleasant. Passengers are herded around like cattle and shoved from pillar to post. We'd booked an off-site parking company who ferried us to the airport and would pick us up on our return. By the time we joined the queue for passport control there was less than an hour until take-off. The queue was short and free flowing. Five minutes after joining it we were given the all-clear and sent on our way.

'Last call for Ryanair passengers flying on flight FR2835 to Liverpool John Lennon Airport. Please proceed to gate twelve immediately,' echoed through the departure lounge.

I glanced at my watch: 8:30 pm.

'Why do Ryanair flights always depart from the gate furthest away from the terminal?' moaned Melanie.

'You get what you pay for.'

When we arrived at the boarding gate the inbound flight hadn't yet landed. Last call indeed.

'I knew it,' said Melanie, staring out of the window at an empty parking bay.

Half an hour later the aircraft landed and the passengers disembarked. Within minutes, two members of the cabin crew appeared at the boarding gate desk. Passengers jostled for position, each wanting to be first to board. Melanie and I have a more relaxed approach to boarding. We had our tickets and were happy to wait for the mêlée to subside.

Once on board the full extent of the mayhem was there for all to see. The central aisle was a battleground. Passengers were wrestling their oversized and overweight carry-ons into the overhead lockers. I slipped my case into the first available space and then helped Melanie with hers.

The plane touched down in Liverpool ten minutes earlier than scheduled. By the time we'd fought our way off, the clock had ticked around to 22:46. Time was of the essence.

'This way,' I said, pointing at the exit marked "EU citizen".

Walking through Customs provokes the same emotions as being followed by a police car. You know you've done nothing wrong but feel guilty nonetheless. The harder you try to look innocent the guiltier you feel. Pace is key: too fast and you might attract someone's attention; too slow and you've definitely got something to hide.

'Look straight ahead and pretend you're innocent,' I said.

'We are innocent,' replied Melanie.

Despite never having been stopped, it's always a relief to reach the arrivals hall unchallenged. We stared at the information board and searched for bus departures.

'There,' said Melanie, pointing at the sign.

I glanced at my watch: 22:50.

'We've got five minutes,' I said, as we raced through the exit.

Outside on the pavement we paused to get our bearings. The chill of an October evening stung my cheeks but at least it wasn't raining.

'It's this way,' said Melanie, dragging her carry-on across the road.

I chased after her.

'That's it over there,' I said.

A single decker bus with the logo Terravision emblazoned along its length was waiting to depart. We dashed up to the door which opened with a familiar whoosh of piston-driven hydraulics. Clumsily we boarded. I showed the driver our tickets. A handful of passengers were scattered randomly throughout the bus. We took a seat close to the entrance.

'Made it,' I sighed, as I slumped into the seat.

I checked the time: 22:56. We'd boarded with two minutes to spare.

Next stop Manchester Bus Terminal, a thirty-four-minute ride that would leave us fifteen minutes to walk the five hundred metres to Manchester Piccadilly Railway Station, find the platform, and board the train. Everything was going to plan.

We arrived in Manchester exactly as scheduled.

'This way,' I said.

Before leaving home, I'd checked and double checked the route. There was no margin for error. All we could do now was walk as quickly as possible. Pausing to check the time was not an option. The street outside the railway station was quieter than I'd expected.

'Over there,' said Melanie, tipping her head.

This was our first visit to the station. We entered and paused, searching for an information board.

'There it is,' I said, grabbing the handle of my carry-on and rushing towards it.

Manchester to Huddersfield departing from platform three at 23:47 … Cancelled.

'You've got to be kidding. Cancelled!' said Melanie.

What were we going to do now?

The 23:47 was the last train to Huddersfield. The next service didn't leave Manchester until 05:30.

'Surely they can't just cancel the last train without providing an alternative,' I replied.

'Over there.'

Melanie was pointing at the information desk. Wearily we walked across in the hope of finding a solution.

'Essential maintenance. We've laid on a service bus. It departs at 00:30 from outside the station,' said the staff member.

'Out there?' I asked, pointing towards the main entrance.

'That's right.'

'At half past midnight?'

'Yes.'

His casual attitude fell far short of an apology.

'The station cafeteria is closed but there's a café around the corner,' he added.

His remark was a polite way of telling us to sling our hook.

'Thanks,' I replied, with a hint of sarcasm, and off we sloped.

On the pavement outside, I checked the time.

'Let's grab a coffee and a bite to eat. We've got forty minutes to kill.'

An illuminated sign guided us to a greasy spoon eatery. The glass frontage was misted with condensation and droplets of water dribbled down the inside of the window. I pushed open the door and we stepped inside. Warm, fatty aromas greeted our arrival. The place was busy with night-time revellers taking a break. Some were clearly the worse for wear.

'What do you want?' I asked Melanie, who was reading the menu hanging above the serving counter.

'I don't know, what are you having?'

I studied the board.

'The all-day full English breakfast looks value for money.'

'It's nearly midnight.'

'I'm starving.'

'In that case I'll have a cheeseburger.'

'And to drink?'

'Fanta orange.'

I approached the counter.

'Yes?' asked the assistant.

Her accent sounded Eastern European. I gave her our order. It seemed ironic that this much maligned section of British society were the very people helping travellers in need.

'Anything to drink?' she asked.

'Fanta orange and coffee with milk.'

She served our drinks and told us to take a seat. Melanie sent a message to her mum. Her reply cut to the chase, 'The key is under the doormat. Let yourselves in and I'll see you tomorrow.' Minutes later our order was called.

'One burger and one full English.'

'I guess that means come and get it,' I whispered to Melanie.

Neither dish was the best we'd ever had but it filled a gap and killed some time.

'Come on, let's go. We don't want to miss the bus.'

The bus arrived precisely on time. What the rail employee had failed to tell us was that it stopped at every town and village between Manchester and Huddersfield. What was scheduled as a fifty-minute train journey became a two-hour bus ride. By the time we reached St. George's Square, Huddersfield, the clock had ticked around to 2:30 am and we were completely fed up and absolutely knackered. To make matters worse, there wasn't a single cab at the taxi rank.

'Come on, we'll have to get a mini-cab.'

Wearily, we dragged our carry-ons across the square to the mini-cab office on the corner. We flung ourselves at the mercy of the Pakistani-owned cab company, another minority group providing an indispensable service. Within fifteen minutes we were rummaging around in the dark searching for the door key.

A journey which would usually take about six hours had taken over nine. We left our luggage in the kitchen, climbed the stairs, and collapsed into bed.

The things we do to support our team.

8

Time Waits for No Man

Living in the Spanish countryside is nothing if not peaceful. The Canabal rush hour starts at 9:00 am when Toño drives past the house to check the status of the council sewerage plant and ends at 9:30 am when he returns home for his breakfast. That first morning at Melanie's mum's couldn't have been more different. I'd been awake for hours listening to the noise of traffic rumbling past the house.

'Are you awake?' whispered Melanie.

'I've been awake for ages. What time is it?'

'Eight-thirty. Would you like a coffee?'

'Yes please.'

Five minutes later she returned carrying two steaming mugs.

'Mum's gone,' she said.

'Gone where?'

'To work. She left a note on the kitchen table. We're to help ourselves to breakfast.'

'I thought we might nip up to the village butcher's for a pork pie.'

'You did, did you?'

Half an hour later we were washed, dressed, and ready for off.

'We'd better take Rusty,' said Melanie.

Rusty is Jennifer's Cairn Terrier. He's a vicious little bugger who'd bite you as soon as look at you. The last time we'd taken him to the village, we tied him up outside a shop and while we were inside the rascal had slipped his collar and done a runner. The idiom once bitten twice shy sprang to mind.

'I'll wait here with him,' I said, as we stood outside the butcher's.

'OK. How many shall I get?'

'Get half a dozen. We can eat one on the way home.'

The pies were delicious: crisp pastry, roughly minced pork generously seasoned with pepper, and a succulent jelly filling.

At 11:00 am there was a knock at the door. We'd arranged a home pickup to collect the hire car. When we arrived at the rental office they were waiting for the vehicle we'd booked to be returned by the previous user.

'It should have been back by now,' insisted the manager.

He glared at the wall clock to emphasise his frustration.

'Have you got anything else?' I asked.

We'd booked the cheapest super-mini but the last thing we wanted to do was waste time hanging around the office.

'Only the car we picked you up in but that's more expensive.'

The vehicle in question was a very nice Chevrolet Captiva, a large and luxurious SUV. I glanced at Melanie to get her approval. A nod was all I needed.

'How much more?' I asked.

The manager tapped on the computer.

'I can do you that one for another four quid a day.'

'What do you think?' I whispered to Melanie.

'Let's go for it.'

Ten minutes later we were heading out on the open road or, more accurately, the congested road.

'What are we going to have for lunch?' I asked.

'What about fish and chips?'

'That's a great idea.'

'Let's take a drive out to Compo's Café,' suggested Melanie.

Compo's Café is a fish and chips restaurant situated seven miles outside Huddersfield in the village of Holmfirth. It's named after a character from the hit TV series *Last of the Summer Wine* which was filmed in the area. Having lived most of my life in Huddersfield it seemed ironic that my first visit to Compo's would be as a tourist. Not so Melanie who had eaten there many times with her granny, a former resident of Holmfirth.

Half an hour later we were pulling into the carpark. I felt even more like a tourist when we stepped inside. With the exception of two young mothers with preschool infants the rest of the patrons were pensioners. Hardly surprising given that most people our age would be at work on a Friday lunchtime. Compo's fish and chips were everything I'd hoped for: crisp, light batter, succulent cod, and proper chips.

This self-indulgent feeding frenzy continued into the evening with an Indian feast from a local takeaway. By midnight, Melanie and I conceded defeat and turned in.

A bacon butty for breakfast set us up for the day ahead. *Football Focus* on the BBC whetted my appetite for the afternoon's match. Melanie dropped me outside the ground and I met Mark as arranged. The new all seater stadium was great. Before kick-off we enjoyed a pint of John Smith's bitter from one of the on-site food and drink kiosks housed in wide corridors below the stands.

I always feel a sense of anticipation when I climb the concrete steps onto the terraces. Grey clouds gave way to a theatre of dreams as we stared out across the bright green turf to the opposite side of the stadium. Today's opponents, Leicester City, were currently top of the league. The size of the crowd reflected the enormity of the challenge. Over sixteen thousand fans waited impatiently for the appearance of their respective teams: not a bad crowd for the third tier of English football. In contrast to their opponents, Town started the day 15th in the table having won just two of their first eight games, drawing three and losing three.

'How are they playing?' I asked Mark, as results don't always reflect performances.

'They're rubbish,' he replied. 'This new manager hasn't got a clue.'

Mark's not one for mincing his words.

Last season, following a run of bad results, the board had dispensed with the services of the manager, Andie Richie, with six fixtures still to play. Academy boss Gerry Murphy stepped in and steadied the ship until the end of the season. The start of the new season saw Stan Ternent appointed as manager.

'What's the problem?'

'Ternent's brought in Dickinson on loan and all they do is hoof the ball upfield and hope he gets on the end of it.'

For his sins, Mark has been a season ticket holder for as long as I can remember. If anyone was entitled to moan about the team's style of play it was him.

From the first whistle Town were on the back foot, outplayed and outperformed in every department. Despite this, they went in at halftime with the score at 0–0.

'I see what you mean,' I said, as we queued to get a pint during the interval.

My affinity for Huddersfield Town AFC began at the tender age of six when Dad first took me. Through good times and bad I've stood on the terraces and cheered them on but this was the worst forty-five minutes of football I'd ever seen.

Five minutes after the restart Leicester took a deserved lead. Ten minutes later they extended it to 2–0. What followed brightened up what had been a very dull afternoon. On sixty-nine minutes Gary Roberts grabbed one back for Town. All of a sudden, the atmosphere inside the Galpharm Stadium changed. Supporters, who minutes earlier had been moaning about every wayward pass and missed tackle, were now cheering them on. On seventy-seven minutes Town's pressure paid dividends and the much-maligned Dickinson drew us level at 2–2.

Levelling the score initiated an immediate response from the away side. Town were now under the cosh. Wave after wave of attacks rained into the home side's box. The anxiety in the crowd was palpable. Could the lads hang on for a famous comeback?

With five minutes of regular time to play, whistles rang out from every section of the home crowd urging the referee to blow his. On ninety minutes the fourth official held up a board announcing four minutes of extra time to a crescendo of disapproval from the home fans. With three minutes left to play, Lloyd Dyer pounced on a loose ball and fired the away side into the lead. The players had given their best but come up short. If truth be told, Leicester City were worthy winners.

I spent Sunday afternoon at an altogether different football match. Mark had invited me to watch his son play. We met at his house and headed off into the Yorkshire Moors. A sloping, windswept field was quite a contrast to yesterday's facilities. Unfortunately, the result was the same: a resounding win for the away side. While I battled the weather and listened to partisan parents hurling abuse at the referee, Melanie visited her granny.

That evening our gastronomic festival continued with a doner kebab from the takeaway around the corner. Their high fat content is the stuff of legends which is probably why they taste so good.

Before we knew it, the long weekend was over. Melanie visited her granny for one last time after which we returned the hire car. Our last supper was another portion of fish and chips. A fitting end to a hectic five-day trip. Thank heavens airlines only weigh luggage.

Whining traffic nudged us into a new day. It was surprising how quickly we'd adjusted to our new environment. After a leisurely breakfast we packed our bags.

'This isn't going to fit,' said Melanie.

That was strange; everything had fitted on the way here.

'What have you been buying?'

'Nothing, Mum gave me this fleece but it won't fit.'

'If you want it, wear it.'

Problem solved.

The trip home was the reverse of the journey here. Train from Huddersfield to Manchester, bus from Manchester to Liverpool, and the flight from Liverpool to Santiago de Compostela. Mel's mum would drop us at the railway station and the carparking company would collect us from the airport. What could go wrong?

The timings of each transfer had pretty much picked themselves with the exception of the train from Huddersfield. The service ran hourly at a quarter to the hour. The flight from Liverpool departed at 18:50 which gave us two options: catch the 14:45 and arrive two hours early or take the 15:45 and have just over an hour to wait.

'What do you think?' I'd asked Melanie.

'Perhaps we ought to catch the earlier train.'

'Are you sure? We don't have to check in our luggage and we'll already have our boarding passes.'

After a short deliberation we'd opted for the later train.

A tearful farewell signalled our departure from Huddersfield Station. The rolling stock on the Cross Pennine route could have come out of a museum. It was noisy, drafty, and uncomfortable. Despite this we arrived at Manchester Piccadilly Station on time. The station clock read 16:35.

'It's this way,' I said, as we stepped outside.

It's remarkable how different a place looks in the daylight. The pavement was much busier than on our arrival.

Buses to Liverpool Airport were scheduled to depart every half hour and the next one was due at 17:00. We found the bus stop with fifteen minutes to spare and joined a short queue.

'Are you waiting for the bus to Liverpool Airport?' I asked a young man.

It couldn't harm to make sure.

'That's right,' he replied.

Everything was going to plan.

Buses came and went but the one to the airport was conspicuous by its absence. I checked my watch, 17:08.

'The bus is late,' I said to Melanie.

'It's probably the traffic at this time of day.'

Five minutes later, I checked it again.

'What time is it now?' asked Melanie.

'Twelve, no, thirteen minutes past.'

By twenty past I started weighing up our options. Only one sprang to mind: hailing a taxi. The thought of having to pay for a thirty-five minute cab ride shocked us into waiting. I stared down the street, willing the bus to appear. Each passing minute felt like five. The 17:00 service must have been cancelled. If the 17:30 didn't arrive we'd have to bite the bullet and get a taxi.

'At last,' sighed Melanie.

I'd been distracted by a group of school kids opposite. I glanced down the road. Our ride had arrived. The time read 17:32. We'd allowed thirty-four minutes for the journey. With a bit of luck, we would get to the airport at 18:10 which would give us forty minutes to pass through security, find the departure gate, and board the aircraft. Tight but achievable.

What we hadn't taken into account was the Manchester rush hour. As soon as the bus moved away from the bus stop the traffic was nose to tail. For the next half an hour it nudged its way through the congested city streets. Melanie looked anxious but neither of us said a word. Eventually the traffic congestion eased.

What followed next can only be described as unbelievable. Completely out of the blue, the driver pulled into a petrol station and started filling up. To make matters worse he filled it to the brim. I'd never seen anything like it. By the time we pulled out onto the main road, what once seemed possible now looked highly unlikely.

Within sight of the airport I manoeuvred my carry-on into the aisle.

'Get ready to move. If you can't keep up shout, otherwise we don't stop for anything,' I said.

By the time the bus had come to a stop and the door hissed open, the time had moved on to 18:35. The plane was scheduled to take off in fifteen minutes.

From the moment we left the bus we didn't stop moving. With five minutes until take-off we reached the boarding gate. Gasping for breath, I handed our boarding passes to a staff member.

'Where are you flying to?' she asked.

'Santiago de Compostela,' I replied, holding out my hand to encourage her to return them.

'One minute please.'

We didn't have a minute. What was going on?

Melanie looked at me with tears in her eyes. The crew member was mumbling to someone on the phone.

'I'm sorry sir, but last call was announced some time ago and the aircraft is preparing for take-off.'

The plane was in its parking bay. We could see it through the window.

'It's there. Can't you let us on?' I asked.

'I'm sorry sir but the aircraft doors have been sealed.'

She made it sound more like a sarcophagus than an aeroplane.

'But it's just there,' protested Melanie.

When it comes to airline operators, resistance is futile.

'I'm sorry but there's nothing I can do.'

Melanie looked ready to explode.

'Come on love,' I said, turning to walk away.

'But what are we going to do now?'

Her rage had turned to despair.

'Don't worry,' I said, trying to reassure her.

Melanie's emotions contrasted sharply with my pragmatism. When reason fails, we can neither dictate nor alter the actions of others; all we can do is react to them. The aircraft hadn't yet taken off but it soon would do and when it did, we wouldn't be on board. No amount of protestation would change that. We'd used our best endeavours to arrive on time but had failed. All we could do was find an alternative.

We'd been cutting it fine for years. Our luck had finally run out. If nothing else we'd learnt an invaluable lesson. Never ever rely on public transport to get you anywhere in a timely manner.

'Let's find the Ryanair information desk and see what they can suggest,' I said.

We trudged back to the departures hall, found the Ryanair desk, and explained our dilemma. The staff's response can best be described as prickly. Their body language was dismissive and unhelpful. Melanie said nothing but I sensed her mounting frustration. Any moment now, someone was going to feel the full force of her pent-up emotions. Just as I sensed she was about to let rip, I stepped in.

'OK, thank you for your help.' I turned and walked away. 'Come on, love.'

Melanie's rage drained from her cheeks.

'Anyone would think it was our fault the bus was late,' she said.

'Over there,' I said, pointing at one of the airport's free to use public computer terminals.

'That woman was so rude, I could have …'

'I know, love.'

'What are we going to do now?'

'Let's check the availability online.'

At least this way we wouldn't have to listen to the sarcastic overtones of a Ryanair jobsworth. The cost of last-minute tickets was extortionate: over three hundred pounds each if we wanted to fly the following day. The day after that, Thursday, they were slightly less.

'What do you think?' I asked.

'Bang goes our cheap getaway.'

We looked at each other and burst out laughing; if we hadn't, we would have cried. What had started out as a short and inexpensive break had turned into an expensive fiasco. There were cheaper flights but that would have meant staying longer in the UK and a longer stay would inevitably have meant more expense. Entering my credit card details over a public network was not my preferred option but we had little choice.

'Done,' I announced.

'So how are we going to get back to Mum's?'

'Well we're not catching a chuffing bus. Come on.'

The car hire offices were at the far end of the terminal. We walked straight over to the Enterprise Car Hire desk and explained the situation. In contrast to the Ryanair staff, the young man at Enterprise couldn't have been more understanding. He even gave us a discount without me having to ask. The company's motto is "UK car hire with US customer service". It's a claim they can be proud of.

Six hours after leaving Melanie's mum's we turned up on her doorstep. Melanie had phoned ahead so our arrival came as no surprise. That evening we rang Roy and Maria to explain.

'Don't worry, stay as long as you like. Jazz is no bother at all,' said Maria.

This short extension gave Melanie another opportunity to visit her granny who, unlike her previous visit, was awake and able to chat. That alone justified the additional expense. The following day we securely locked the stable door and left Huddersfield with more than enough time to get to the airport. A trouble-free journey home had come at quite a cost.

9

Sowing the Seeds of Success

Waking up in our own bed felt quite strange. The silence was bliss but something was amiss. It's often said that you don't know what you've got until it's gone. That was definitely true this morning. A wet nose and a wagging tail are a great way to start the day. Mornings aren't the same without a four-legged friend to greet you.

'Right then, let's get cracking,' I said.

'What's the hurry?'

'We've got to collect Jazz from Roy and Maria's and I want to get the grapes harvested this afternoon.'

'Are we making the wine today?'

If we hadn't been to England, we would have picked them by now.

'It shouldn't take us long,' I replied.

Within ten minutes of leaving home we were pulling up outside Roy and Maria's farmhouse. I rang the outside bell and pushed open the gate. No sooner had we entered the courtyard than the back door opened and Jazz came sprinting down the steps. She was delighted to see us.

'Come in,' called Roy.

Jazz led the way and Melanie and I followed. We walked through the hall and into the large, open plan lounge.

'Sit down,' said Maria. 'Coffee?'

It would have been rude not to.

'Yes please.'

When Maria walked off Melanie nudged my leg.

'What?' I mouthed.

'Look,' she whispered, tipping her head towards the corner of the room.

Maria's would-be outdoor mouse catcher was snuggled up asleep in a brand-new cat bed. There was a new scratching post and a lovingly crafted playhouse in the opposite corner of the room. Any doubts that Snowflake might one day find her way back to *El Sueño* were instantly forgotten. Moments later Maria returned.

'Remind me again, Maria, is this the same cat that was going to live outside and catch mice?' joked Melanie.

'That's Roy's fault,' she replied.

Roy said nothing but his sly wink said it all.

We sipped our coffees and recounted the story of our missed flight. In the space of two days a personal trauma had become a farcical tale.

Later that afternoon, Melanie and I began the *vendimia*. I picked the grapes and she crushed them. The final count was 142 kilos. Not our best year but far from being the worst. Once again, we combined the red and white grapes in the same vat. Fermentation would take anywhere from a few days to several weeks depending on the temperature. The weather forecast suggested somewhere in between. I couldn't help thinking that if my winemaking skills were ever going to improve, I would need to expand my knowledge beyond the boundaries of the village.

A weekend of rest and relaxation left us raring to go on Monday morning. The restoration project was nearing an end. All we had to do now was finish the garden. There were two jobs still to do: the gravel bed and seeding the lawns. Before we could seed, we needed to weed.

'What have we got planned for today?' asked Melanie.

'Weeding. We also need to call at the garden centre and the builder's merchant.'

'What for?'

'We need some weed-proof membrane from the garden centre and I want to order two tonnes of gravel from the builder's merchant. Before we set off, can you ring José Digger and find out when he can deliver the soil?'

She scrolled through her contacts and dialled.

'He can bring it this afternoon,' she said.

'That just leaves Ramón,' I replied.

We hadn't heard from the plumber since he had declared a two-week bout of influenza.

'I suppose you want me to give him a ring?' asked Melanie.

'If you wouldn't mind.'

After a short conversation she ended the call.

'He can make a start tomorrow afternoon.'

That was excellent news. Everything was falling into place.

En route to *Campo Verde* we called at the garden centre and Ramón Otero the builder's merchant. The weed-proof membrane fitted easily into the back of the car. The gravel would have to be delivered.

'Can you bring it tomorrow?' I asked.

'Yes, but it'll be in the afternoon.'

'That's OK. Can you make it the first drop after lunch?'

'Sure, no problem.'

Ten minutes later we were trundling through the narrow lanes of Vilatán.

Weeding the stone-free soil was a doddle. By the time we headed home for lunch, the area to the left of the driveway was free of weeds and ready to seed.

The house felt toasty warm on our return. A bowl of soup would keep us going until dinner.

'Right then, we'd better be making a move,' I said.

'But it's only a quarter to two.'

'I know, but if we're not there when the soil is delivered you can bet your bottom dollar José will dump it in the wrong place.'

The thought of shovelling seven tonnes of earth from one end of the garden to the other had Melanie reaching for her coat.

'I told you it was too early. Where is he?' she moaned.

We'd been waiting for almost an hour and hadn't seen sight nor sound of him. I was beginning to think he wouldn't show.

'You'd better give him a ring,' I said.

Melanie rang. Her response didn't bode well.

'What did he say?' I asked.

'He said he'll be here first thing in the morning.'

Situations like this call for deep breaths and a measured response. If only he'd rung earlier, we could have saved ourselves the drive and stayed at home. We didn't want to seem ungrateful, especially as he was supplying the soil for free, but that cut both ways. Disposing of earth and hardcore is quite a problem for Spanish contractors. Finding someone willing to take it for free was a bonus.

The following day he turned up as promised with seven tonnes of freshly excavated earth and dumped it adjacent to the driveway.

'Do you want any more?' he asked, eager to get rid of another load.

Deciding that before levelling this pile would have been a mistake. It's much easier to ask for more than it is to get rid of too much.

'If we need any more, I'll give you a call.'

Within ten minutes of José leaving, Ramón arrived. All we needed now was the builder's merchant to deliver the gravel and we'd have a full house.

Ramón made a start on the top garden digging out the channels for the water pipes. Melanie and I unfolded the weed-proof membrane and laid it out over the soakaway. If the gravel arrived as promised it could be tipped exactly where it was needed.

'Right then, let's get this soil shifted.'

Levelling the earth was much easier than I'd anticipated. An hour after starting we'd finished and not a moment too soon. The sound of a reversing alarm signalled the arrival of the gravel.

'Where do you want it?' asked the driver, having manoeuvred his tipper truck through the narrow entrance and onto the driveway.

'Here,' I said, pointing at the membrane.

The driver climbed back into his cab and reversed up to the edge of the soakaway. Melanie and I stood back as he jumped out and unlatched the rear doors. A lever on the side triggered the hydraulics and the flatbed began to rise. Higher and higher it rose until the two-tonne load reached tipping point and thundered down the flatbed like an express train. The few pieces that remained were jerked free when the driver bunny-hopped his vehicle back from the edge. As he did, the remaining chips scattered across the granite driveway like marbles on a tiled floor.

The gravel was easier to level out than the soil. While all this was going on Ramón had started work on the freshly levelled soil in the lower garden. Things were going so well I couldn't help thinking that something was bound to go wrong.

'What time is it?'

Melanie had noticed me looking at my watch.

'Ten past twelve.'

'What's next?'

'Let's assemble the frame of the gazebo.'

Earlier in the year we'd bought a steel-framed gazebo in an end-of-season sale from BricoKing in Monforte. The label on the packaging read "Made in China". We'd given the display model the once-over and if nothing else it seemed like value for money. The instructions were easy to follow and all the bits were present and correct.

We hadn't long made a start when the unmistakable hiss of water cut through the silence. Ramón was testing the sprinkler system. After a few tweaks he called me over and explained how to set the digital programmer.

'If you have any problems just let me know,' he said.

Before Melanie and I headed home for lunch we finished bolting together the frame. Little by little the project was edging towards completion. The final job, seeding, would have to wait. Bob and Janet were flying out at the weekend to celebrate Bob's 60th birthday and we were tasked with preparing *Casa Bon Vista* for their arrival. It seemed inevitable that a project beset with delays would end that way.

Like us, they too had dreamt of living a new life in Galicia but their dream had quickly turned into a nightmare. Within months of arriving they'd repacked their belongings and moved back to the UK. At the time they were unsure what to do with their Spanish property. To ease their concerns, we'd offered to look after it for them. Rather than leaving it standing empty, we suggested advertising it as a holiday rental property and offered to manage it on their behalf. After due consideration they accepted our offer and three years down the line we'd enjoyed our busiest season to date.

'What are we going to do next year?' asked Melanie, as we drove to *Casa Bon Vista*.

'What do you mean?'

'I mean how are we going to clean two properties at once?'

The question hadn't escaped me but I hadn't yet found a satisfactory solution.

'I'm not sure. We might have to employ some cleaners.'

'Perhaps we could have two different changeover days,' suggested Melanie.

At the moment, the changeover day for *Casa Bon Vista* was Saturday. Departing guests had to leave the property by 10:00 am and new arrivals could enter the house from 2:30 pm onwards. That gave us plenty of time to get the place looking spick and span. Having a different changeover day for each house would give us more flexibility but there were drawbacks.

'We could do, but Meet and Greet might get in the way.'

'Mmm.'

Solving that conundrum could wait for another day as we had work to do. Two and a half hours after arriving the place looked spotless.

Plans for Bob's birthday party had been taking shape for some time. Janet had asked Melanie to make the arrangements and invite the guests. The evening would begin at Mulligan's, an Irish themed bar in Monforte, before moving on to La Maja, a bistro style restaurant, for dinner.

On Saturday evening Melanie and I left home early and called at the restaurant to dress the table with balloons and hang celebratory bunting. By the time we got to Mulligan's all the guests had arrived. The topic of conversation soon got around to *Campo Verde*.

'How's it going?' asked Bob.

'We're nearly there, just the lawns to seed.'

'And what happened with the flight?'

Everyone was keen to hear our tale. Needless to say, sympathy was in short supply.

'OK, enough of the wisecracks. Is anyone hungry?' I asked.

We'd booked the table for 9:00 pm and time was ticking by. Five minutes after leaving Mulligan's we were sitting around the dinner table playing balloon volleyball. As usual the food was excellent and the wine flowed freely.

'Are you alright?' Melanie asked Janet.

All of a sudden, the colour had drained from her face and droplets of sweat were trickling down her brow.

'I don't feel very well.'

Bob looked concerned. They'd been up early to catch the flight and hadn't stopped since. A large meal, copious amounts of wine, and a warm, busy restaurant were taking their toll.

'What's the matter?' asked Bob.

'I'll be alright, I just feel really warm.'

Janet was clearly struggling.

'I think I'll nip outside for a few minutes to cool down,' she added.

Bob took her hand and they walked out together. Five minutes later they returned.

'She's not feeling any better,' said Bob. 'I think she needs to lie down.'

Bill and Di had driven them into town to save Bob from driving so the four of them left together. Their untimely departure halved the numbers. No sooner had they left than the waiter brought a bottle of cava to the table.

'Compliments of the house,' he said.

It seemed a shame to waste it so I proposed a toast. Raising a glass to absent friends didn't seem appropriate so I settled for, 'To Bob, happy birthday'.

'To Bob,' echoed the reply.

After a good night's sleep Janet had fully recovered and the two of them popped in to say thank you for organising the party.

'You're very welcome,' said Melanie.

'I particularly enjoyed the bubbly,' I joked.

Bob looked bemused so I explained.

'Lucky you,' he quipped. 'There's something else we wanted to discuss with you.'

That sounded ominous.

Reaching sixty qualified Bob for his company pension and Janet would soon be eligible for hers. With that in mind they'd quit their part-time jobs and officially retired. In retirement they planned to visit Galicia more often and stay for longer.

'We'd like to make the house more homely and have decided not to rent it out any more. I hope you don't mind?' asked Bob.

Mind? We were delighted. The problems of managing two properties had disappeared. We'd be able to concentrate all our efforts on making *Campo Verde* a success.

'That's fine. To be honest we've been agonising over how to look after two properties,' I confessed.

'Are you sure?' asked Janet.

'Certain,' replied Melanie, 'besides which, it'll be lovely to see more of you.'

Bob and Janet's decision couldn't have come at a more opportune time.

Monday morning was a day for keeping out of the shadows and staying in the sunshine. It wasn't frosty but it was chuffing cold.

'Right then, I'm off,' I announced.

'Will you be late back?'

'I don't think so. It shouldn't take long to seed the lawns.'

Twenty minutes later I arrived in Vilatán. The position of the sun cast a long shadow across the top garden so I made a start on the bottom. After lightly raking the earth I scattered the seeds as evenly as possible. Using the back of the rake I caressed the surface level. By the time I'd finished the bottom garden, the sun had risen above the roofline and the long shadow had all but disappeared. I repeated the process of raking, seeding, and levelling. The watering system would ensure the new seeds got the best possible start.

To be sure everything worked properly, I set the programme running and sat on the garden wall to wait for each zone of sprinklers to complete its twenty-minute cycle. Small rainbows floated on the watery mist and skipped across the garden. Bright sunshine illuminated our beautiful farmhouse and I couldn't help but marvel at our achievement.

Choosing the house had been easy. The first time we clapped eyes on the place we'd fallen in love. Had we known then what we know now, that love affair might never have blossomed.

Hindsight is a wonderful thing but nothing can alter the past. Discovering the house had never been registered started a catalogue of challenges no one could have anticipated. By the time we'd resolved that problem, fourteen months had passed. The next two hurdles were water and electricity. Buying a house without either wasn't the smartest move. Drilling for water had proved problematic but paled into insignificance when compared to acquiring an electricity supply. By the time we'd achieved those goals twenty-seven months had elapsed. The house restoration could finally begin. Hard work and determination carried us through a rollercoaster of emotions. At times we'd hung on for dear life but I wouldn't have missed it for the world. Thirty-nine months of blood, sweat, tears, and laughter had produced a legacy to be proud of and a home that would stand the test of time.

We'd finally achieved our goal of creating quality accommodation for the discerning traveller. All we had to do now was attract those travellers in sufficient numbers to provide an income.

That thought coincided with a loud burp as the pop-up sprinklers finished their cycle and shot into the ground.

'All done,' I announced, when I arrived home. 'All we have to do now is find some punters.'

10

Sister Julie

Two of the most challenging questions when welcoming visitors to *El Sueño* are: where to go and what to do? The same can't be said when my sister visits. She sends an itinerary long before her arrival and woe betide anyone who interferes with it.

Beep! Beep! Beep! Beep!

The sound of the alarm clock shocked us into a new day. My sister Julie and her husband Jeremy were scheduled to touch down in Santiago de Compostela in less than three hours and yours truly was tasked with picking them up.

'It feels cold,' moaned Melanie, as she pulled on her winter dressing gown.

She wasn't kidding.

While Melanie went to put the kettle on, I ventured out of bed and pushed open the window shutters. A thin layer of frost was clinging to the car. Quickly, I closed the window and scampered back under the duvet. Moments later Jazz nudged open the bedroom door and leapt onto the bed. Melanie followed her in carrying two mugs of steaming coffee.

'It's icy outside,' she remarked.

'I noticed.'

Within the hour we were washed, dressed and ready to go. Shards of ice clung to my wrist as I cleared the windscreen using a bank card.

From home we drove through the Val de Lemos and followed the signs to Chantada. As we climbed out of the valley the mist cleared revealing a cloudless, powder-blue sky. From Chantada we headed towards the town of Lalín. The route took us up and over the mountain of Monte Faro. Once through Lalín we joined the AP-53 toll road all the way to Santiago. The airport is situated thirteen kilometres outside the city centre.

We parked in the airport carpark and made our way to the arrivals hall.

'Fancy seeing you here,' said a familiar voice.

We'd been so focused on the information board we hadn't noticed Bob and Janet.

'What are you doing here?' I asked.

'We're waiting for Sue and R'mam (our mum),' said Janet.

'Are they on the Ryanair flight from Stansted?'

'Yes. It landed five minutes ago,' said Bob.

'We're here to pick up my sister and her husband.'

It seemed we were just in time.

Before long, passengers began wandering through the arrivals doors. Julie and Jeremy were amongst the first to appear. As usual, her greeting was very reserved.

'Hiya,' she said.

'Hello. Good flight?'

At that point she noticed Bob and Janet standing next to us.

'Oh hello, I didn't expect to see you.'

Julie's tone lacked assurance. Was her itinerary under threat?

The devil in me wanted to tell her they'd be joining us for the day but I couldn't bring myself to say it.

'They're here to pick up Janet's sister Sue, and their mum. We'd like to wait for them and say hello, if that's OK?' I added.

'That's fine,' said Julie, clearly relieved that her plans weren't about to be gate-crashed.

It wasn't long before Sue and R'mam walked through the doors dragging their luggage. In stark contrast to Julie's greeting, Sue flung her arms around Melanie, hugged her tightly, and kissed her on both cheeks before doing exactly the same to me. Her mum was equally as warm and sincere. I sensed the irony wasn't lost on Julie.

'Right then, we'll be off,' I said. Julie was becoming restless.

'I'm sure we'll see you during our stay. We're here for a week,' said Sue.

'We look forward to it,' replied Melanie.

As soon as we exited the airport, Julie's plan kicked into action. First stop was the pilgrimage city of Santiago de Compostela.

The drive from the airport to the historic centre took less than ten minutes. The cathedral of Santiago de Compostela is the second most visited tourist attraction in Spain after the Alhambra Palace in Granada. A fact made all the more astounding by the availability of parking within a few minutes' walk of the cathedral.

From the carpark on Avenida de Xoán XXIII we strolled along Rúa de San Francisco towards the Praza do Obradoiro, site of the iconic cathedral. The Rúa has restricted access to traffic but it pays to stay alert. Lining one side of the Rúa are a number of confectionery shops selling the world-famous Tarta de Santiago (an almond flavoured cake with citric overtones of oranges and lemons) and others selling the less well-known Pedras de Santiago (toasted almond pieces coated in milk or plain chocolate). The latter is Julie's favourite and one of the reasons we were here. To encourage shoppers to buy, confectioners offer samples to passers-by.

'I'll buy some on our way back to the car,' said Julie.

'Where are you going?' I asked.

'To sample some. Are you coming?'

'I am not.'

Some people have more cheek than a baboon's backside.

After tasting everything on offer at every establishment en route, we continued on to the next destination on Julie's tourist checklist, the Hostal dos Reis Católicos.

Built in 1499, it was designed to accommodate pilgrims who had completed the Camino de Santiago (Way of St. James). Today it's part of the prestigious Parador Hotel group and is internationally recognised as the oldest continuously operated hotel in the world. On a sunny day, the ground floor cafeteria is the perfect venue from which to view the façade of the cathedral and enjoy a glass of regional wine or a cup of freshly brewed coffee.

We took a seat on the terrace and watched as travel-weary pilgrims hobbled into the square.

'Let's look around the cathedral,' suggested Julie.

'OK.'

'I'll get these,' said Jeremy, whipping the tab off the table.

He wouldn't hear any complaints from me.

On our way out, Julie spotted a poster advertising a lunchtime special. A three-course meal for two people including bread and a beverage for thirty euros.

'Look at this,' she said.

Fifteen euros per head was more than we were used to paying but it seemed like excellent value for lunch at one of the most prestigious hotels in Spain.

'Not bad,' I remarked.

We walked out of the hotel and across the square to the steps of the cathedral. We mingled with pilgrims, some of whom had walked over eight hundred kilometres to climb the steps; we'd strolled less than eight hundred metres.

Legend has it that the remains of Saint James, or Santiago as he's called in Spanish, are housed there. The apostle is credited with bringing Christianity to the Iberian Peninsula before returning to Jerusalem to be beheaded in 44 AD. Some time later his remains were brought back to Galicia where they lay undiscovered for almost five hundred years. Through accident or design, his tomb was rediscovered around 814 AD and quickly became a site of pilgrimage. Thousands of Christians flooded into the area at exactly the same time as the Islamic Moors were being forcibly evicted from the region; how convenient.

Whatever your religious persuasion, the construction and adornment of this Catholic temple stands as a testament to the ingenuity and imagination of mankind and is definitely worth a visit.

We'd entered through the front door or Pórtico de la Gloria and departed at the rear through Puerta de las Platerías, bypassing the gift shop on the way out. I wonder what Christ would have made of that?

The Puerta de las Platerías leads into the Plaza de la Quintana. A street busker was playing haunting tunes on an electric guitar. He was standing outside a row of cafés and eateries. The clock had ticked around to lunchtime so we browsed the menu of each one, searching for a suitable venue.

'What do you think?' I asked.

I knew what Julie would say.

'Let's go back to the Parador,' she replied.

We all agreed and wandered back to the hotel. The signs to the restaurant took us through an opulent lounge. Oil paintings were hanging on the walls and the thick carpet pile felt like marshmallows underfoot. Stylishly dressed guests relaxed in sumptuous armchairs. Some were reading the daily news and others chatted quietly. From there we descended a flight of stairs into a narrow corridor. The restaurant was on the right. A smoked glass door hinted at what lay beyond. Julie pushed it open and we followed her inside. The dining room occupied an elegant and luxurious hall. Stone arches supported a vaulted ceiling. All the tables were set. Starched white tablecloths formed the perfect canvas for the precisely placed silver-plated cutlery and large wine glasses sparkled under the artificial lighting. The only things missing from this high-class eatery were customers and staff. Given our attire I couldn't help thinking we were somewhat underdressed for our surroundings.

'Do you think it's closed?' whispered Julie.

How were we supposed to know? I shrugged my shoulders.

We were just about to leave when an immaculately dressed waiter appeared as if by magic.

'How many are you?' he asked.

I felt like asking him to guess but thought better of it.

'Four,' I replied.

'This way,' he said, leading us to a table in the centre of the room.

While we made ourselves comfortable, he fetched the menus. He handed them out, ladies first, and placed the wine menu on the table between Jeremy and me. I opened the leather-bound cover to find an à la carte offering. By the time I'd flicked through the pages the waiter had returned.

'What would you like to drink?' he asked.

I glanced at Julie who had come to the same conclusion as me.

'Is there a special lunchtime menu?' she asked.

'The thirty-euro menu?'

'Yes.'

'That's in the cafeteria along the hall.'

We giggled nervously, unhooked our coats from the chair backs, and left. Talk about embarrassment. Out in the hall our chuckles turned into laughter.

The meal in the cafeteria was edible but disappointing. As for the surroundings, the less said about them the better. On our way out we checked the advert. Hidden in the small print was the word "cafeteria". Perhaps one day we'll return, suitably dressed and with enough cash to dine in style.

The following day's itinerary included a trip to Chaves in Portugal. We parked close to the *torre* and wandered around the old town to build up an appetite before lunch at the Jing Huà Chinese restaurant.

'Let's go somewhere else for coffee,' I suggested, after we'd eaten.

The food at the Jing Huà is always delicious. Their coffee, however, is not.

'Where to?'

Julie just had to know.

'It's a castle that's been converted into a hotel. It's not far.'

She liked the sound of that.

We settled the bill and drove through the town centre to a public carpark on Rua Pedisqueira. Directly opposite are the impressive castle walls of the Forte de São Francisco Hotel. Two cannons stand guard over an arched entrance which leads into the gardens beyond. Autumn leaves had created a golden carpet over the cobbled pathway leading to the hotel reception.

'This looks very nice,' remarked Julie.

The building dates back to the 16th century and was originally a Franciscan convent. During the Portuguese War of Restoration (1640–1668) the convent was converted into a fortress to defend the town from Spanish invasion. Today the fifteen thousand square metre site is a luxury hotel.

Melanie and I led the way. The interior retains many original features; however, the bar area has a contemporary feel. We took a seat overlooking the gardens and ordered coffee. Service was swift and the coffee was excellent.

Before heading home we stopped at E. Leclerc, the main supermarket in Chaves, to stock up on wine and port. Julie couldn't resist making a few purchases. Melanie and I said nothing.

Despite having a big lunch Julie insisted on going out for dinner to La Maja, her favourite pizzeria in Monforte de Lemos. As usual the food was first class.

'When can we look at the house?' asked Julie over dinner.

'We can go tomorrow afternoon if you like?'

'Can't we go in the morning?'

Whether intentional or not, Julie's egoism can be quite annoying at times.

'I'd prefer it if we went in the afternoon.'

Tomorrow's weather forecast promised bright sunshine. Ideal conditions for snapping a few promotional photos of the exterior.

'Why?' she asked.

'I want to take some photos of the outside for the website and the sun doesn't reach the front until after lunch,' I replied.

Begrudgingly she agreed.

For once the weather predictions proved correct. A misty start quickly gave way to bright sunshine. After lunch we drove to Vilatán. Melanie showed them around while I took some snaps. When I'd finished, I went inside.

'What do you think?' I asked.

'It's lovely,' said Julie.

Her comment was reassuring. If she hadn't liked it, she would have said. Jeremy, who's an architect by profession, was far more interested in the materials we'd used and the method of construction.

'All the walls are original, so too these roof joists,' I explained.

To emphasise the point, I reached up and knocked on one of the large chestnut beams.

'Other than that, it's basically a new build,' I added.

Jeremy thought the builder had done a great job and couldn't believe how little it had cost. Prices in central London are considerably higher than central Galicia.

That evening Julie asked to return to her favourite pizzeria for their final dinner in Galicia and we were happy to oblige.

The next day they readied to leave. Melanie and I prepared ourselves for the inevitable disappointment.

'Chuff me!' said Julie, as she burst into the lounge.

'What's the matter?' I asked.

'I'm not going to be able to take my chuffing port home.'

Melanie bit her lip as I innocently asked, 'Why?'

'You're only allowed one hundred millilitres of liquid on the flight.'

'Oh dear. Don't worry, we'll look after it for you.'

'Did you know?'

'It must have slipped my mind.'

My reply had Melanie laughing out loud.

'I can see you're really upset. Here you go then, enjoy,' said Julie, holding out a bottle of port and a red wine from the Douro.

'Thanks.'

Saying goodbye at the airport felt as awkward as saying hello. Julie stood on the pavement at the drop-off point while Jeremy and I lifted the luggage out of the back of the car. She kept her distance and waved. Jeremy and I shook hands.

'Have a safe flight,' I said.

'And give us a call when you get home,' added Melanie.

On that note we jumped back in the car and drove off.

The roads around Santiago de Compostela are excellent and the traffic was free-flowing. Before long we'd joined the AP-53 heading towards Ourense.

'Are we going to organise an Office Party this year?' asked Melanie.

Last year Melanie and I organised a Christmas party for a group of friends. We christened the event the Office Party. It was a throwback to the days when I used to organise a festive party for my staff. The event had been a great success. We'd spent the night in Chaves and had a banquet at the Chinese.

'I don't see why not,' I replied.

'We ought to do something different this year.'

'Like what?'

'I don't know.'

'What about renting a *casa rural* and ordering an Indian takeaway?' I suggested.

A *casa rural* is a privately owned holiday let. More often than not they're situated in the beautiful Galician countryside. Most are old properties that have been lovingly restored.

'Takeaway?'

Takeaway food brings back memories of a knock on the door and fumbling around in the dark for the correct change.

'I used the term loosely,' I admitted.

In reality it meant pre-ordering the food and collecting it at lunchtime to be reheated later in the day.

'More like click and collect than a takeaway,' quipped Melanie.

'You've got it. What do you think?'

'I think it's a great idea.'

'In that case, will you have a phone around when we get home?'

A few calls later and the usual suspects had been rounded up, seven in total. Party games were suggested for entertainment and one of the group volunteered herself and her husband to cook a full English for breakfast. This was shaping up to be a great event.

Having confirmed the numbers, I began my search for a suitable venue. The nearest Indian restaurant is in the city of Vigo, 140 kilometres from home. A house close to that would be preferable and a party of seven would require a minimum of four bedrooms. One property caught my eye, *Casa Aranza* in the province of Pontevedra. The photos of the house showed a tastefully restored, four-bedroom farmhouse twenty kilometres from the centre of Vigo.

'Come and look at this and tell me what you think,' I said to Melanie.

She studied the photos and read the description.

'It looks perfect.'

I checked the online calendar for availability.

'How does Monday the 15th sound?' I asked.

'When do we go to the Costa del Sol?'

'You're asking me?'

'Well you booked it.'

'I can't remember things like that. Isn't it in the diary?'

Melanie went to check.

Our diary is actually a calendar fixed to the kitchen wall. The butcher at Carnicería Real in Monforte de Lemos gives one to his customers in the run-up to Christmas.

'The 15th is fine,' she confirmed.

'When do we head south?' I asked.

'On the 22nd.'

Things couldn't have worked out better.

Since harvesting the grapes, daily temperatures had been colder than predicted. As a result, the fermentation process had taken longer than I'd expected. Twenty days after crushing them the grumbling grapes fell silent, signalling an end to the primary fermentation.

'I'm going to clean the wine this morning,' I said, as we sat up in bed sipping our morning coffee.

'Will you need my help?'

'I might do at some point. I'll give you a shout if I do.'

Cleaning or racking the wine is my least favourite part of the winemaking process. The system I've developed is rudimentary to say the least. It involves scooping the solids out of the vat using a small frying pan and filtering them through a muslin sieve into buckets. After cleaning the vat, the wine is poured back in. On cold, damp days the work is soul-destroying, made all the worse by the fact that to date, none of my wine has been very good. Nevertheless, my goal remained the same, to one day produce wine I'd be happy to pay for.

Three hours after starting, and with a little help from Melanie, I sealed the vat. For better or worse Mother Nature would do the rest.

The next morning Melanie received a devastating phone call. Her mum rang with news that her granny was gravely ill. It wasn't unexpected as she'd been in poor health for some time but even so, it shocked her to the core.

Melanie has always been very close to her granny. When her parents separated their relationship became even stronger. To take her mind off things I suggested a drive into the countryside.

'Would you like to go to A Rúa?' I asked, after lunch.

Jazz pricked up her ears.

'It looks like someone would,' she remarked.

Throughout autumn and winter the reservoir at A Rúa is one of our favourite dog walking locations. It's known to some as the oasis of the river Sil. During the 1950s, under Franco's dictatorship, the government began a series of ambitious civil engineering projects to create hydroelectric dams in Galicia. One such scheme created a manmade lake in the town of A Rúa, seventy kilometres east of Canabal. The oasis has become a magnet for migrating birds and a wide variety of flora and fauna has developed on the wide floodplain.

Daily temperatures had been dropping slowly since the beginning of October. By November the mercury rarely reached double figures. On a clear day the wintry sunshine made it feel much warmer but out of the sunlight the air had quite a bite.

As usual Jazz leapt into the back of the car and curled into a ball. Hats, coats, and gloves went onto the back seat. The drive took us along one of my favourite stretches of road: the *carretera nacional* N-120. Less than an hour after leaving home we were pulling up on the edge of the reservoir. Jazz knew exactly where we were and whined with excitement.

'Just wait,' said Melanie, as she lifted the tailgate.

Jazz was having none of it. She leapt out and ran to the water's edge. A wide promenade, lined with wrought iron railings, runs along the northern edge of the reservoir. Jazz was pacing back and forth searching for a way to get nearer to the water.

'Come on,' I called, as we made our way eastwards along the prom.

Plane trees line both sides of the walkway. Careful pruning has created a weblike sculpture of interlocking branches. In spring and summer, new foliage provides a shady canopy. The end of the walkway marks the start of the floodplain. Halfway between the two is a slipway where small boats are launched during the busy summer months. Jazz ran ahead, searching for the incline. By the time we'd caught up with her she was paddling in the shallows and whining with nervous energy, desperate to venture further into the water but terrified to do so. I teased her by throwing sticks that landed tantalisingly close but far enough away to be out of her depth.

'What is he doing to you?' said Melanie.

'Go on, fetch it,' I replied, encouraging her to swim.

We knew she could. On the few occasions she'd unwittingly found herself doing the doggy paddle she even seemed to enjoy it.

We watched her paddling for a while before walking on.

'Come on,' I called.

Reluctantly she followed.

At the end of the promenade we entered a wooded area where the local council have built a number of granite picnic tables and benches, and some stone barbecues. Needless to say, it would be some time before they were used again. An hour and a half after arriving, we made our way back to the car and headed home.

Within ten minutes of getting back the phone rang. Melanie answered it. Her face said it all. At 5:33 pm on Sunday the 9th of November, aged 95, Melanie's granny, Kathleen Delbridge, had passed away peacefully.

11

Open for Business

For the third time in three years we were hurriedly making plans to fly to England for a family funeral.

'I've found a flight. It departs on Sunday the 16th and returns a week later,' I said.

The funeral had been arranged for Monday the 17th.

'Where from?'

'Santiago to Stansted. Do you want me to book it?'

Given the short notice, availability was limited and prices were high.

'How will we get to Huddersfield?'

'We'll have to hire a car.'

'You'd better book them both.'

The travel arrangements ran smoothly and the funeral went as well as could be expected. Tears were shed and the eulogy shone a light on a different era.

As a young woman, Kathleen had worked in service. Following the outbreak of World War II, she married

Donald who she had outlived by twenty-four years. Life had been a struggle for Kathleen and her legacy resides not in wealth and possessions but in her two daughters and their three children. Her estate covered the cost of the funeral and left a balance of sixty pounds for each grandchild.

The wake was a quiet affair. Melanie made a tortilla and Jennifer laid on a buffet. By late afternoon family and friends had left.

'What have you got planned for Christmas?' asked Jennifer.

Her question cut through the silence of personal reflection.

'I've already told you. We're going to the Costa del Sol over Christmas and New Year,' replied Melanie.

'Oh yes, of course you are.'

'And don't forget the Office Party,' I added.

'Are you doing it again this year?'

Melanie explained our idea which kept the conversation moving along.

'There is one thing I wanted to ask you,' said Melanie.

'What?'

'Have you got any ideas for a party game?'

It just so happened that Jennifer had recently organised a racing evening to celebrate a friend's birthday.

'What about a race meeting?' she suggested.

'Race meeting?'

'That's right, dog racing.'

'Dogs? We're the only ones with a dog and I can't see Jazz taking up the challenge.'

'Not Jazz, greyhounds.'

'Greyhounds?'

Jennifer explained that the races were on a pre-recorded DVD. Party guests have to place a bet on each race based on previous form and the betting odds. After a series of races, the person with the highest winnings gets a prize.

'That sounds perfect.'

Before leaving I pirated the DVD and photocopied the betting slips.

The flight home passed without a hitch. We cleared immigration and caught the service bus to the off-site carpark.

'Will you take notes of the route home?' I asked Melanie, before we set off.

'What for?'

'For *Campo Verde*.'

The drive back to Canabal would follow the same route guests would have to take to *Campo Verde*. We knew from experience that there's nothing worse than landing in a foreign country and not knowing where you're going. First impressions count and accurate driving instructions were an essential part of our customer service.

For many people, sorrow is a private emotion which seldom spills out into the public domain. Since Granny's passing Melanie had been quiet and subdued. Occasionally her mood would manifest itself in tears over something unrelated and for no apparent reason. My role was to support her through this difficult time and try to take her mind off things.

'Would you like to go out for lunch?' I asked.

'Where to?'

'I thought we might go to Vigo and try the food at the Taj Mahal.'

'That sounds nice.'

'Let's give the owner of *Casa Aranza* a call before we set off and see if we can view the house while we're out that way,' I suggested.

Melanie agreed and the owner was more than happy to meet up and show us around.

'If we can't find the house, we can ring him and he'll come and meet us,' said Melanie.

'He sent me directions by email when I confirmed the booking.'

'I know but he said it's not easy to find.'

Lunch at the Taj Mahal Indian Restaurant lived up to expectations despite the owners being from Pakistan. Next stop *Casa Aranza*.

We found the village of Aranza without any problem. Locating the house was an altogether different proposition. The centre of the village was a rabbit warren of narrow streets and blind alleys.

'This can't be right,' said Melanie.

The lane we'd taken veered away at a right angle and climbed steeply.

'It must be. We've followed the directions to the letter.'

The higher we climbed the narrower it became.

'Watch out,' said Melanie.

Three stone steps jutted out into the lane at its narrowest point. Opposite them was a stone-built retaining wall which sloped inwards. This didn't look good. The door mirror was so close to the wall that I stopped, lowered the window, and pulled it in. As I did, the car started to roll backwards. The gradient was too steep for the handbrake to hold it. Quickly, I hit the accelerator, revved the engine, and slipped the clutch. The front wheels spun as the car edged forwards. I winced, expecting to hear the sound of grating metal. Thankfully, we squeezed through the gap and continued upwards.

'That was tight,' I remarked.

Melanie had kept silent throughout.

When we pulled up outside the house the owner looked surprised to see us.

'You managed to find it then,' he said, stating the obvious.

'Your directions were excellent.'

'Still, not many people do.'

The day proved to be a welcome distraction and for a short time lifted Melanie's mood.

The day after our trip to the coast, the weather provided the diversion.

'Is that snow?' asked Melanie.

We were en route to *Campo Verde* to dress the house for a photo shoot. The shots I'd taken of the exterior were better than I expected but making the interior look appealing would require the skills of a professional. As we climbed out of the Val de Lemos the rainfall turned into sleet and then snow. By the time we reached the plateau, the flakes had started to settle. Within minutes, the road and the countryside merged into a seamless blanket of virgin white snow.

'I don't believe it,' I remarked.

Yesterday had been beautifully sunny. What a difference a day makes.

As quickly as it had started it stopped, and before we reached Vilatán the roads had cleared. We spent the next few hours making sure every room looked exactly how we wanted it to. On our way home we called into Monforte to make an appointment with the photographer. He introduced himself as Miguel.

'I can come on Wednesday at 3:30 pm,' he said.

'That's fine,' I replied.

'Do you know where Vilatán is?' asked Melanie.

'Vila Cha?'

If we had a euro for every time someone had said that we'd be worth a fortune.

'No, Vilatán,' I replied.

Miguel looked puzzled.

'Do you know the petrol station in Escairón?' I added.

'Yes.'

'We'll meet you there at 3:25 pm.'

'OK. What car do you have?'

'A blue Renault Mégane.'

When we arrived home, Melanie checked the post box.

'I can guess who this is from,' she said, waving an envelope in the air.

'What is it?'

'I think it's our first Christmas card.'

'You're joking, it's the 1st of December.'

'I bet it's Ray and Lesley.'

Ray and Lesley were Melanie's next-door neighbours when she was growing up. Even after she'd left home, they still sent her a Christmas card and it was always the first to arrive. We had thought they might stop when we moved to Spain but no.

I unlocked the door and Melanie ripped open the envelope.

'Yep. Merry Christmas love Ray and Lesley.'

Christmas was on its way but before then I had work to do.

It's a well-known fact that more holidays are booked in January than any other month. With this in mind it was vital to build the website for *Campo Verde* before the new year.

Online research had steered me towards Weebly.com, a free to use website creator. After careful consideration, and a lot of trial and error, I decided to have five main sections: Home Page, About Campo Verde, About Galicia, Prices & Availability, and Contact Us.

My first job was to photoshop the picture of the exterior and replace the patches of earth with lush green grass. As soon as the newly seeded lawns had grown, I would swap the touched-up photo for a new one.

'What do you think to this?' I asked Melanie when I'd finished manipulating the image.

'You'd never know it wasn't real.'

'It is real. Everything belongs to us. The lawns are from here and the house is from Vilatán.'

'They just don't belong together.'

'A minor detail.'

My next task was to write the copy. I'd been working on a few tag lines for the home page and settled on:

Direct from the owners
Campo Verde – Luxury Farmhouse
Where luxury and affordability combine to form the
perfect holiday retreat

Quality accommodation for the discerning traveller

After meandering through leafy lanes into the sleepy village of Vilatán, you'll discover the recently restored farmhouse of Campo Verde. In the charming interior of the house, open stone walls and solid beams combine to create a traditional feel. With its tiled floors, stylish soft furnishings, and homely finishing touches, this is a home that exudes comfort and quality to such an extent that guests are unlikely to want to leave.

This same quality and thoughtful care is echoed outside the house. A long granite driveway is flanked on both sides by manicured lawns. A steel-framed gazebo nestles in one corner of the garden providing welcome shade from the mid-day sun and provides the perfect place to enjoy the rural views over afternoon tea. At one end of the house a fully enclosed, stone-flagged sun terrace is ideally situated for enjoying alfresco dining.

I asked Melanie to give it the once-over.
'Manicured lawns?'
'They are in the photo,' I joked. 'What do you think?'
'It sounds idyllic.'
'It is idyllic.'
The website was starting to take shape.
My attention turned to the section headed "About Campo Verde". Scrolling over this header revealed a dropdown menu with the following subsections: Guestbook Comments, Meet the Owners, Location, and Photo Gallery. The aim of including a guestbook was to encourage visitors to leave a review.
"Meet the Owners" came next. I felt it was important for guests to know who they were dealing with when handing over their hard-earned cash.

Meet the Owners – Craig and Melanie

Craig and his wife Melanie moved to Galicia in May 2002. Originally from Huddersfield in West Yorkshire, they sold a small printing business to pursue their dream of living abroad.
Since their move to Spain, Craig has turned his hand to writing, penning a weekly column for an online magazine. As well as writing, both Craig and Melanie are keen winemakers and produce wine using grapes from their own vineyard.

What year did you buy the property? 2006

Why this location?

Campo Verde is situated in the heart of the Galician countryside in the village of Vilatán. It's an ideal location from which to explore Galicia and northern Portugal. We bought the house as a ruin, without water or electricity. Using local craftsmen, we have painstakingly converted it into the luxury farmhouse it is today. The attention to detail and desire to retain as many original features as possible can be seen throughout the property.

What are the unique benefits of Campo Verde?

There are wonderful walks right outside the front door along paths and *caminos*. Tiny hamlets are scattered throughout the countryside along with pastures for sheep and cattle. It's a wonderful place for bird watchers and in spring, wildflowers blanket the landscape. Perhaps Campo Verde's main attraction is its central location providing visitors with quick and easy access to Galicia's main attractions including: Santiago de Compostela, Lugo, Ourense, the rugged coastline, the *Camino de Santiago*, and the fjordlike canyon of the river Sil, to name but a few.

Finding a royalty-free map for the section headed "Location" proved harder than I'd expected. Eventually I found what I was looking for and indicated the location of the house in relation to Galicia and Galicia in relation to the rest of Spain. With a bit of luck, we'd soon have the interior photos to upload to "The Gallery".

The next tab on the home page was "About Galicia", which included a dropdown menu of two headings, "How To Get There", and "Photo Gallery".

The "About Galicia" page gave me the opportunity to indulge my creative writing skills.

A magical, unspoilt paradise just two hours from the UK

Visitors to Galicia will enjoy a spectacular landscape of deep river valleys, high mountain peaks, and a rugged natural coastline. A patchwork of lush green meadows, ancient deciduous forests, and small conifer plantations are stitched together with a network of drystone walls, wooden fencing, and unkempt thickets. Sprinkled over this idyllic landscape are the white washed walls of tiny hamlets and weathered granite blocks of stone-built farmhouses.

Where culture and history walk hand in hand

From the pilgrimage city of Santiago de Compostela to the Roman walls surrounding Lugo, Galicia is steeped in history. There are castles and cathedrals, monasteries and manor houses. Even in the height of summer, Galicia's modern infrastructure offers visitors stress-free driving on traffic-free highways.

Under the heading "How To Get There", I wrote information about local airports, and the ferry crossing from the UK to Santander. The main emphasis was on the road infrastructure and the ease with which visitors could get around the region at any time of year. The catchphrase, "stress-free driving on traffic-free highways", was perfect.

I spent the next few hours trawling through my digital photo albums choosing the best shots of the region and uploading them to the website. I finished off a good day's work by creating a simple contact form that would automatically forward to the email account I'd set up.

On Wednesday afternoon we met Miguel as arranged. He followed us to *Campo Verde* and we parked on the driveway. I'd expected to see a tripod, lighting, and bounce boards when he opened the back of his car, but Miguel had none of these. Instead, he lifted a tatty camera case out of the back and flung it over his shoulder.

Properties like ours were designed to be warm in winter and cool in summer. They have thick stone walls, small windows, low ceilings, and solid wood doors. All of this makes the interior very dark. The lack of natural light didn't faze Miguel and within half an hour he'd finished his work and was ready to leave.

'When will they be ready?' I asked.

'Do you want hard copies or a CD?'

'CD.'

'In that case, you can pick them up tomorrow.'

'What time?'

'The final hour of the morning.'

We thanked him for his time and drove home.

Naming our website had been on my mind for a few days. Campoverde.com seemed like the obvious choice, but was it? Online marketing and search engine optimisation seemed like the dark arts to me. I combed the internet searching for inspiration. One theme kept recurring. The addition of the word 'go' to a destination seemed very popular (GoGreece, GoFrance, and GoSpain), so why not GoGalicia?

When I checked, one of our competitors had already bagged it. That's when the word "getaway" sprang to mind and Getaway Galicia was born.

We picked up the CD as arranged and sped home, impatient to view the results. I booted up the computer and inserted the disc. My concerns about the lack of natural light proved ill-founded. Miguel's well-trained eye had perfectly captured the romantic beauty of our charming farmhouse and we couldn't have been happier.

Creating our own website added credibility to our fledgling enterprise. Established holiday rental portals would give us the global reach we needed. Marketing Bob and Janet's property had given us valuable insight into the most cost-effective providers. To give us the best possible chance of success, without breaking the bank, we placed our listing on three sites: Holiday Rentals, Owners Direct, and Holiday Lettings. After completing the online submissions and uploading the photos, I contacted each one to negotiate the best possible deal. All we could do now was cross our fingers and wait for the enquiries to hit the inbox.

Campo Verde was open for business.

12

Lecoq-a-hoop

Emigrating throws up many challenges. Some are anticipated but others are completely unexpected. Take family Christmas shopping, for example. Who would have thought that this would pose a problem? It wasn't so much a question of what to buy as how much it weighed. If we weren't careful the cost of postage could far exceed the value of the gifts.

'Can we nip up to the post office this morning?' asked Melanie over breakfast.

'No problem, I'll just check the emails before we set off.'

The adverts for *Campo Verde* had been live for a week and we were still waiting for our first enquiry. I knew it was early days but had hoped to have at least one in the first week. Such was my concern that I'd even sent myself an enquiry from each platform to make sure they were working. Needless to say, they were.

'Anything?' asked Melanie, when I came back into the lounge.

'Not yet, but it's early days,' I replied, doing my best to sound upbeat.

The post office in Sober operates from a tiny office inside the Casa de Cultura or community centre.

'*Buenos días*,' said Melanie.

'*Buenos días, pasa* (Come in),' replied the post-lady.

The postlady is responsible for every aspect of the service within the municipality of Sober. First thing in the morning she collects the mail from the main post office in Monforte de Lemos. Back in her office she sorts it and serves the general public. At exactly 11:00 am she closes the office and drives around the area delivering the mail and stopping en route to make collections from public post boxes. Later in the day she returns to Monforte with the day's collections. It's hardly surprising they chose a woman for this multitasking role.

'How much will these cost to send to England?' asked Melanie.

She handed over two packages, one addressed to her mother and the other to my sister. The postlady placed the first parcel on the weighing scale.

'This one is six euros.'

'And the other?'

'The same, six euros.'

Melanie's expression said it all.

'What's the matter?' I asked.

'I'm not paying six euros to send my mum a tortilla turner that only cost one. She'll have to put it in her case the next time she visits.'

Melanie smiled at the postlady and politely asked for them back.

'Here,' she said, handing me the parcel for her mum.

'What are you doing now?'

Melanie was carefully peeling the Sellotape off the other package.

'This can wait until your sister next visits,' she replied, pulling out a weighty fridge magnet.

'How much is it now?' she asked, handing back the parcel.

The postlady placed it back onto the scale.

'Three euros sixty-five.'

'That's better. Do you have some Sellotape I can borrow?'

Some people love Christmas; personally, I'm not a great fan.

Clang, clang, clang, clang!

For one brief moment my heart stopped. Surely that wasn't Penelope? Talk about being caught with your pants down. I was standing on the bathmat, dripping wet. Muffled voices emanated from the lounge. I looked out of the window. Penelope's car was parked on the driveway. Suddenly, the bedroom door opened and Melanie dashed in.

'Penelope's here,' she whispered.

'What time is it?'

'A quarter past.'

'She's early.'

Melanie pulled off her clothes and left them where they lay.

'I'm going in the shower,' she said, hurrying into the bathroom.

Penelope was one of seven attendees at this year's Office Party. The others were Roy and Maria, Peter and Veronica, and Melanie and me. Jazz was travelling with us so we'd offered to take Penelope. Peter and Veronica were riding with Roy and Maria.

By the time I'd dressed, Melanie had showered. Drips of water followed her around the bedroom.

'I'll occupy Penelope,' I whispered, and left Melanie to get ready.

Penelope and I caught up. Five minutes later Melanie walked into the lounge.

'I'll ring and order the food before we set off,' she said, picking up a note pad from the dining room table and thumbing through the pages.

She rang the restaurant and placed the order.

'How long will we be?' she whispered, holding her hand over the microphone.

'About an hour and a quarter,' I replied.

By the time we left home the clock had ticked around to 1:10 pm. We'd arranged to pick up the food and meet the others at junction 294 on the A-52 highway at 3:00 pm. As we reached the outskirts of Vigo, Melanie's mobile rang.

'We're about five minutes away,' she said to the caller. 'That was the Taj Mahal. The food is ready to collect.'

Parking near the restaurant proved impossible. I found a safe place to double-park and Melanie hopped out.

'Are you sure you'll be alright?' I asked.

I couldn't risk leaving the car unattended.

'I'll be fine.'

'If I'm not here when you get back, wait and I'll pick you up as soon as I can.'

'OK.'

Within five minutes of disappearing around the corner Melanie returned, accompanied by a waiter from the restaurant. Over-ordering an Indian takeaway is hardly headline news, but five carrier bags of food between seven seemed a little excessive.

'Are you sure you've got everything?' I quipped.

Melanie paused for a moment before the penny dropped.

'Very funny,' she replied.

We arrived at our rendezvous with five minutes to spare. Two minutes later Roy's Hyundai pulled up behind us. After a quick exchange we were off, heading towards our overnight hideaway.

The lane leading to the house hadn't got any wider since our last visit but we all made it safely up the hill. The owner had left the gates open so I drove straight through and Roy followed.

'Crikey!' he said, stepping from his car. 'How on earth did you find this place?'

'It was easy really. Once we'd started climbing that hill there was no turning back.'

We unloaded our overnight bags and chose our rooms. As soon as we were settled, we uncorked a bottle of wine and the party began. The takeaway was a great success. Everything was delicious. So much so that, despite thoughts to the contrary, we ate the lot.

'So Veronica, what party game do you have for us?' I asked.

Veronica looked sheepish.

'I couldn't think of anything,' she confessed.

'Oh. Has anyone else brought anything?'

The room fell silent. It was just as well we'd come prepared.

An hour or so later, Peter was crowned the greyhound race night champion and presented with a box of chocolates which he shared with everyone. By the time we turned in, the clock had ticked around to 2:00 am.

The following morning Melanie and I were the last to rise. Preparations for breakfast were well underway.

'Can we give a hand with anything?' asked Melanie.

'Everything is under control but thanks for asking,' replied Veronica.

Penelope and Maria were sitting in the lounge chatting.

'Where's Roy?' I asked.

'He's taken Jazz outside,' said Maria.

I went to find them. Roy was standing in the garden throwing a stick for Jazz to chase.

'Morning,' I said.

'Morning. She's not very good at bringing it back,' said Roy.

Be it a stick, a ball, or anything else, Jazz loves chasing. As for fetching it back, you might as well forget it.

The view from the hilltop garden was magical. Swathes of cloud created an ethereal mist in the valley below. Whitewashed houses seemed to be floating on a fluffy white haze. The sky above graduated from white to pastel blue as it rose towards the heavens. In the shadows the air had a wintry chill but in the sunshine it felt comfortably warm.

'Breakfast's ready,' called Melanie.

We didn't need telling twice.

Breakfast was a veritable feast. Peter and Veronica make their own sausages and Peter cures and smokes his own bacon. Both were absolutely delicious. Fried eggs came courtesy of Penelope's free-range chickens: a small golden sunshine on every plate. Fried mushrooms, fried tomatoes, baked beans, and fried bread completed the dish. Orange juice and coffee provided the refreshments and we finished off a fabulous full English with a few rounds of toast and marmalade. What a way to start the day.

By the time we'd washed up, tidied the house, and packed our bags the clock had ticked around to 2:30 pm. After such a filling breakfast no one was in a rush for lunch.

That evening Melanie went to bed at 9:30 pm and I wasn't far behind. Perhaps it's our age.

The last six months had flown by. In six days' time we'd be heading south for our Christmas and New Year getaway. Before leaving I wanted to settle all outstanding invoices for the work at *Campo Verde*. A much more difficult task than you might imagine.

'Who's still left to pay?' asked Melanie.

'Just José Metal.'

José Metal had manufactured and fitted the gates for the driveway and side entrance, as well as the handrail for the internal staircase.

'Can you give him a call and see how much we owe him?' I asked.

'Why can't you?'

'I want to check the emails,' I replied, and disappeared into the office before she could respond.

I switched on the laptop and waited. I used to think Windows XP was slow but Vista is a nightmare.

The advertising sites had been live for two weeks. In that time, we'd had a number of false alarms: mainly junk mail from other advertisers. Today's icon indicated two new emails. I clicked on the message to take a look. As I suspected, junk. The second email told a different story.

Holiday-Rentals - Rental Enquiry - Property 410713

Dear Craig Briggs,

You have a booking enquiry about property number 410713 in Galicia.

To respond to this enquiry, simply call the phone number contained in the enquiry or reply to this email. Don't forget - a quick reply will help to secure this booking!

Name: Tanya Rose
Arrival date: Saturday, 02 May 2009
Departure date: Saturday, 09 May 2009
Total no in party: 4
No of children: 0
Further info: please can you advise on price and availability for my dates in May.

A rush of excitement had my heart racing. I read it again to make sure and dashed into the lounge. Melanie was on the phone. I was so desperate to give her the news that my body jiggled from side to side.

'Guess what?' I said, the second she'd finished.

'What?'

'Guess?'

'I don't know.'

'We've got an enquiry.'

Melanie looked bemused.

'For the house,' I added.

'Who's it from?'

Now I was bemused. What did it matter who it was from; it wasn't as if she'd know them!

'Someone called Tracy or Tabatha or something.'

'Is it Tracy or Tabatha?'

'Why does it matter?'

'I don't suppose it does. That was José by the way.'

'Oh yes. How much do we owe him?'

'He's no idea. He said he'll sort out an invoice and call us.'

'Did you tell him we're going away for a month on Monday?'

'I did.'

'And?'

'He said we can pay him when we get back.'

Bang went my ambition of clearing our debts.

Packing the car for a month-long winter break is more challenging than one might think. Squeezing everything in was a real headache. I placed bags in the back and then unloaded them. I put the cases in horizontally and then tried standing them upright. I laid things on the back seat and in the footwell behind the front seats. In the end I unloaded everything and started again.

'Are you sure we need all this stuff?' I asked.

'We are away for a month.'

'That's right, one month, not the rest of our lives. What's in here?'

'Just a few kitchen utensils.'

It felt more like the kitchen sink.

Every time I thought I'd got everything packed, Melanie would find something else we couldn't live without.

'What's this?'

'Shoes.'

'Are you planning on opening a shop?'

'Tsk!' and off she went.

I swapped the shoes for the vanity case and forced that in between two large suitcases and a bag containing the kitchen equipment.

'Is that everything?' I asked, stepping back inside.

'Yes.'

'At last.'

'Apart from toothbrushes and hairbrushes.'

They wouldn't take up too much room.

'Oh, and there's the picnic bag of course,' she added.

'Of course.'

'And our coats.'

Would it ever end?

The following morning a thick layer of frost blanketed the car. I turned the key in the ignition and switched on the fan to maximum. The thermos picnic bag went on top of everything else on the back seat and I laid the coats on top of that. Finally, I pushed my laptop case behind the front seat and that was that. The car was packed and we were ready for off.

'It's chuffing freezing out there.'

Melanie was in the bedroom folding the duvet to the bottom of the bed.

'Are you nearly ready?' I asked.

'Two minutes.'

That could mean anywhere from two minutes to half an hour.

'Can I put the dog in?' I thought it wise to ask.

'Yes, I'm coming now.'

'Come on, lass.'

Jazz was curled up on her bed in the lounge. Slowly she got to her feet and wandered over to the French doors. I picked up her bed. The footwell behind the passenger seat was full. I'd chosen items that were as tall as the seat to give Jazz a little more space. Fortunately, she's much happier squeezed in rather than sliding about every time we go around a bend.

Loading anything into the back of a two-door coupé is awkward at the best of times but leaning across with a fidgeting hound made it even more difficult.

'Have you got everything?' asked Melanie.

If I didn't, it was too late now.

'Yep,' I replied.

Melanie locked the gates and jumped in. The fan had cleared the windscreen sufficiently to risk using the wipers. Like skis across icy snow they swung back and forth. Not exactly clear but good enough to see where I was going.

As we drove through the village the temperature display read -2°C. One thousand kilometres south it read 19°C. Twenty-one excellent reasons for migrating south for the winter.

Our destination was Puebla Aida, a modern take on a whitewashed Andalucian hilltop village which overlooked the seaside resort of Fuengirola. The centrepiece of the village is a mock Moorish-style castle divided into luxury apartments. We were spending the first ten days in *Casa Victor*, a one-bedroom studio apartment on the top floor. This was directly above *Casa Jesse*, the two-bedroom apartment we'd stayed in last year and where we would end our holiday.

'It's amazing how different the view is,' said Melanie, as she stepped out onto the balcony.

We were only three metres higher than the balcony below but the difference was quite remarkable.

'Drink?' I asked.

A Mediterranean sunset is the perfect accompaniment to a Teatime Taster.

'Did you hear any more from that rental enquiry?' asked Melanie, as we sipped our wine and stared out across the Med.

'Not a peep.'

'Oh well, it's early days.'

We quickly settled in to our new surroundings. The underfloor heating was a real bonus. We'd arranged to spend Christmas Day and New Year's Eve with Bill and Di, whom we'd met through a mutual friend. They were lucky enough to own an apartment in the area as well as a house in Galicia.

A traditional Christmas dinner is all well and good, especially when someone else is doing the cooking, but I did miss our seasonal Christmas Day barbecue. After lunch we took a stroll on the beach. Jazz was in her element. She ran in and out of the sea and barked at the breaking waves. The first ten days flew by and before we knew it we were packing our belongings and loading them into the lift. We'd enjoyed our stay at *Casa Victor* but *Casa Jesse* was in a different league.

There's something uplifting about starting the day sitting in bed and staring out across the Mediterranean Sea. The master bedroom at *Casa Jesse* provided such a view.

On New Year's Eve we dined with friends at the Nine Dragons Chinese Restaurant in La Cala de Mijas: great food at a fantastic price.

Bright sunshine welcomed in the new year.

'Are we going to do anything for Los Reyes?' I asked, as I stepped out onto the balcony on New Year's Day.

Día de los Reyes or Three Kings' Day commemorates the visit of the Three Wise Men to the baby Jesús. It's celebrated in many Hispanic countries. Here in Spain it's equally as important as Christmas Day and is the traditional time when presents are exchanged. On the evening prior to Día de los Reyes many towns, cities, and villages host a parade. Children and families line the streets and the kings toss boiled sweets into the crowd.

'I don't know, what do you think?' asked Melanie.

Last year we'd watched the parade in the seaside village of La Cala de Mijas. We'd enjoyed the evening but the size of the venue was reflected in the length of the procession.

'Perhaps we should try a bigger resort this year. What about Fuengirola?'

During the summer months this large seaside town is a popular destination with foreign holidaymakers. Out of season the locals regain control.

'Fuengirola?'

'Why not?'

'I wasn't disagreeing, I just wondered why you suggested there.'

'Given its size there should be a good atmosphere.'

'OK, Fuengirola it is.'

An online search revealed the route and the time it was scheduled to begin.

We spent the next few days lounging around the apartment enjoying the fabulous weather.

'We've had another enquiry,' I announced.

Melanie was outside on the balcony reading a romance novel her mum had given her for Christmas.

'That's good.'

'It sounds like they're French.'

'French?'

'With a name like Lecoq, they're either French or someone is having a laugh.'

To ensure accuracy and consistency I'd formulated a standard reply letter.

Dear Jean-Pierre

Thank you for your enquiry regarding renting our luxury farmhouse, Campo Verde. The house is currently available during your chosen dates 15th until 29th of August.

The weekly rental rate during your chosen stay is 660.00 euros.

What's included in the rental price?

Guests enjoy full and exclusive use of the house and gardens. All linen and towels (excluding leisure towels) are included. All utility expenses are included and we leave guests a welcome grocery starter pack to see them through the first day.

Our TV satellite system receives most UK free-to-air channels including your favourite BBC and ITV programmes.

Owners' website: To help potential visitors make a better-informed choice about visiting Galicia and a stay at our luxury farmhouse, Campo Verde, I have designed a website. On it you'll find comprehensive information about the house and Galicia. Enjoy the stunning photos in our photo galleries and much, much more.

If you wish to make a reservation or require any further information, please don´t hesitate to contact me again.

Kind regards
Craig

Less than twenty-four hours later Jean-Pierre replied.

Hi Craig

It's great, how can I proceed to the reservation?

Regards
Jean-Pierre

I could hardly contain my excitement and hurried outside to tell Melanie.

'I've heard back from Monsieur Lecoq.'

I played down the news, trying not to give the game away. Melanie's response was equally unenthusiastic.

'Oh yes. What did he have to say?'

'He wants to know how to proceed.'

'Proceed?'

'With a booking.'

'He wants to book?'

'That's right. We've got our first booking.'

'That's fantastic.'

Melanie's questioning went into overdrive.

'When is it for?'

'August.'

'For how long?'

'A fortnight.'

'How many people?'

'Four adults and two babies.'

'Babies?'

'Babies, two of them.'

The details were important to Melanie. I on the other hand was just relieved to have our first booking. I'd spent the last three and a half years questioning whether we'd made the right decision. Securing our first reservation went some way towards justifying that.

The next stage in our booking process was a completed booking form and deposit payment. Imagine our surprise when the form came back and Monsieur Lecoq lived in the suburbs of Barcelona.

13

Curvaceous Coastline

On the evening of the fifth we wrapped up warm and drove into Fuengirola. It had been a beautifully sunny day and the pastel shades of twilight seemed reluctant to give way to the darkness of night. The parade would pass along Avenida Ramón y Cajal. We parked nearby and walked the rest of the way. The night sky was clear. A half moon hovered over the town centre apartment blocks. Crowds, both young and old, lined the street waiting for the arrival of the kings.

'Let's walk a bit further,' suggested Melanie.

I glanced at my watch. We had half an hour to kill.

'OK.'

The further we walked the less crowded it became.

'Would you like a drink?' I asked.

We'd reached Henry's Resto Bar: a kerbside hostelry, more shabby than chic. A low wall separated the roadside terrace from the pavement.

'Why not?'

We took a seat and waited for service. A few minutes later a young waiter came to the table.

'*Sí* (Yes).'

We've learnt not to read too much into someone's abruptness.

'A small beer and a glass of white wine.'

He jotted down the order and wandered back inside. I checked my watch. There were fifteen minutes to go. Our drinks soon arrived. We sipped them slowly and watched as families wandered back and forth.

'They're late.'

I'd been keeping an eye on the time.

'Now there's a surprise,' said Melanie.

Before long the sound of Latino rhythms echoed down the street. The tall buildings amplified the sound. Two minutes later the flashing blue lights of the lead police car danced from side to side. The kings were on their way.

Following the police car came a procession of fantasy-themed floats pulled by large four-wheel drive vehicles. There were mythical beasts, elves sitting on toadstools, and a Roman chariot to name but a few. Aboard each float were groups of children tossing boiled sweets into the excited crowd. The three largest floats hosted a king sitting on a golden throne. Some of the older, more mischievous kids hurled the marble-sized treats with such velocity they shattered glasses on the tables around us.

Twenty-seven floats took over half an hour to roll past. Within minutes of them passing, street cleaners began the clear-up. Half an hour later and no one would have known the event had taken place.

Wandering back to the car we recalled the evening's events.

'The way some of those kids were throwing the sweets, I'm surprised no one lost an eye,' remarked Melanie.

'I know. Perhaps we'll try somewhere different next year.'

This was our fourth Three Kings parade in four different towns. Each was uniquely special thanks to the imagination and hard work of all those involved.

Día de los Reyes marked the halfway point of our winter getaway. The days were slipping by and we hadn't yet been exploring.

'Would you like to go to Granada?' I asked, as we sipped our morning coffee.

The weather was glorious, warm and sunny without a cloud in the sky.

'When?'

'Today.'

'How far is it?'

'About 150 kilometres.'

'And how long will it take us to get there?'

'A couple of hours.'

'Is that where the Alhambra Palace is?'

'That's right.'

'OK, let's go.'

Half an hour later we were on the road heading towards Granada. We drove past Málaga before turning inland on the A-45. It wasn't until we joined the A-92 that I noticed the temperature. Along the coast the mercury had reached a very comfortable 22°C; inland it had fallen to 2°C.

'Have you seen the temperature?' I said.

'Crikey, it's freezing.'

We'd left the apartment without a coat between us. If it didn't warm up, we certainly wouldn't be wandering around a 13th century palace.

It took us an hour and forty-five minutes to reach the outskirts of Granada. All we had to do now was find the Alhambra. The temperature hadn't budged a degree and by the look of the snow-capped peaks of the Sierra Nevada mountain range, it wasn't likely to.

'Keep an eye out for a signpost,' I said, as we followed the traffic around the outskirts of the city.

'We can't wander around in this. We'll freeze to death,' said Melanie.

A slight over-exaggeration but I agreed with the sentiment. In these conditions we needed more than just a coat to go exploring. A hat, scarf, and thermal underwear wouldn't go amiss.

'Let's find out how to get there and come back another day,' I suggested.

It seemed an awful long way to drive to have to turn around and go back but anything was preferable to hypothermia.

'There,' said Melanie, pointing at a signpost, 'take the next right.'

Within five minutes of exiting the city the magnificent Alhambra Palace appeared on the horizon.

'Over there,' said Melanie.

I pulled into a layby to get a better view. Even from afar it looked impressive.

'Stand over there,' I said, pointing towards the palace.

The least I could do was snap a record of the trip.

'Would you like me to take one of you both?'

We weren't the only ones taking advantage of this vantage point.

'If you wouldn't mind?' I replied.

The wind was biting cold. I put on a brave face, smiled, and tried to look warm. We thanked our kind stranger and jumped back in the car before we got frostbite.

'Let's take a different route back to the apartment,' I suggested, as we rejoined the main road.

From Granada we headed straight for the coast along the E-902. Forty minutes after leaving Granada the Mediterranean came into view.

'That's better,' I said, pointing at the temperature gauge, now a comfortable 24°C.

At the town of Motril we headed west along the N-340, a highway which has the distinction of being the longest road in Spain. It runs from Barcelona in the north to the southern city of Cádiz, a distance of one thousand kilometres.

The first place we came across was the town of Salobreña. It's described by some as the Jewel of the Costa Tropical. A labyrinth of narrow streets and whitewashed houses clings to a large rocky outcrop set back from the sea and topped with a Moorish castle. I made a mental note. This was one destination that deserved a closer look.

West of Salobreña the road hugs the contours of the coast, weaving in and out of tiny bays and around rocky outcrops. The one constant is the cool blue water of the Mediterranean Sea. Every so often a tight curve offers fleeting glimpses of white-crested waves breaking on the cliffs below. The drive conjures up images of a bygone era, a time when sixties Hollywood movie stars would race an open top sports car along the coast. Our little French coupé lacked that wind in the hair appeal but its performance and handling were far better than anything the sixties had to offer.

We skipped past the coastal town of Almuñécar and on towards the village of Cotobro. It wasn't until we'd driven past that I wished we'd stopped for a closer look.

'Look at that,' said Melanie. 'It's beautiful.'

Whitewashed houses were huddled around a small, steep-sided bay which flowed down the cliff to the edge of the Mediterranean. It looked idyllic.

The next place of note was La Herradura. The town occupies a sweeping, sandy bay. The headlands on both sides are dotted with exclusive villas. Each has a fabulous view over the Med. We continued on and into the Acantilados de Maro-Cerro Gordo Natural Park. The previous thirty kilometres of coastline had been spectacular but this was something else.

The natural park covers an area of 395 hectares along an eight-kilometre stretch of the N-340. It's unspoilt and undeveloped and reminds visitors exactly how beautiful this part of Spain once was. It harks back to a time before mass tourism and greedy property developers. Around every bend lies a scene of untouched beauty.

'I'm going to pull over,' I said.

It's fair to say that the N-340 is showing its age but sections of an older incarnation still exist. Short fragments of road that once looped around the tightest bends have been abandoned in favour of less acute curves but have survived as laybys. Drivers who choose to stop are treated to some of the most spectacular views along the coast. I couldn't resist and pulled off the road.

The sharp bend of the old carriageway was lined with concrete blocks, the length of a coffin and twice as deep. Back in the day, road safety was more concerned with preventing vehicles leaving the road and falling hundreds of metres to the beach below than causing impact injuries.

'Come on, let's go for a walk,' I suggested.

The air felt warm as we stepped from the airconditioned car, quite a contrast to earlier in the day. I opened the tailgate and Jazz leapt out, tail in the air and nose to the ground. The views from the parking area were breathtaking. Facing east, rocky headlands jutted out into the sea one after another and below us undulating waves lapped gently onto a sandy beach. The old road curved around a headland. We strolled along to find out what lay beyond.

'It rejoins the main road,' I said.

'I wonder what's down there.'

Melanie had spotted a dusty track running parallel to the highway.

'Let's take a look,' I suggested.

Up ahead was a Mediterranean-style villa perched on the clifftop. We ambled along the track. After twenty metres it merged with another section of the old coast road. As we passed the villa the panorama opened out, giving us an unrestricted view of the sea. Mirrored sunlight skipped across the crest of the waves as they rolled towards the coast. On the beach below were the remnants of a 15th century watchtower or *torre*.

The southern coast of Spain is littered with *torres*. Many are very well preserved, unlike the one below us. In general, square based *torres* are of Moorish origin while round ones were built after the Reconquista (the name given to the defeat of the Moors by Christian Crusaders). Regardless of their origin, they were built for one purpose: to keep a watchful eye out for invaders from the sea.

We continued on down the shallow incline until the road curved around the contours of the cliff and dropped down into a small bay. The apex of the corner provided an unrestricted view along the coast. In the distance a sizeable town of whitewashed houses occupied a sweeping bay.

'I wonder where that is,' said Melanie.

'I'm not sure. It could be Nerja.'

'I think it is. Nerja appeared on some of the signposts we've passed.'

The bay was home to a small hamlet consisting of half a dozen cottages, none of which looked occupied. The one we'd reached had views to die for.

'What do you think?' I asked, tipping my head towards a sun-bleached sign pinned to the roof.

'It's beautiful,' she replied.

Melanie was soaking up the fabulous seascape.

'Not that, *that*.'

This time I pointed at the sign which read "To Rent" and had a mobile telephone number stencilled underneath in faded red ink.

'What about it?'

'This would be a fabulous place to stay.'

'We've already got somewhere to stay.'

'Not this year, next.'

Melanie paused for thought.

'I bet it costs a fortune,' she said.

'We won't know unless we ask.'

I could tell from her silence she was giving it due consideration.

'Well, what do you think?' I asked.

'It can't harm to find out.'

Before heading back to the car, I photographed the sign.

Shortly after rejoining the N-340 we reached the outskirts of the coastal town of Nerja.

'I'm going to go back to Fuengirola on the A-7,' I said.

Time was ticking by and we were more than one hundred kilometres from Fuengirola. The A-7 whisks traffic along the coast and links all the main tourist resorts. It's an excellent road and despite passing through a number of overdeveloped urban areas, it affords stunning views along the Costa del Sol.

Within an hour and a half we were pulling into the carpark below the apartment in Puebla Aida. Our day trip hadn't gone exactly to plan, but who cares? We'd had a great day out and seen lots of new places which had left us eager to experience more of this part of Spain. We'd been away for almost six hours and covered over 360 kilometres. Throughout the journey Jazz had been as good as gold.

That evening I booted up the laptop and Googled the telephone number of the cottage we'd seen. To my surprise the property was listed on a Spanish letting site. The name of the bay was Playa del Río de la Miel.

'That's it,' I blurted.

Melanie lifted her head from the pages of her novel.

'That's what?'

'The cottage next to the sea.'

'Let's have a look.'

Melanie dumped her open book on the coffee table and came to look.

'That is it,' she acknowledged.

I flicked through the photos on the website.

'What do you think?'

'It looks alright.'

Her lukewarm response was understandable. Compared to the modern apartment we were currently staying in, the interior décor looked dated. That aside, it had everything anyone would need for a self-catering holiday.

'How much is it?' she asked.

I scrolled through the blurb to the bottom of the page.

'Is that all?'

The price listed was eight hundred euros per month.

'It does say *from* eight hundred a month,' I replied.

'What do you think?'

'I think it's worth enquiring about and if the price is right, we should ask to take a look. What do you think?'

'Why not? What do we have to lose?' Melanie paused for a moment. 'Does that mean you want me to give them a call?'

'That's a brilliant idea.'

Melanie dialled the number and a man called Francisco answered. Spanish telephone conversations tend to be short and to the point.

'What did he say?' I asked.

'The price at this time of year would be eight hundred euros and we can view it next Wednesday.'

That was excellent news. It hardly seemed possible we could afford to stay at a property in such an outstanding location.

Yesterday's adventures had unleashed a desire for further exploration.

'Let's take a drive down the coast today,' I suggested.

What I actually meant was west but that wouldn't mean anything to Melanie. To her we either travel up the coast or down.

'Where to?'

'Wherever the wind takes us.'

'OK.'

The month was flying by. A week tomorrow and we would be heading back to Galicia. There was no time to lose but then again, why hurry?

'What would you like for breakfast?' asked Melanie.

'Would you like me to rustle up a couple of sausage butties?'

'Yes please. Sounds delicious.'

By the time I'd cooked the sausages, breakfast had turned into lunch. We sat outside on the balcony, bathing in the warm sunshine.

'Are you ready for off?' I asked.

'Ready when you are.'

Jazz had been lying in the sun all morning but knew exactly what was going on. She rose lazily to her feet and wandered inside.

'Are you ready as well?'

She shook herself from nose to tail and stared at me through her big brown eyes.

'Come on then,' and off we went.

From the hills overlooking Fuengirola, we joined the A-7 coast road heading west in the direction of Cádiz. We passed through La Cala de Mijas before skirting the outskirts of Marbella. We continued along the A-7, through the district of Nueva Andalucía and on past the exclusive marina resort of Puerta Banús. A band of cloud had drifted in from the west, obscuring the sun. The temperature remained warm but the earlier sunshine had disappeared. The next town of note was Estepona where we unwittingly merged onto the AP-7.

'This is the toll road,' said Melanie.

The last thing we wanted was to pay for our impromptu driving excursion.

'I'll come off at the next exit.'

At junction 153 we left the main road.

'Where now?' I asked.

Craig Briggs

'I don't know.'

The slip road had ended at a roundabout. The first exit would take us back from where we'd come. A signpost at the second exit offered five options. One was Casares which seemed as good a destination as any. At a second roundabout, twenty metres from the first, all reference to Casares had mysteriously disappeared. I drove around the roundabout a second time in case we'd missed it but nothing.

'If you don't make your mind up soon, I'm going to throw up,' said Melanie, as I navigated the roundabout for a third time.

'Hang on, Yedra here we come.'

The road climbed steadily into the foothills of the Sierra Bermeja and merged into the MA8300 where the sign for Yedra disappeared but the one for Casares reappeared. The road continued upwards into the Sierra Crestellina mountain range. Higher and higher we climbed, twisting and turning to compensate for the steepness.

All of a sudden the town of Casares came into view. The focal point of the village is a hilltop church. Below that, whitewashed village houses fan out down the valley. We stopped on the road overlooking the village to take a few snaps and let Jazz out for a wander before driving on. At the junction with the A-377 we had two options, right to the village of Gaucín or left towards Manilva and the coast. We'd been driving for almost two hours so decided to head back to the coast.

From a distance, the village of Manilva looked interesting. The 16th century church was very different to the one in Casares. Exploring Manilva would have to wait; it was time to find a sandy beach for Jazz to stretch her legs.

Back at the coast we drove towards Estepona. At one of the many roundabouts I pulled off the highway into a beachside carpark at Bahía de Casares. Jazz was on her feet, whining at the smell of the sea.

We followed a footpath from the carpark to a promenade which curved around a small bay. On one side was a narrow beach and the Mediterranean Sea and on the other a rather stylish apartment complex. Watching over both was another *torre*. This was very different to the one at Playa del Río de la Miel. Not only did it have a square base, indicating its Moorish origin, but it was also in excellent condition.

Jazz was itching to get onto the sand and paddle in the sea. She'd been cooped up in the back of the car for over two hours.

'OK, just hold your horses,' I said.

As soon as I unhooked her leash, she sprinted down onto the beach and ran into the sea. The sound of breaking waves had her barking with excitement. Whatever she wanted them to do, they weren't paying a blind bit of notice.

We'd started the day enjoying the irresistible aromas of pan-fried sausages and ended it with the unmistakable pong of a soggy pooch festering in the back. At least someone was happy.

14

Second Best

Feeding Melanie's insatiable appetite for the written word is an ongoing challenge. English language books are a rare breed in the Galician countryside. She regularly exchanges books with friends, and her mum chips in with at least one new title a month. Even so, it's a struggle to keep pace with my word-eating leviathan. Imagine our euphoria when we stumbled across the La Cala Lions charity shop. It's a veritable emporium of secondhand goods including books. At the cost of one euro per title we can satisfy Melanie's craving while donating to a very worthy cause. Perfect.

'Can we call into the charity shop this morning?' asked Melanie over breakfast.

'No problem.'

To help with their fundraising Melanie had brought back half the titles she'd purchased last year. We dropped those off and bought over thirty new ones.

We spent the rest of the day lounging on the terrace and soaking up the rays. Summer sunshine in January was one of the reasons we'd chosen the Costa del Sol for our winter escape and so far, it hadn't disappointed. As much as we enjoy exploring, it seemed a shame not to take advantage of the weather.

By Sunday my wanderlust had returned. A day sunbathing is quite enough for me.

'Let's take a drive up the coast today and find somewhere for Sunday lunch,' I said.

Adding lunch to my suggestion increased the chances of finding a willing participant.

'Where to?'

'I'm not sure. We drove past it the other day. I can't remember the name, but I'll know it when I see it.'

'OK. What time do you want to set off?'

'As soon as we're ready.'

Sunday lunch in Spain tends to start a little later than during the week. Families often converge on their favourite restaurant and enjoy a long, lazy meal together. With that in mind, there was no rush.

By the time we set off the clock had ticked past eleven. We joined the A-7 heading east. The highway was much quieter than during the week, especially around Málaga. We made good progress and reached Nerja in less than an hour. I was fairly confident the place I had in mind was somewhere between there and Salobreña. We left the A-7 and joined the N-340. I kept my eyes peeled.

'This looks familiar,' I said.

By the time I'd slowed down, I'd driven straight past the exit.

'That was it, Cotobro, Playa de Cotobro.'

I checked my rear-view mirror, indicated, and pulled into the side of the road. Making a U-turn seemed preferable to finding somewhere to turn around. I waited until the coast was clear and doubled back. The exit was positioned on the crest of a sweeping bend which was why I'd missed it.

The view of the bay from the main road was nothing compared to the panorama that opened out within fifty metres of exiting it.

'Oh wow! Look at that,' said Melanie.

I had one eye on the view and the other on the narrow road in front. I pulled over to get a better look.

'That is stunning,' I replied.

From our high vantage point the hills surrounding the bay undulated along the coast like a pleated skirt. Luxury villas, separated by patches of vegetation and tall palm trees, clung to the side of the cliff. Every property had unrestricted views around the bay and out to sea. With a blue sky overhead, the Mediterranean looked deceptively inviting. Mad dogs and Englishmen might venture out in the midday sun but only madcap Scandinavians go for a dip in the Med in January.

The road to the beach narrowed as it tumbled down the hillside, twisting and turning to ease the steep descent. Strategically positioned roadside mirrors guide drivers around the tightest bends.

'What happens if we meet someone coming up?' asked Melanie.

It didn't bear thinking about.

Eventually we reached the sea. Jazz had been whining for the last few minutes.

'Shall we stop?' I asked.

'We'd better let her out.'

I pulled into a carpark next to the beach. Low rise apartment blocks ran along the front. I opened the tailgate and Jazz jumped out. She had one thing on her mind, the sea. Bright sunlight bounced off the blue water like a disco strobe light. Jazz paddled in the shallows as we walked along the seashore.

'I wonder if there are any places to rent here,' I said.

My idle musing had unwittingly become speech.

'I thought we were going to look at that other place.'

'We are, but if we're driving up this way it wouldn't harm to find out if there's anything available here.'

'I suppose not.'

'I'll take a look online when we get back. Come on Jazz,' I called.

Reluctantly, she came.

It was too early to stop for lunch so we drove around a headland and on into the coastal town of Almuñécar. From there we rejoined the N-340 heading east. We continued on past Salobreña and through the coastal villages of Torrenueva Costa, Playa La Rijana, and Castell de Ferro.

'Why is there never a restaurant when you want one?' I remarked.

'Perhaps there'll be one here.'

The road sign read "Castillo de Baños". A hundred metres further along we entered the coastal village and passed the Hornabeque de Baños, an 18th century fort and watchtower built specifically to deter Berber pirates from landing and raiding the Alpujarras.

'There,' said Melanie.

Twenty metres past the watchtower was the Restaurante el Paraiso. Finally, we'd found a place to eat. A waiter greeted our entry and guided us to a sunny terrace at the rear. The situation was idyllic. The only thing separating the terrace from the sea was a ten-metre-wide promenade. We couldn't have wished for a better location. We took a seat and the waiter handed us menus.

'What are you going to have?' asked Melanie.

I think she knew my answer before she'd asked.

'*Lubina a la plancha* (Grilled sea bass).'

Melanie opted for the chicken. The fish was delicious, moist and meaty and topped with thinly sliced garlic and olive oil. After lunch we went for a stroll along the front before heading home.

We arrived back just in time to watch the sun setting over the distant hills.

'Teatime Taster?' I asked.

'That sounds like an excellent idea.'

We retired to the balcony and reflected on the day's events. As the sun dipped over the horizon so did the temperature. We braved the elements for half an hour or so before settling in for the evening. Watching TV was quite a novelty. Finding something worth watching was far more challenging.

The following morning I began my search for a holiday rental property in Cotobro. It didn't take long to find somewhere of interest.

'What do you think to this?' I asked.

Melanie was sitting outside with her nose in one of her charity shop finds and enjoying the morning sunshine. She marked the page and wandered inside.

'It looks nice,' she said, as I flicked through the online photos.

'Let's give the owner a call and see if we can view it on Wednesday.'

'Yes let's.'

Melanie was teasing but I didn't mind. After a short conversation she held her hand over the microphone and turned to me.

'The only day she can show us the house is next Saturday,' she whispered.

That was a shame. It meant we would have to make two trips up the coast.

'OK, that'll have to do.'

Melanie agreed.

'Is two o'clock OK?' she asked.

I nodded, and the appointment was set.

After lunch on the terrace we enjoyed an afternoon snooze in the sun. We spent the rest of the day lounging around the apartment.

'When are we going back to Granada?' asked Melanie over dinner.

'What about tomorrow?'

'Why not?'

This time we'd go prepared.

Mornings at *Casa Jesse* are a real treat. Bright sunlight angles into the bedroom through large sliding doors which lead out onto the terrace. In the distance the morning sun reflects off the Mediterranean as if it were a sheet of glass. Tiny wrens fly around outside and perch on the iron railings surrounding the terrace.

It was a view worth staying in bed for but not that morning. We had a two-hour drive ahead of us. Unlike our previous trip to Granada, we wrapped up warm and threw our winter coats, scarves, and gloves onto the back seat. By midday we'd reached our destination. The size of the carpark underlined the Alhambra Palace's status as Spain's premier tourist attraction.

'I'm glad we brought our coats,' remarked Melanie, as we stepped from the car.

She wasn't kidding. The air felt bitterly cold.

Entry into the grounds of the palace cost twelve euros each. The ticket office was very organised although I wouldn't want to put it to the test during peak season. We followed the crowds through the gardens towards the palace, access to which is carefully controlled. Groups of approximately twenty are admitted at regular intervals. It's a slick operation and we didn't have to wait long.

The Alhambra Palace is undoubtedly an architectural treasure but I couldn't help feeling a little disappointed. Unlike most museums there are no exhibits or artefacts to indicate how the inhabitants lived. There are a number of fountains and interesting water features but the main fountain was undergoing restoration work and some of the others weren't working. The layout of the palace is interesting and the views over the old city are stunning. In season, I'm sure the gardens are beautiful too but the empty building lacked soul.

Within the grounds is a Parador Hotel. We took a break for refreshments. Even that was disappointing. The décor was reminiscent of a sixties Bond movie. I half-expected to bump into Odd Job on the way out.

We were glad we'd visited but won't be in a hurry to return. Faced with a choice between Spain's first or second most visited tourist destination, I know which I would choose. As for the Paradors at each location, it's hard to believe they belong to the same hotel group.

Why is it the final week of a holiday seems to pass twice as quickly as the previous weeks? We'd arranged to meet Francisco, the owner of the cottage in Playa del Río de la Miel, in the morning.

'Give me a call when you get there,' he'd said. 'I can be there in five minutes.'

We knew from experience that five minutes can mean anywhere from five to fifty, but it was another gloriously sunny day so we didn't mind waiting. Upon arrival we parked adjacent to the cottage in the shade of a carefully manicured blue jacaranda. Its foliage provided a natural carport. There were a few lilac-coloured flowers clinging to the tree but most had already fallen, carpeting the ground around it. Melanie rang Francisco and to our surprise his five-minute estimate turned out to be accurate.

'Casa María,' he said, pointing at a nameplate mounted on the wall outside the entrance.

The sign had been made out of the individually lettered ceramic tiles so typical of the area. Francisco unlocked a tall gate which led into a small enclosed courtyard.

'The house is owned by my wife,' he said.

Unlike the UK, assets held within a marriage are not jointly owned. The adage, "What's yours is ours and what's mine is my own" certainly doesn't apply in Spain.

The charming courtyard was enclosed by a high wall topped with terracotta tiles. On the left stood a brick-built barbecue with a large chimney that easily cleared the two-metre-high wall.

Francisco unlocked the front door and we followed him inside. The main living area was open plan with a small kitchen divided from the lounge by a marble-topped breakfast bar. The main feature of the lounge was an open fireplace. My eyes were drawn to French doors on the adjacent wall which opened out onto a narrow balcony. The cottage was perched on the clifftop with nothing but the Mediterranean Sea for company. Two bedrooms, one double and one twin, and a small bathroom completed the accommodation. The phrase "compact and bijou" sprang to mind. We wandered into the lounge and stared out of the French doors.

'What do you think?' I asked.

'It's a bit different to what we're used to but I like it, and look at that,' she said, tipping her head towards the sea.

There was no denying its main selling point: an unrestricted view of the Med, less than a stone's throw away.

Francisco explained that the TV received English channels which was nice to know but wouldn't have been a deal breaker. Utilities weren't included in the rental price.

'But the water heater is solar powered,' he added.

'What if the sun doesn't shine?' I asked.

Francisco smiled.

'Don't worry,' he said, 'the heater can be switched to the mains supply if needed.'

The cottage was simply furnished but fully equipped.

'Is there a dishwasher?' asked Melanie.

'No dishwasher,' replied Francisco.

Well, nearly everything.

We could live without a TV but a dishwasher was a different matter. This really could be a deal breaker. I stared at Melanie. She looked disappointed but not devastated. Francisco led us back outside into the courtyard.

'Do you swim?' he asked.

'Not at this time of year,' I replied.

'Come this way.'

Francisco opened a door in the corner of the courtyard and led us down a flight of steps to a compact terrace below. What we hadn't expected to find was a small but perfectly formed swimming pool. The view from the terrace added a new dimension to the panorama. We stood in silence, staring out to sea. Francisco brought our daydream to an end.

'What do you think?' he asked.

'It's lovely but can we think about it and let you know at the weekend?' I asked.

'No problem, I'll be here on Saturday until about eight o'clock.'

We thanked him for showing us around and headed back to Puebla Aida.

'What did you think?' I asked, on the drive home.

'The view from that balcony is out of this world.'

'What about the dishwasher?'

'I'm sure we can manage to wash a few dishes between us. What do you think?'

'I love it. The location is unbelievable. Can you image sitting on that balcony with a Teatime Taster and watching the sun setting over the Mediterranean?'

Casa María had stolen our hearts. The house we'd arranged to view in Cotobro would have its work cut out to trump that little place.

Our winter break was drawing to a close. It was difficult to believe we'd been here for nearly a month. How time flies when you're having fun.

'We've got another,' I called from the dining table.

Melanie was sitting outside enjoying the morning sun.

'Another what?'

'Booking,' I said, getting to my feet and dashing outside.

'Another! That's great news. Who is it this time?'

'A Dr Gerald Cann from Strathclyde.'

Melanie looked at me as if I was stupid.

'Don't you get it?' she asked.

'Get what?'

'Gerald Cann … Gerry can.'

'I bet he got some ribbing at school.'

'How big is the party?'

'Just two.'

'Perfect.'

We'd learnt from managing Bob and Janet's holiday rental that two guests are less work than four and when kids are involved the cleaning is a nightmare. We'd joked about adding "Pets welcome, kids not allowed" to the advertising but thought better of it.

'How long have they booked for?'

'Two weeks, from the 23rd of May until the 6th of June.'

We were really pleased. We hadn't reached the halfway point in January and we already had four weeks booked.

On Saturday afternoon we headed back up the coast to Cotobro. We'd arranged to meet the property owner at the entrance to the village. We followed her down the narrow street and stopped outside a new development of townhouses about halfway down the hillside.

'This looks very nice,' remarked Melanie.

Nice? It looked brand new.

The only blot on an otherwise excellent first impression was the number of steps leading from the road to the house. When our host pointed out that her property was on the row above that, I began to question the practicality of living halfway up a hillside. It wasn't so much the necessity of ascending and descending forty-plus steps every time we arrived and departed that bothered me, although that in itself was a pain in the quadriceps; it was the thought of hauling a week's shopping up them.

In contrast to *Casa María*, the house was very well appointed. It even had a dishwasher. However, unlike *Casa María*, the views over the bay, although stunning, were not unrestricted. Rooftops flowed down to the beach like a terracotta waterfall but our biggest concern was access.

'Is there any other way to get to the house?' I asked.

'You can park at the top of the hill and walk down but it's about the same distance,' she admitted.

That confession sealed this beautiful property's fate. For a week or two we could have put up with the inconvenience but not for a month. We thanked her for showing us the house and said we'd be in touch if we decided to stay.

'What did you think?' I asked, as we made our way back up the hill to the main road.

'It's a beautiful house but those steps would be a killer.'

I had to agree.

'And what about *Casa María*?'

'I like it. It's a bit basic but has everything we'd need and that view is to die for.'

Not for the first time we were in total agreement.

'Right then, let's call in on the way back and pay the man.'

Francisco had asked for a deposit of 150 euros to secure the booking. As we drove down the track towards the house, I spotted his car parked in the shade of the jacaranda. We rang the doorbell and waited. He opened the gate and invited us into the courtyard.

'We'd like to reserve the house,' I said, '12th of December until the 9th of January.'

I handed him the deposit. He counted it and we sealed the deal with a handshake.

'That's next year sorted,' I said, as we drove back to the apartment.

Two days later a 6:15 am alarm call jolted us into a new day. We'd packed all but the essentials the evening before. By 7:20 am we were on the road heading home to Galicia. We started the journey in bright sunshine. Before reaching Madrid, the clouds had closed in and it had started to rain. Eight hours into the journey we made our first stop. Melanie couldn't hold out any longer. By now the rain was bouncing down. I offered Jazz the option of a toilet break. She took one look at the weather and decided to stay put.

Despite the rain we'd made good progress and managed to drive all the way without topping up. One thousand one hundred kilometres on a tank of fuel. Beat that for efficiency.

15

Scaling the Heights

On a cold, damp morning the snuggle factor of a warm duvet is irresistible. The thought of having to abandon it was agonising. I sensed that Melanie was awake but resisted opening my eyes. Anything to delay the inevitable.

'It's twenty-five past nine,' she said.

Her surprise was understandable. We'd been asleep for over ten hours.

'Are you awake?' she asked.

'I am now.'

'Did I wake you?'

I resisted the temptation to lie.

'No, but it feels cold out there.'

'Coffee?'

'Yes please.'

Melanie slid out of bed and pulled on her fleecy dressing gown.

'It's freezing,' she said.

While Melanie wandered off into the kitchen, I dragged myself out of bed and pushed open the window shutters. The tiled floor felt like I'd stepped onto an ice rink. The view from the window perfectly illustrated the contrasting climate between the southern Mediterranean coast and the highlands of Galicia. The car and lawn were covered with a fresh dusting of snow. It hadn't settled on the driveway or the lane outside but all the vegetation was blanketed with a fresh coat of virgin white. Little wonder it felt so cold.

By lunchtime, all signs of the earlier flurry had disappeared thanks to torrential rain and high winds. The wind was so severe it uprooted trees along the N-120, causing traffic chaos. A week earlier we'd been staring out across the Mediterranean Sea and soaking up the sun's rays.

On the evening of the 28th of January, we were about to sit down to dinner when the phone rang. Melanie answered it.

'Who's speaking? … Oh hello, I thought I recognised the voice. Just one minute and I'll pass you over.'

'Who is it?' I mouthed.

'Edward,' she whispered, holding her hand over the microphone.

'Edward?'

'You know, Edward …' she said, thrusting the phone at me.

I was none the wiser.

'Hello.'

My confident greeting belied my ignorance.

'Hi Craig, it's Edward.'

My silence prompted a response.

'Edward from Singapore.'

The penny dropped immediately.

Three years ago, Edward and his wife Roberta had been guests at Bob and Janet's holiday rental property. Roberta had arrived at the house with their two young children. Edward would be joining them in a few days. By the time we went to conduct the Meet and Greet, Roberta was in quite a state. She and the kids had flown into Santiago de Compostela from Belgium where they'd spent a week with Roberta's parents before flying on to Galicia. When they left Singapore, they were a party of four: Roberta, the two kids, and a Filipino maid. What Roberta hadn't anticipated was the maid doing a runner less than twenty-four hours after landing in Belgium. It was difficult not to feel sorry for her. She was clearly stressed with her additional responsibilities.

'Hello Edward, how are you and the family?'

Pleasantries over, Edward announced that they'd bought a house in the area. The news wasn't a complete surprise as he'd quizzed us about the property market on their previous visit.

'Actually, it's more of a ruin than a house,' he confessed.

They were planning to visit this summer and were looking for somewhere to stay. Lucky for us; we had just the place. Without further ado he booked *Campo Verde* from the 4th until the 10th of July.

'Perhaps we can get together during our stay so we can pick your brains.'

At least his intentions were clear.

'No problem. I'm sure we can work something out.'

I only wished he'd spoken to us before buying the house. Only time would tell if he'd made the right decision.

The weather had been awful since our return from Andalucía. Pumping water out of the swimming pool had become a weekly chore. On the 6th of February we had another flurry of snow. Thankfully it melted almost as quickly as it had fallen. By the end of our third week back we were thoroughly fed up.

'Let's go out for Sunday lunch.'

Enthusiasm was in short supply.

'Where to?'

'What about Portugal?'

'Portugal?'

Did I hear a modicum of interest in her reply?

'Yes, I thought we might take a look at Melgaço.'

Six years ago, on one of our impromptu road trips, we had almost visited this Portuguese border town. On that occasion, time got the better of us and we returned home without having set foot in the place. We'd promised to return one day. I don't think either of us thought it would be so long. My suggestion sowed the seeds of anticipation; rainfall did the rest.

'That's a good idea. It's ages since we nearly visited,' said Melanie.

We set off early and took the scenic route. From Ourense we followed the OU-402. The road twists and turns as it follows the meandering course of the river Miño, falling and rising over the undulating terrain. Downstream the road merges into the OU-801 before crossing the border into Portugal and joining the N202 into Melgaço. We followed a signpost for the *castelo* and found a parking space opposite the town hall.

Even on an overcast day the beauty of the old town is undeniable and typically Portuguese. Narrow cobbled streets create a labyrinth of crisscrossing alleyways and tracks. Almost every twist and turn reveals another picturesque chapel. A mismatch of individually designed properties line the streets. Some have been painstakingly restored while others are in various stages of dereliction. Hidden treasures lie around every corner.

'What about here?' I said, standing outside the Cantinho do Adro restaurant.

The building looked charming, a throwback to a bygone era.

'Why not?'

I pushed open the door and we stepped inside. The first thing to greet us was warm air. Most restaurateurs in our local area seem reluctant to light a fire, but here the atmosphere felt snug and inviting. A young waitress came to greet us.

'*Para dos* (For two),' I said with a lisp.

Hello, goodbye, please, thank you, and *não faz mal* (it doesn't matter) are the extent of my Portuguese vocabulary. For everything else I speak in Spanish and add a lisp. She led us through into the restaurant which was separated from the bar area by a thick stone wall. Moments later she returned with menus.

'Did you bring the dictionary?' I asked.

Fifteen years ago we bought an English/Portuguese dictionary but never seem to have it with us when it's needed.

'No, did you?'

That told me.

Relying on potluck wasn't such a bad idea. What the food lacked in taste was more than made up for by the warm surroundings, convivial atmosphere, and helpful staff.

After lunch we wrapped up and headed for the castle. The fortifications date back to the 12th century. At the time of its construction it represented Portugal's most northerly defences. Within the walls is an impressive castle keep. The walls themselves can be accessed via stone steps located at regular intervals along its length. The height of each step was quite extraordinary, matched only by the narrowness of the tread.

'Come on,' I said, placing my foot on the first step.

'Do be careful,' cautioned Melanie.

I kept my eyes fixed firmly on the top and climbed.

'Are you coming, or not?' I called, having reached the summit.

Melanie looked nervous. Carefully she began her ascent, one step at a time.

'Someone is going break their neck one day,' she said.

It's rare to find such blatant disregard for health and safety.

'I bet more soldiers died going up and down those steps than in battle,' I joked.

In terms of public safety, the top of the ramparts fared little better. The merlons had long since disappeared along with the battlements they'd been sitting on. All that remained was an uneven stone surface, most of which was covered with a bright green moss. On such a damp day it made the surface as slippery as a skating rink. It seemed inconceivable that there wasn't a single safety rail.

'I'm not sure I like it up here,' said Melanie.

Since climbing she'd been standing motionless in the centre of the wall with her arms slightly open to assist her balance.

'Don't worry. It's as safe as houses.'

A ridiculous statement given the situation.

In an attempt to reassure her I wandered along the wall without a care in the world. Reluctantly she followed, stopping occasionally on the pretext of taking in the scenery.

'Let's have a look inside the keep,' I suggested.

Melanie was eager to get off the ramparts but less keen to negotiate the descent.

'It might be an idea to go down backwards,' I said.

Melanie took my advice. One step at a time she made her way back to terra firma. I followed her example. On balance, my undignified descent was preferable to a life-changing fall.

An elevated doorway is a design feature of 12th and 13th century castle keeps. The entrance to this one was about three metres above ground level. Fortunately, the council had spared further blushes by installing a metal staircase which bore more than a passing resemblance to a fire escape.

We climbed the steps and entered the tower. What seven hundred years ago would have cost countless lives to access is now available for the princely sum of three euros. On days like this I couldn't help wondering if it was worth anyone's time to hold the fort.

The tower houses a museum and other exhibitions which Portuguese speaking visitors will undoubtedly find interesting. A lack of translation sped our ascent to the roof. The final few steps led to a closed metal door about the size of an attic skylight. I went first and pushed it open. A gust of icy wind swept through the opening. Miserable clouds did their best to dampen our experience. Undeterred, I climbed the last few stairs and stepped out onto the roof. Melanie followed.

'Wow! I bet the views are lovely on a nice day,' said Melanie.

Pale grey clouds clung to the horizon. Gentle winds nudged them along, affording fleeting glimpses of pastures and forests.

'I bet they are,' I replied.

The best views were of the surrounding town. From our lofty position it reminded me of one of those model villages Mum and Dad would drag me and my sister around when we were kids.

'It's freezing up here,' said Melanie.

'Perhaps it's time to head back.'

She didn't need asking twice and bolted for the exit.

'I can't lift this,' she said, tugging on the handle of the steel door.

'Let me have a go.'

Opening it against the elements was much harder than pushing it from inside.

'Stop messing around.'

If only that were the case. With one almighty tug I lifted the door and held it open for Melanie. She climbed through and I followed, lowering the door as I climbed down the steps.

Once on the ground we made our way back to the car.

'Where are you going?' I asked.

'Isn't it this way?'

The streets of the old town are a maze of narrow alleyways. That said, Melanie was heading in completely the opposite direction to where we'd parked.

'No, it's down here.'

Left to her own devices, I'm sure she'd still be wandering the streets of Melgaço.

'I really enjoyed that,' said Melanie on the drive home.

'We'll have to do it again when the weather improves.'

That evening the phone rang and once again Melanie answered it.

'Just one minute and I'll pass you over,' she said, holding the receiver towards me.

'Who is it?' I whispered.

'It's about the house,' she mouthed.

The caller, a Mr Robert Panton, wanted to check the availability of *Campo Verde*. Two people for a fortnight in June. I rushed through into the office to look at the calendar.

'Yes, the house is available.'

'In that case I'd like to make a reservation. Will you need a deposit?'

I took Mr Panton's email address and forwarded him the details.

'That's seven weeks we've got now,' I said.

'That's great.'

Bookings had been a little slower than we'd hoped for but this one brought us to within three weeks of our ten-week target.

It's remarkable how a ray of sunshine can put a spring in your step. There's nothing more frustrating than being cooped up indoors when there's work to do in the garden. Melanie nudged open the bedroom door and Jazz sprinted past her and leapt onto the bed.

'Good morning, how are you this bright and sunny day?'

Pet owners will appreciate this one-sided conversation. For the rest of you, the answer is yes, we are stark raving mad.

'Here you go,' said Melanie, handing me two dog treats and placing a mug of steaming coffee on the bedside table.

Jazz sat to attention, waiting patiently for her reward.

'Please,' I said.

Her response was to offer me a paw.

'And the other.'

She swapped legs and offered up the other.

'Good girl.'

Gently she took the treat and wolfed it down. Without request, she offered her paw again.

'Here you go.'

She took the second treat and quickly ate that one. Despite never getting a third, she always tries again.

'That's it, there's no more.'

Without fuss she retired to the foot of the bed, walked around in a tight circle, dropped down, and curled up into a ball.

'I'm going to make a start on the bamboo today,' I announced.

Six years ago, when we first moved into *El Sueño*, we spent a small fortune on garden plants. We ordered them from a large garden centre near the coast. What we failed to appreciate was the difference in the climate between there and our inland home. Winter casualties were high. We lost a lemon tree and a small palm tree in the first year. The orange tree and camellia fared a little better but even they gave up the ghost after three winters. That said, if the weather hadn't killed them our lack of husbandry probably would have. Neither Melanie nor I know the first thing about gardening and lack the inclination to learn.

One species that not only survived but positively flourished was the bamboo. We'd bought two plants for no other reason than we got a lot of greenery for our money. We planted them in the back garden, one in the gravel bed and the other on the edge of the lawn. For the first three years we couldn't have been happier. They were low maintenance and eye-catching. It wasn't until year four that things started to get out of control.

The ground under the gravel was covered with a weed-proof membrane. What we hadn't counted on was the strength and determination of young bamboo shoots. We were oblivious to the plant's fearsome reputation as one of the fastest growing plants known to man. Rampant didn't come close. The gravel bed covers an area of roughly forty-five square metres. Young shoots were popping up everywhere, punching their way through the membrane and heading skyward at a rate of thirty centimetres a day. Something had to be done.

'What are you going to do?' asked Melanie.

'We're going to have to dig it up.'

'What, all of it?'

I could hear the disappointment in her voice.

'I think so.'

Melanie's bottom lip dropped.

'I'll tell you what, before we make a decision, I'll remove the gravel and find out what's happening under the weed-proof membrane.'

Melanie's face lit up.

It felt good to be outside in the sunlight. The air temperature was quite cool but shovelling a few tonnes of gravel soon warmed me up. By lunchtime I'd had enough. Most of the membrane was now exposed and the gravel was piled up on the terrace.

The following day I continued. The weed-proof membrane was in remarkably good condition. Starting from the corner furthest away from the bamboo, I began peeling it back to expose the earth below. To my amazement, the roots had spread out across the underside of the membrane like the endoskeleton of a mythical hydra. The extent of its growth was phenomenal.

'Come and look at this,' I called from the kitchen door.

Melanie came to look.

'Oh my word!'

'Exactly. We're going to have to dig it up.'

'Can't we keep a little bit?' she pleaded.

When a light breeze drifts through the garden on a warm summer's day, the sound of its rustling leaves was very relaxing, but what choice did we have?

'Look how quickly it's grown. If we don't remove it all, I'll be forever digging it up.'

'What about the other?' she asked, pointing to the clump on the edge of the lawn.

At some point, that too would have to go, but for the time being I could keep new shoots under control with the lawnmower.

'We'll leave that one for now.'

My response lifted her mood.

'But it's going to have to come out at some point,' I added.

Melanie was happy with the compromise and wandered back inside.

Before I could completely remove the membrane I had to lop the canes that had forced their way through it. By the time I'd finished, I had quite a pile.

'Do you need a hand?'

I'd been so busy I hadn't noticed Melanie step outside.

'Just in time.'

Each cane, or culm as they are called, was covered with long, thin branches that would have to be removed before we could use them as garden canes.

'What do you want me to do?'

'Can you get another pair of secateurs and help me remove these?'

'All of them!'

'One day you'll thank me for all these garden canes.'

Melanie rolled her eyes and fetched a pair of secateurs. Bamboo is much tougher than it looks and within the hour we were both feeling the pain.

'Ouch!'

'What's the matter?'

'I can't do this any more,' she moaned, pulling off her gardening gloves. 'Look.'

The palms of her hands were red and blisters had started to bubble below her fingers.

'Haven't we got enough yet?' she added.

We had sufficient to open a garden centre but I hated the thought of wasting any.

'You put the kettle on and I'll finish off,' I said.

By the time Melanie had brewed up, I'd all but finished.

After a quick coffee break, I pulled up the remaining membrane. With the exception of the area around the original plant, it came up quite easily. Only then did we see the full extent of its incursion. At the base of each culm was a bulbous root or rhizome. From there, a tangled mass of roots had spread out across the entire area.

'Right, that's enough for one day,' I said.

'Is it time for a Teatime Taster?'

'I think we've earned one.'

A quick wash and change and we retired to the far end of the garden to catch the last few rays of the spring sunshine before it dipped below the horizon. Digging up the bamboo was going to be much harder than I'd expected.

16

Taking the Piste

Adult advice is never far away when you're growing up. Take school attendance for example. The number of times I'd heard the phrase, "Make the most of it; they're the best days of your life". I didn't believe it then and don't endorse it now. Memories of school life are few and far between. I excelled at maths but preferred English; however, it's teachers who influence pupils, not subjects.

In my second year at secondary school we had a particularly inspirational English teacher. Her name escapes me but her lessons don't. She posed questions that challenged our preconceptions. 'Is pain good or bad?' she asked on one occasion. As someone who's lived with pain all their life, my instinct was to answer 'Bad'. After debating the topic, I changed my opinion. Pain is a gauge which limits the damage we might otherwise inflict on ourselves.

Tackling the bamboo had sent my gauge soaring. What used to be blamed on a build-up of lactic acid is now referred to as DOMS: delayed onset muscle soreness. Whatever its title, the day after my exertions I felt as stiff as a board.

'I can't move,' I said, as I lay motionless in bed.

A slight exaggeration but my whole body felt like it had been used as a punchbag.

'My fingers ache,' replied Melanie.

I knew exactly how she felt. Hours of pruning with secateurs had taken its toll on both of us. Shovelling tonnes of gravel had been my downfall.

Melanie went to put the kettle on and I dragged my aching frame out of bed and pushed open the window shutters. Bright sunlight angled across the driveway. What better tonic than a glorious spring morning. I crawled back into bed and waited for Melanie to return. Jazz dashed in and launched herself onto the bed.

'Jazz … Be careful.'

Her paws found all the wrong places and my plea fell on deaf ears.

'Here you go,' said Melanie, placing a mug of coffee on the bedside table and handing me two dog biscuits.

Jazz finally sat still, waiting for her morning treats. Melanie slumped back into bed and the morning feeding ritual could begin.

'It's a lovely morning.'

'Yes,' I replied.

We couldn't have wished for better gardening weather, but I had other ideas.

'I thought we might drive out to Cabeza de Manzaneda today. What do you think?'

Cabeza de Manzaneda is a ski resort an hour's drive from home. Neither of us are skiers but we'd often talked about driving up there to take a look. What better time than on a clear spring day?

'What about the bamboo?'

'It's not going anywhere and I could do with a day off.'

'In that case, let's do it.'

We left home and drove east towards Monforte de Lemos before travelling south along the OU-903 to the village of Doade. From there the road tumbles down the valley of the river Sil. Dormant vineyards occupied the southern slopes. They grow on narrow terraces or *bancales* which hug the contours of the valley and climb from the riverbank like a giant staircase.

After crossing the river, we began our ascent to the town of Castro Caldelas and then followed the OU-536 to A Pobra de Trives. In the centre of town, we took a right turn onto the OU-0703 and caught our first glimpse of the snow-covered peak. Anticipation grew as we neared our destination. After nine tantalising kilometres we came to the intersection with the OUR-CV-652. At this point the landscape changed from green to white as the road climbed steeply towards the resort hotel of Oca Nova. Parked cars lined both sides of the approach road.

'What now?' asked Melanie.

'I'm not sure.'

This was our first visit to a ski resort. I found a space and parked. The place was a hive of activity. Well-equipped skiers marched past carrying their skis. Everyone seemed to know exactly what they were doing and where they were going. Talk about ducks out of water, or should that be penguins? We drifted along following the general direction of travel.

'Over there,' said Melanie, pointing at a building some thirty metres away.

A sign read *taquilla* (ticket office). To get to it we would have to cross an open area of compacted snow. How inconsiderate not to clear a path.

'It looks a bit slippery,' said Melanie.

Her observation highlighted our lack of preparedness for a day trip to a ski resort. Gloves and a woolly hat wouldn't stop us falling head over heels. When it comes to footwear, I have the perfect excuse. The only design option I get when choosing a new pair of bespoke orthopaedic footwear is black or tan. Melanie had no such defence. Slick-soled leather boots were hardly suitable attire for scaling a ski run.

To make matters worse, seven days earlier Melanie's mum had slipped on ice and broken her wrist. What had initially been diagnosed as a straightforward break turned out to be a more complex fracture which required surgery. I sensed this was playing on her mind.

'Just follow me,' I said.

My goal was a flight of icy steps thirty metres from the edge of the carpark. Cautiously, I made my move, one short step at a time. Halfway across I turned to check on Melanie's progress. She was using the flailing penguin method of locomotion. Hardly the most glamorous stance but it seemed to be working.

'Are you alright?'

I can't imagine why I asked. If she answered no I couldn't do anything to help her.

'No, not really.'

'Use short steps and keep as upright as possible.'

Sound advice but not exactly helpful.

The reason a footpath hadn't been cleared became blatantly obvious when I turned to continue. Out of nowhere a brightly-clad skier flashed past and came within a whisker of sweeping me off my feet. My sudden recoil almost resulted in a Bambi on ice moment. I regained my balance just in time to avoid a second and then a third speeding skier. I felt like a lone skittle in a bowling alley. I'd hardly had time to catch my breath when three young snowboarders came hurtling towards me on a direct collision course. My mind was a confusion of options. What should I do? Running was out of the question. I stood my ground, wide eyed and motionless. My fate was in their hands. One by one they "caught an edge" and swerved around my trembling frame. With the coast clear I made a beeline for the steps.

Melanie had made it to the halfway point. I glanced across at the adjacent slope. The coast was clear. All she had to do was stay on her feet and keep moving. I crossed my fingers and hoped for the best. I wanted to hold out a helping hand but thought better of it. The last thing we needed was the pair of us in a heap on the snow.

The steps to the ticket office were a little easier to negotiate. Heavy footfall had turned white snow into grey slush. The banister came in handy as we clawed our way to the top. I felt a sense of euphoria after successfully completing stage one of our arctic expedition with all my limbs intact.

'We'd like to go to the summit,' I said to the young lady manning the ticket booth.

She looked at us and smiled.

'And back down?' she asked.

What a strange question; did it look like we were intending to spend a night on the mountain? That's when it dawned on me that all but a few inadequately dressed and poorly shod lunatics would be skiing back down.

'Yes,' I replied.

'That'll be six euros each.'

That didn't seem bad.

As I handed her the money a party of three skiers joined the queue. The young lady handed me the tickets and looked to her next customers. Melanie and I stared at each other and then at the tickets.

'Where next?' whispered Melanie, as we skidded off.

'Let's see where these three go,' I replied.

The three young men bought their tickets and marched off without a care in the world. We watched as they scaled a three-metre-high, snow-covered banking to the chairlift: no drama, no fuss.

'It's up there.'

Melanie looked petrified.

'Let's go this way,' I said.

The snow to the right of us was fresh and crisp. The route was slightly longer but it hadn't been trampled by hordes of impatient skiers. Fresh snow should give us the traction we needed to reach the top. At least that was the idea.

'There's loads of snow over there,' said Melanie.

'Trust me, it'll be much easier to climb.'

At the rear of the ticket office was a cafeteria. Thermal-clad patrons were sitting outside sipping hot chocolate and relaxing in the spring sunshine. Melanie and I seemed destined to become the afternoon's entertainment. Talk about living in a fishbowl.

'Come on,' I said, heading off towards the deeper snow.

At the foot of the banking I turned sideways and began the ascent. My first step sank six inches into the virgin snow. Arms outstretched, I levered myself upwards one footstep at a time. Melanie followed in mine before realising the footholes were a little short for her size eights. After a few hair-raising moments we made it safely to the top. Thankfully, our audience refrained from applauding.

We gathered our breath and watched in horror as the six-seater chairlift swept down the mountainside, swung around the end terminal, and bolted back up the run at a frightening speed. I thought it best not to dwell on the scene as Melanie has a weak constitution for such things. She once collapsed after going on a mild-mannered kiddies' ride at Disneyland Paris. She was twenty-six at the time.

'See, I told you that way would be easier. Come on.'

I headed off towards the boarding station.

'Watch where you're putting your feet,' I added.

Anything to distract her from the chairlift.

Many years ago, as part of Melanie's thirty-fifth birthday celebrations, I booked a trip on the London Eye Ferris wheel. That too is boarded while in motion. Given her disposition, secrecy had been paramount but everything went to plan and Melanie really enjoyed the experience. That said, this was an altogether different beast. The London Eye rotates at a leisurely 0.9 kilometres an hour. This contraption was travelling at closer to thirty. I didn't know about her but I was more than a little apprehensive.

The concrete boarding area was covered in slippery grey sludge. A member of staff was supervising the loading.

'Come on,' he said, gesturing us towards him.

I thought we might at least have time to prepare ourselves but no such luck.

'There and there,' he instructed, pointing at an imaginary X on the concrete.

Melanie and I shuffled into position. We stared at each other in horror as the six-seater swing clattered into the disembarking area, swung through 360 degrees, and headed straight towards us. In one seamless motion it swooped us off our feet and headed up the mountainside. The pair of us let out a nervous laugh.

'Are you alright?' I asked.

'That was brilliant. It's a bit scary though.'

It felt like we were hanging in mid-air.

'I think we're meant to pull this down,' I said, reaching overhead and pulling the guardrail towards us.

'That's better.'

Welded to the guardrail were footrests. We lifted our feet up and grabbed hold of the handrail.

'This is wonderful,' beamed Melanie.

Not only were the views breathtaking but travelling by chairlift felt exhilarating. All I could think of were the Honey Bus lyrics to the classic 1970s Nimble advert. We might not have been harnessed to a red and white striped hot air balloon but it felt pretty close.

My nostalgic daydream was brought to a shuddering halt as the chairlift rumbled over the first of a series of towers supporting the steel cable. Melanie grabbed my hand.

'What was that?'

'Don't worry, we'll be fine,' I reassured her.

The ski run below weaved its way through a picturesque pine forest. Snow-covered trees gave it Christmas card appeal. Skiers slipped past beneath us, slaloming from side to side to keep their speed under control. They made it look easy but I doubt it is. Young snowboarders, dressed in designer gear, used any imperfection to practise their moves, some more successfully than others. Over the tops of the trees were other more open ski runs. I turned in my seat to take in the views. Stretched out behind us was an endless panorama of rolling hills and mountains. An overlapping collage of differing shades of blue, fading into the distant horizon.

'Look at that.'

'Just be careful,' cautioned Melanie.

The lift floated onward and upward towards a blazing sun. The higher we climbed the more outstanding the views. The snow below looked close enough to jump into, but even I'm not that stupid. In places the actions of skiers had created abstract patterns on the mountainside and in others the snow shone like a sheet of glass. As we rose the air cooled and snow-capped peaks of distant mountains came into view. The ride to the summit seemed to take forever but was probably less than five minutes.

Boarding the chairlift had been terrifying; alighting looked even worse. As the chairlift hurtled towards the summit, we prepared to disembark. A shallow mound of snow marked the point of exit. As skiers approached, they raised the guardrail, lifted their skis over the mound, and stood up. The gentle incline and force of gravity swept them clear of the speeding seats. That was all well and good for those lucky enough to have two fibreglass floorboards strapped to their feet. With nothing more than a pair of orthopaedic boots for company, this was going to be devilishly more challenging.

'Are you ready?' I asked, as I prepared to raise the guardrail.

'No.'

'As soon as we clear the mound, jump off and walk away at an angle of forty-five degrees,' I instructed.

'What?'

'Veer off to the left. Whatever you do, don't walk straight ahead.'

'What do you mean?'

'Are you ready?'

'No! What do you mean?'

'Here we go.'

'But what do you mean?'

I pushed the guardrail upwards and readied my escape. The end of the ride was approaching at an alarming speed.

'Ready.'

'No.'

'Remember to walk away at an angle.'

'I don't know what you mean.'

Melanie's shrill tone highlighted her fear.

'Go, go, go!'

I stepped off the seat and scuttled away like a sprinting penguin. Thank heavens no one was watching. Melanie did exactly what I'd told her not to do and dashed forwards. How the row of seats missed whisking her up and carrying her back down the mountain is anyone's guess.

I skidded across to see if she was alright. By the time I'd reached her, four skiers riding on the row of seats behind us were about to disembark. We were standing directly in their path. I grabbed Melanie and closed my eyes. I needn't have worried. Their skiing prowess far outweighed our lack of chairlift etiquette.

'Are you alright?' I asked.

'Fine.'

Before we'd had chance to move, two snowboarders jumped off the next row of seats and whizzed past.

'Come on, let's get out of the way.'

I would have offered to help her but I was struggling to keep myself upright. Ten metres from the lift the snow had a bit more bite. Cautiously, we moved away from the danger zone.

'That was a bit scary,' said Melanie.

'To say the least, but look at those views.'

It felt as if we were standing on top of the world and, depending on where we cast our gaze, we could almost believe were alone. For as far as the eye could see, not another peak came close to our altitude. Standing there, staring out across that endless landscape, I could only imagine how Edmund Hillary felt when he conquered Everest.

The scenery was breathtaking but other than that, there's very little to do on top of a mountain except descend it.

'Shall we go back down?' I asked.

'I think so.'

We made our way towards the chairlift. Unlike the well-trodden approach at the base station, the path at the summit wasn't immediately obvious. Given that most people ski back down, this was hardly surprising.

'This way looks the best,' I said, heading out in front.

Half a dozen steps later, I was up to my knees in snow.

Unbeknown to me, Melanie had taken a different route. I retraced my steps and tagged onto her footprints. Staff members at the summit are surplus to requirement. Deciding which chair to board, and when and where to position ourselves, was down to us.

'Ready?' I asked.

'Ready when you are.'

'We'll take the one after the next one.'

'Not this one?'

'No, the next one after that.'

We had one chance to get it right. The consequences of failure could be life-changing. Speed was important but balance was essential.

'This one, go, go, go.'

Like two penguins we shuffled into position. The row of chairs clattered into the station and catapulted around the terminal. Like the embrace of a professional ballroom dancer, it whisked us off our feet and up, up, and down we went.

The ride back seemed shorter than the ascent but of course it wasn't. At the bottom we alighted like old pros, with the emphasis on old. The next challenge was descending the snow-covered banking to the carpark. A difficult job made more daunting by the spectre of speeding skiers. I chose the kamikaze approach: head down and full tilt ahead. Miraculously, I reached the bottom unscathed and managed to stop without ending up on my backside. Melanie took a more cautious approach. She crouched as low as possible and used her hands as stabilisers. If she did fall, her backside was so close to the ground that only her pride would feel the impact. I couldn't resist taking a few snaps.

'Aw, don't,' she complained, but the moment was captured for posterity.

We chose a different route home. Why waste such a beautiful spring day?

On leaving A Pobra de Trives we took the OU-CV-65 towards Montefurado. The scenery en route was spectacular: an overlapping landscape of rolling hills and deep river valleys. Shades of blue and grey faded into the distance as the earth merged with a hazy blue sky. The final descent into the village of Montefurado was particularly stunning. The dam on the outskirts has created a lochlike reservoir nestling in the valley. It's fed by the rivers Navea and Bibei. At that time of year, it was full to capacity.

Eventually, the road merges with the N-120. We headed west and within an hour were trundling through Canabal and pulling into the driveway. As usual, Jazz was delighted to see us.

'That was brilliant,' said Melanie, as we enjoyed a well-deserved Teatime Taster.

I couldn't have agreed more.

17

The Lonesome Pine

It took six days to clear the gravel bed of bamboo. A battle of attrition that ended in victory.

'Done,' I said, as I tossed the last shovelful of gravel onto the bed.

'It's a bit bare,' remarked Melanie.

Personally, I like the minimalist look, to say nothing of the low maintenance.

Our gardening conquest coincided with confirmation of our fifth booking at *Campo Verde*, a party of three (two adults and a child). That brought our total to nine weeks, one short of our target. Each new booking filled us with confidence. We'd taken a risk, and in many respects still were, but we couldn't have asked for a better start to our fledgling enterprise.

On the 28th of the month, three weeks of unseasonably good weather came to an abrupt end. Being cooped up inside gave me the opportunity to reflect on my next project. April would mark the second anniversary of the creation of our *huerta* or vegetable garden. Melanie's initial enthusiasm for gardening had quickly waned. It was much easier to cadge a lettuce off a neighbour than grow our own, especially as they're more than happy to oblige. To avoid it becoming an overgrown eyesore, repurposing was required.

'What about a vineyard?' I asked.

Once again, my musings had translated into speech. Melanie raised an eyebrow.

'What about a vineyard?'

'In the *huerta*. What about planting a vineyard?'

'If that's what you want, then go ahead.'

Her willingness to secede the *huerta* without a fight reinforced my rationale for change.

Between rain showers I measured up and made plans. The *huerta* was a little over a hundred square metres with the potential to extend. Overshadowing the plot was a ten-metre-tall pine tree that would have to go. When we first moved here it provided a pleasant focal point at the end of the garden. Since then it had grown several metres taller and much wider. It had also developed an easterly lean. Felling this giant wouldn't be easy. What I needed was a chainsaw.

'I've been thinking about this vineyard,' I said, over lunch.

'Oh yes, and what have you been thinking?'

'The pine tree will have to go.'

'Aw, why?'

'It creates too much shade and it's not very pretty.'

Her disappointment was short-lived.

'Who's going to cut it down?' she asked.

The hook had been baited and the line cast.

'I thought I'd give it a go.'

'You? Give it a go? What with?'

The catch was hooked. All I had to do now was reel it in.

'You're right. The tools I've got are no good for that job. What I need is a chainsaw.'

Before she could say another word, I continued.

'Without one I'll have to climb the tree and fell it in stages.'

If that didn't do the trick nothing would.

Three years ago, we'd watched in horror as José the lumberjack fell out of the plane tree in the front garden. A combination of luck and quick thinking resulted in him catching one of the lower branches on his way down which saved him from hitting the ground. If it could happen to a professional tree surgeon, what chance did I have?

'Do you know how to use a chainsaw?'

I hadn't a clue but how difficult could it be? I thought it best to sidestep that question and moved on.

'I was thinking I might get an electric one.'

'That's a good idea.'

Melanie was warming to the idea.

'The next time we go into town we'll see what BricoKing have to offer.'

'OK.'

Job done. I gave myself a metaphorical pat on the back for delivering another successful pitch.

Over the next few days the weather worsened. Intermittent showers turned into a continuous downpour and the wind strengthened.

'Aw Jazz, did you have to?'

Melanie had gone to make our morning coffee and was clearly unhappy with the dog. When she returned, Jazz was nowhere to be seen.

'Where's Jazz?'

'She's on her bed.'

'What's she done?'

'Left a puddle by the French doors.'

That was really out of character. She'd never given us any problems in that respect.

'Do you think she's unwell?' I asked.

'She seems alright.'

'Jazz, come on lass!' I called.

She wandered into the bedroom looking very sheepish.

'Come on,' I said, patting the duvet.

She leapt up and sat between us.

'Have you been a naughty girl?'

Her facial expression dropped. If she wasn't guilty, she was doing a good impersonation.

The morning after we were woken by the sound of garden furniture sliding across the front porch and colliding with the iron railings. Strong winds were howling around the house and the rain was lashing down. I pulled the duvet over my ears and tried to block out the noise.

'Are you asleep?' asked Melanie.

'As if. It sounds like the end of days out there.'

'Shall we have a coffee?'

'Why not.'

Melanie hopped out of bed and pulled on her fleecy dressing gown. No sooner had she opened the doors than Jazz sprinted into the bedroom and jumped onto the bed. She was clearly upset by the storm.

'You're alright now,' I said.

When Melanie returned it was her turn to look sheepish.

'What's matter?' I asked.

'Do you remember what happened yesterday?'

'Yes.'

'Well, it's happened again.'

Jazz was staring right at me waiting for her morning treats.

'Jazz?'

Her ears dropped and she dipped her head.

'It's not her fault,' said Melanie.

'Not her?'

'No.'

I hoped she wasn't accusing me.

'Who then?'

'It's the rain.'

I had visions of water dripping through the ceiling.

'The rain?'

'The wind is forcing it through the seal on the French doors.'

In one respect we were pleased. On the other hand, leaking doors weren't ideal. I turned to Jazz.

'I think she owes you an apology, lass.'

Her ears pricked and her eyes lit up.

'Here you go,' I said, handing her a treat.

Within no time, all was forgiven.

When it came to choosing a chainsaw, I opted for the least expensive. It wasn't as if it would get much use. I settled on a Garland sixteen inch. It had a durable, bright yellow plastic body with black trim and bore more than a passing resemblance to a child's toy. Despite its appearance this was a serious piece of kit that demanded respect. According to statistics, there are over thirty-six thousand chainsaw related injuries every year.

'What do you think?' I asked Melanie, proudly displaying my new toy.

'I think you need to be careful.'

I was gripping it firmly in both hands and making wild slashing motions in the air.

'It's not plugged in,' I replied.

'Stop waving it around.'

That told me. I placed it back in the box and went to investigate my intended victim.

The tree was located just outside the garden wall which suggested it had self-seeded. A strong wind or passing bird were the most likely culprits. Over the years it had developed a Pisa-like stance and the roots were in danger of breaking the boundary wall.

Predicting where it might fall was difficult. Doubts began to surface. I had the tool for the job but did I have the skill? Any mistake could have serious repercussions. Putting personal injury to one side, it could easily destroy the garden wall. If things went disastrously wrong, the swimming pool was well within the drop zone. Perhaps a plan B was called for.

'I might ask Roy to give me a hand,' I said on my return.

'That's a good idea.'

It seemed Melanie had already considered the possibility.

'Yes, I'll give him a ring and see if he can help.'

I knew full well that the term "help" meant asking Roy to do the job for me. Thankfully, he was more than happy to give me a hand.

'I'll call in tomorrow morning. Have you got a chainsaw?' he asked.

'Brand new. Still in the box.'

Before Roy arrived, I ran an extension cable from the shed to the tree and made sure the chainsaw was working properly. Everything seemed fine, so much so that Melanie came dashing out of the kitchen as soon as she heard the motor.

'What are you doing?' she called.

'Just making sure it works.'

Within minutes of Roy's arrival, I knew I'd made the right decision. From the back of his van he handed me two heavy-duty ratchet straps and a length of rope. There was obviously more to felling a tree than owning a chainsaw.

'What do you think?' I asked, tipping my head towards the Garland.

'It's electric.'

'Is that alright?'

'Yeah, that'll do the job.'

That was a relief.

Roy began by looping one of the straps around the pine tree and securing the end to the base of an oak tree. He did the same with the second strap but secured the end of that one to the garden wall. When tensioned, the two straps created a right angle. In theory, the pine would fall equidistant between the two. As an insurance policy he tied a rope around the pine and gave me the other end.

'Take this and stand over there,' he said, pointing to a patch of ground between the two tensioned straps, 'and whatever you do, don't pull until I tell you to.'

Roy double checked the tension on the straps before picking up the chainsaw. He didn't give much away but seemed happy with the setup. The new saw ripped through the trunk. A second cut created a wedge-shaped gash.

'OK, take the strain but don't pull,' he called.

I gripped the rope tightly but resisted the urged to wrap it around my hand. If anything went wrong, I didn't want to be leashed to an unstoppable force. That's when it dawned on me, the glaring paradox in Roy's methodology. The mug holding the rope, namely me, would soon be encouraged to pull a great big pine tree towards himself. Was I mad?

Roy began the critical cut. If the tree toppled backwards, we could say goodbye to the swimming pool. If it fell to the right or left, one of the boundary walls would cop it. Any of those outcomes was bad enough but if this piece of rope was shorter than the height of the tree it was curtains for me. Nervously, I stared at the top of the tree, trying to judge my fate.

'OK, pull!' shouted Roy.

Time for thinking was over; action was required. I tugged on the rope and the pine let out a thunderous crack before surrendering to my encouragement.

'Timber!' called Roy.

I watched in horror as the towering pine toppled towards me. Anxiety turned to joy as it crashed to the ground a few metres from my feet. We'd done it. The tree had fallen exactly as intended. Roy set about removing the branches before sawing the trunk into foot-long rounds. A phone call from Maria brought his day to an end.

'Will you be alright to finish off?' he asked.

If truth be known I couldn't wait to get my hands on my new toy.

'No problem Roy. I'll take it from here. Thanks for your help. I couldn't have done it without you.'

Roy's departure coincided with Melanie calling me in for lunch.

'We're going to need permission to burn,' I said.

Trimming the trunk had left a mountain of waste to dispose of. Burning rubbish is a serious business in Galicia. The danger to life and property is so great that a licence is needed. Applicants are required to call a dedicated premium rate number and explain where, when, and what they wish to burn. The licence is valid for one week from Wednesday to the following Tuesday so timing is important. During spells of unseasonably good weather and throughout the summer, open fires are strictly forbidden due to the risk of them spreading and penalties for breaching the rules include time behind bars.

'*We* are, are we?'

'Would you mind ringing up, you're much better on the phone than I am.'

'When?'

'If you call them today, we might be able to make a start on Wednesday.'

'OK, I'll ring up after lunch.'

Permission was granted and a licence number issued. By the end of the day, our lonesome pine had been reduced to two piles: one of neatly cut logs ready to be transported to the *bodega* at *Campo Verde*, and the other of spindly twigs awaiting burning.

'A couple of trips should do it,' I said, as I stepped into the kitchen.

'Do what?'

'Get those logs shipped to *Campo Verde*.'

'You're not going to do it now, are you?'

'No. I'll make a start in the morning.'

'Will you need me?'

'If you don't mind.'

When it comes to moving heavy loads, Melanie and I complement each other perfectly. I lift and she pushes. My body isn't designed for travelling over rough terrain. Upper body strength compensates for a lack of mobility. In contrast, what Melanie lacks in strength is more than made up for in her ability to wheel a barrow. Whether it's a load of concrete or in this case logs, working as a team we get the job done.

On Tuesday morning I hitched the trailer to the car and we made a start. I loaded and unloaded, and Melanie wheeled the barrow from back to front. Weight rather than volume dictated the load size. My prediction of two trips proved correct. Unloading at *Campo Verde* was easy. I unhitched the trailer and wheeled it straight into the *bodega*. The freshly cut wood would need time to season but once it had I would split it for firewood.

It's said that burning wood warms you three times, when you cut it, when you split it, and when you burn it. If anything, the last two days had called into question that wisdom. There's no mention of the sweaty palms generated by the prospect of a ten-metre-tall pine tree falling on your head or the fiery ardour of getting your hands on a chainsaw for the first time. And what about the warm glow of humping the wood from one side of the house to the other and the sticky heat of loading and unloading? In short, the whole idea of burning wood harks back to prehistoric times and to think that some folk find it romantic. Give me electric storage radiators any day of the week.

On the drive home I had another bright idea.

'I think we ought to stay at the house before the start of the season,' I suggested.

'What for?'

'To make sure everything works properly and people have got what they need.'

'That's a great idea, when?'

'Let's take a look at the weather forecast and then decide.'

'How long for?'

'I don't know, what do you think?'

'A week or two should be long enough to make sure everything works properly.'

'Let's say ten days then.'

'OK, perfect.'

'There's one other thing, well two, actually.'

'What?' asked Melanie.

'Perhaps we ought to produce a self-drive tour guide.'

When it comes to marketing, Galicia is a shrinking violet. As for this immediate area, the Ribeira Sacra, talk about hiding your light under a bushel. Most of the tourist information we'd collected so far wasn't even printed in Spanish, the Galician language of galego being the preferred choice.

The house's central location makes it the perfect base for exploring the region's main tourist attractions, all of which can be found in glossy travel guides. What I had in mind was those off the beaten track destinations. Anything we could do to encourage people to return to *Campo Verde* had to be a good thing.

'A tour guide?'

'Yes, we could visit a few of our favourite places, write detailed driving instructions, and provide some background information.'

Melanie looked unconvinced.

'We could include suggestions for lunchtime stopovers and highlight which *bodegas* offer free tastings.'

That got her attention.

'How many places were you thinking of going to?'

'Eight should be enough. Even if people are staying for a fortnight they won't want to be touring every day.'

'Actually, that's a really good idea.'

High praise indeed.

'And what's the second thing?' she added.

'You'll love this one.'

'Go on then?'

'Restaurant reviews.'

'Huh?'

'Let's visit some local restaurants and write a review. We can include directions and phone numbers, and encourage guests to do the same.'

When staying in a holiday rental property it's not uncommon to find a stash of tatty old menus and business cards stuffed in a sideboard drawer, most of which are neither use nor ornament. What I had in mind was an organised folder with information about which restaurants served what type of food, an indication of price, contact information, and detailed driving instructions.

'I'm all for that idea,' said Melanie.

'It'll be work, you know, not just going out for a slap-up meal.'

'Of course,' she replied, with a cheeky smile. 'Work it is. When do we start?'

18

A Leap in the Dark

Who can resist the allure of a garden bonfire with its intoxicating scent of wood smoke and the comforting heat from skipping flames? Wednesday provided the perfect weather conditions to rid ourselves of the remnants of our fallen pine. The freshly cut waste proved difficult to light but once ablaze burnt quickly. A steady plume of smoke blended seamlessly into the ashen clouds. It had been a cool start to the day but the glowing embers had kept me toasty warm. By lunchtime the fire was on the wane.

'Lunch is ready when you are,' called Melanie from the kitchen.

After lunch the cloud cover broke. Patches of blue sky created puddles of sunlight in the garden. I spent the afternoon working outside to keep an eye on the fire.

'All done,' I said, as I stepped into the kitchen.

The clock had ticked around to 7:30 pm. The sun had set and the temperature had started to drop.

'Is the fire out?' asked Melanie.

'More or less.'

'It's not dangerous, is it?'

'No, it'll be fine.'

After dinner I picked a DVD out of our ever-expanding collection and slotted it into the laptop. On nights like this you question the merits of not having a TV.

'Not this one again,' moaned Melanie.

'Is there anything you'd like to watch?'

'Is there anything we haven't seen before?'

'No.'

'In that case, watch what you want. I'm going to read.'

I didn't know why she was complaining. Melanie rarely watches a film to the end. She usually falls asleep in the chair or takes herself off to bed to read. True to form, halfway through the movie she made her excuses and wandered off into the bedroom. Ninety-nine times out of a hundred, she's fast asleep by the time I join her.

For the umpteenth time the hero won the day. I ejected the DVD and powered down the laptop.

'Come on lass,' I said.

Jazz jumped to her feet and trotted off towards the French doors. One final toilet break before bedtime. I pulled my jacket on and opened the door. Cold air kissed my cheeks as I followed Jazz down the driveway. In the light of a full moon we wandered up the lane towards the cemetery. Jazz had her nose to the ground and tail in the air, searching for exactly the right place to go. As we neared the cemetery carpark, something in the darkness caught her eye. She leapt across the roadside drainage ditch and sprinted full tilt across the tarmac. Suddenly, she let out a terrifying scream and collapsed to the ground. My heart sank. What had she done?

I ran towards her, my mind a muddle of chaotic thoughts. I'd never heard such a harrowing squeal. By the time I'd reached her she was trying to walk but her back legs weren't responding. Fear and confusion brought a tear to her eye.

'What's matter?' I asked, stroking her coat and trying to reassure her.

Her crying stopped but she was panting heavily. I needed to get her home as quickly as possible. I looped my arms around her chest, lifted gently, and hurried back to the house.

'Melanie!' I shouted as I lowered her onto the dining room floor. 'Melanie!'

I ran into the bedroom. Melanie had woken and was dragging herself out of bed.

'Jazz has had an accident,' I said.

'What kind of accident?'

'I don't know, she saw something in the carpark and gave chase. The next thing I heard was a horrific scream and she collapsed to the ground.'

Melanie rushed into the dining room and crouched beside her.

'What's matter?' she said, stroking her head and doing her best to comfort her.

'It's her back legs. It's as if they're paralysed.'

'We'll have to take her to the vets'. What time is it?'

I glanced at the clock.

'Half past twelve.'

'There's an emergency telephone number in her passport.'

'You stay there. I'll get it.'

I needed to do something. I dashed into the office, yanked open the filing cabinet and pulled out the file marked Jazz. The contact details were in the front of her pet passport.

'It's here,' I said, handing it to Melanie.

Jazz seemed a little calmer but was still panting heavily. The phone rang and rang before someone finally picked up. Melanie explained what had happened.

'She'll be there in five minutes,' said Melanie, as she replaced the receiver.

'Right then, let's go.'

Melanie scooped Jazz off the floor and carried her to the car. She slipped into the front seat with Jazz on her lap. I locked the door, opened the driveway gates, and we were off.

The surgery in Monforte de Lemos is thirteen kilometres from home. It was time to find out exactly how fast this little Renault could go.

Within seconds of us arriving, the vet pulled up alongside. She introduced herself as Jacie, unlocked the doors and led us through into a treatment room. Melanie and I looked on anxiously as she began her examination. The tests confirmed a lack of reflex response from her back legs.

'I need to take an X-ray. Can you carry her?' asked Jacie.

As gently as possible, I lifted her off the examination table and followed Jacie into the X-ray room. Jazz looked desperately sad. I lowered her onto the X-ray table.

'You'll need to keep her perfectly still. Here, put this on.'

Jacie handed me a heavy tabard which I looped over my head.

'Remember, perfectly still,' she repeated, before closing the door behind her.

Keeping her motionless wasn't a problem. My concern was her heavy panting. A green light above the door went out and a red one illuminated. Moments later they changed back. The door opened and Jacie entered.

'OK, bring her back into the treatment room,' she said.

From the moment we'd arrived at the surgery, Jacie had been calm and professional which was more than could be said for Melanie and me. I lowered Jazz onto the examination table. Jacie viewed the X-ray.

'Mmm.'

Was that a good mmm or a bad mmm? The suspense was awful.

'This is where the damage is,' she said, pointing at the grainy transparency.

She explained that two vertebrae in her spinal column had crashed together, trapping the spinal cord.

'It probably happened when she leapt across the drainage ditch,' she added.

Jacie made fists with her hands and closed them together to demonstrate her theory. Her actions sent a shiver down my spine. We could only imagine the pain Jazz was in.

'Will she recover?' I asked.

Diagnosing the problem was one thing but remedying it was far more important.

'It's too early to say but you did the right thing bringing her here straightaway.'

My heart sank. This wasn't what we wanted to hear. If her paralysis was permanent our options were limited.

'I'll give her an injection for the pain and an anti-inflammatory to reduce the swelling. We'll keep her here overnight to monitor her,' she added.

The medication would be administered through a canula. We looked on helplessly as Jacie struggled to find a vein. After failing for a second time Melanie had to sit down for fear of fainting. On her third attempt she found a vein and the treatment could begin.

Saying goodbye was heart-wrenching. We knew she was in good hands but logic counts for nothing in such circumstances. By the time we got home the clock had ticked around to 2:00 am.

Despite feeling exhausted we hardly slept a wink. First thing in the morning we were back at the surgery. Jacie was already there when we arrived.

'Come through,' she said, leading us into the recovery room.

Jazz was lying motionless in a large cage looking very sorry for herself. Jacie reassured us that her lacklustre mood was a result of the cocktail of drugs they'd administered. We crouched beside the cage and stroked her coat.

'Has she eaten anything?' asked Melanie.

'Not yet but she will do when she's ready.'

'When will we be able to take her home?' I asked.

'Come back at closing time and we'll see how she is. Bring a travel case with you.'

That sounded encouraging.

The clinic closed at 8:00 pm. We returned ten minutes early. Jacie had been relieved by the practice owners, husband and wife team Honario and María Jesús. María Jesús greeted us and ushered us into the recovery room. In contrast to this morning, Jazz pricked up her ears and lifted her head. María Jesús opened the cage and Jazz hauled herself to her feet and wobbled out. She was clearly struggling but the progress she'd made was amazing and our relief was overwhelming. We dropped to our knees and helped to steady her. There was a long way to go but she had a sparkle in her eyes and I could have sworn she was beaming from ear to ear.

'The change is remarkable,' said Melanie.

'It's a big improvement but you'll need to keep her completely still for the next two weeks.'

'Will she fully recover?' I asked.

'We're hopeful her mobility will improve but she's unlikely to move as freely as she did. From now on there'll be no chasing and definitely no jumping,' María Jesús said, directing her final comments at Jazz.

Her remarks were welcome but our relief was tinged with sadness. Jazz enjoyed her freedom and loved nothing more than running around the garden. She'd had a difficult start to life, having been rescued from a property in the

UK where she'd spent the first eighteen months of her life locked in a damp, dark cellar. Perhaps that was why she loved to run. We had found her at the RSPCA rescue centre in Halifax. Since moving to Spain she'd enjoyed even more freedom. This accident looked set to change her life forever.

Jazz's exertion had left her collapsed on the floor and panting for breath. Between us, we lifted her into the travel case and closed the grill.

'You can take this to any pharmacy,' said María Jesús, handing Melanie a prescription, 'and remember, toilet breaks only. The rest of the time she needs to remain as still as possible.'

We thanked her for their efforts and asked her to pass on our appreciation to Jacie. Carefully, we lifted the case into the back of the car and headed home.

Jazz stayed in our bedroom that night. Sleep was a luxury none of us achieved. Heavy panting was briefly interrupted with short periods of silence and despite efforts to the contrary, Jazz spent the entire night in the travel case. At 5:00 am she woke again. Unsure why, we chose the safest option and helped her outside for a toilet break.

'No.' Jazz was heading for her bed in the lounge. 'Come on lass. I know it's difficult but it's for your own good.'

I doubt she understood a word but it couldn't harm to explain. Reluctantly, she obeyed and waddled back into her travel case.

At 9:00 am we set off for the pharmacy to fill the prescription.

'Have you seen what this is for?' asked Melanie, en route.

'No, what?'

'Valium.'

'Valium! Crikey, that should keep her quiet.'

The nearest pharmacy is in the village of Sober, two kilometres from home. The drive took us out of the valley and into the surrounding hills. As we climbed, the early morning mist gave way to bright sunshine and a clear blue sky.

'It looks like it's closed,' said Melanie.

She hopped out of the car and went to check.

'It doesn't open until ten,' she said on her return.

'Let's try the one in Ferreira,' I suggested.

The village of Ferreira de Pantón is about ten minutes from home. I drove back down into the mist and out again on the other side of the valley. The high street was quiet. I parked outside the pharmacy and we went in together.

'*Buenas días,*' we said as we entered.

The place was busy. More customers joined the queue as others left. Finally, it was our turn to be served.

'Can I have this please?' asked Melanie, sliding the prescription across the counter.

The pharmacist picked it up and read the details.

'You'll have to register in order to get Valium,' she said.

Her announcement hushed the waiting customers. I could feel them staring at us. An explanation was called for.

'It's not for me, it's for my dog,' said Melanie.

I bet they all say that, I thought to myself.

Her pleas fell on deaf ears.

'You'll still have to register,' she said, sliding a pen across the counter.

While Melanie filled out the form, the pharmacist served the next customer. Once completed she slid it back across.

'You live in Sober?' asked the pharmacist.

This revelation sent idle tongues into overdrive. A whisper of intrigue spread around the shop. I hadn't a clue what they were mumbling but could imagine. 'First she said it was for her dog and now she's getting it here instead of her local pharmacy.'

Melanie and I stood to one side while the pharmacist filled the prescription. We avoided direct eye contact with our accusers. Eventually, she returned and passed the drugs to Melanie.

'*Gracias*,' we said, before sprinting outside.

'Can you believe that?' said Melanie, as we set off home. 'Everyone will think I'm a manic depressive or something.'

I was certain they wouldn't but couldn't resist teasing.

'You know what they say, good news travels fast but bad news travels faster.'

To ensure Jazz's cooperation I pushed the pill into a piece of cheddar. She wolfed it down and the effects were nigh on instantaneous. Her panting stopped. We could only hope the pain had too.

The drugs kept her calm and she slept for long periods. Thankfully, the physical trauma hadn't affected her appetite. It was our responsibility to keep her still and hope that Mother Nature would do the rest.

While Jazz began her convalescence, I turned my attention to preparing the ground for our vineyard.

'I'm going to have a word with Roy and see if I can borrow his garden rotavator,' I said, over morning coffee.

As a rule, I avoid borrowing mechanical equipment. You're never sure what condition it's in before you get your hands on it. If it breaks down, who's responsible? But the thought of turning over a hundred square metres of land with a garden fork had me reaching for the phone.

'No problem, but I'll need it back by the weekend. When do you want to collect it?' asked Roy.

'Can I come now?'

'OK. See you in a quarter of an hour.'

Roy and Maria live in Pinol, a remote village in the hills above Canabal. I hooked up the trailer and headed off. Roy was in the courtyard when I arrived.

'This is it,' he said.

The petrol powered rotavator had six tilling blades. Its rotary action turned the soil and propelled it across the ground. What caught my attention was its condition. It looked as if it hadn't been cleaned since the day it was bought. Lumps of hard-baked soil covered the drive shaft and dried weeds were wrapped around the blades.

'It's easy to use,' said Roy. 'All you do is raise the transport wheel, open the choke, and yank the starter cord.'

'How are we going to get it into the trailer?' I asked.

It looked far too heavy for the two of us to lift.

'You open the back and I'll drive it on.'

When it comes to mechanical equipment, Roy is the kind of man who tests things to destruction. I didn't for one minute believe the operating instructions recommended driving it over hard surfaces, quite the contrary.

I removed the swing panel off the back of the trailer and Roy used two wooden planks to form a ramp. He walked over to the rotavator, raised the transport wheel, opened the choke, and tugged the starter cord. Clouds of blue smoke ejected into the air from the exhaust as the beast fired into life. He squeezed the throttle and the machine leapt forward, bouncing across the gravel courtyard and onto the road. As it hit the wooden planks the tilling blades clawed their way onto the trailer. Roy's abuse only fuelled my concerns about its reliability.

'Have you got a rope?'

I was delighted he'd asked. I've never been a Boy Scout and my knot-tying skills are non-existent.

'Here you go,' I said, handing it to him.

'Rope? I've seen thicker washing line.'

Many a true word …

'There you go,' he said, tying off the loose end.

'Thanks. I'll have it back to you before the weekend,' I confirmed, and on that note I was off.

Under normal circumstances rural roads are more than adequate for getting from A to B. When you're pulling a trailer, they're less than ideal. It wasn't until I glanced in the rear-view mirror that I noticed the washing line had loosened and the rotavator was bouncing around. Quickly, I pulled over to investigate. Roy's knots left a lot to be desired.

I untied the sagging rope, adjusted the position of the rotavator, and bound it as tightly as I could. Nervously I continued, one eye on the road and the other fixed on the mirror. After a nerve-racking journey I pulled into the driveway.

'That was a nightmare,' I said, as I entered the house.

'Why?'

'The chuffing rope came loose and it nearly ended up in the road. Anyway, can you give me a hand to get it out of the trailer?'

Melanie nodded and followed me outside.

'I can't lift that,' she said, staring at the contraption.

Until then, it hadn't crossed my mind how we'd get it out.

'Just wait here.'

What I needed was a plank. I went around to the shed and picked out the longest I had. Melanie was sitting on the front steps when I returned. I leant the plank up against the trailer.

'That doesn't look very safe,' she remarked.

The plank was much shorter than I thought, a point highlighted by the severity of the incline.

'This is the longest one I've got,' I replied. 'Can you put your foot here and make sure it doesn't slip off the trailer?'

Melanie looked apprehensive.

I climbed into the trailer. From my lofty position the drop looked daunting. One wrong move and Melanie, the rotavator, and I would end up in a bloody pile on the driveway. On second thoughts, there had to be a better way.

'I know.'

'What?' asked Melanie.

'I'll bring it down backwards. Just make sure the plank doesn't slip away,' I added.

'Do be careful.'

Gently, I nudged the rotavator this way then that, dragging the heavy machine to the lip of the trailer. Progress was slow but steady. Carefully, I lined up the centre of the rotavator with the plank. The two inner tines rested on the wood as I tilted it backwards.

'You'd better step to one side now,' I said.

If anything went wrong there was no point in both of us ending up in A&E.

I'd reached the point of no return. As soon as the transport wheel hit the top of the plank, gravity would take control. The steepness of the incline and the weight of the machine would do the rest. Melanie stepped to one side.

As predicted, the rotavator took on a mind of its own and I was powerless to stop it. With a scrape and a bump, it careered down the plank and came to a rapid halt on the driveway.

'There you go, that wasn't too bad, was it?'

Under a calm exterior my heart was beating like a drum.

'If you say so,' she replied.

Phase one was complete. I'd successfully transported this indispensable horticultural machine from A to B without loss of life, limb, or machine. Tomorrow, phase two could begin.

19

Pushmi-Pullyu

Believing something is true doesn't make it so. Not for the first time the March weather brought false hope of an early summer. Clear blue sky and bright sunshine ushered in a new day. In the shadows, a light frost blanketed the ground. Down in the village, thin columns of smoke rose vertically from rooftop chimneys and the scent of wood smoke filled the crisp air.

'I'm going to make a start in the garden,' I said, as I wandered through the kitchen and out of the back door.

The rotavator was in the shed. I wheeled it out and onto the waste ground. Roy's instructions were clear: open the choke and pull the starter cord. As I yanked the cord the engine recoiled, almost ripping my arm out of its socket. Crikey, I felt that. I prepared for a second attempt, and then a third, and a fourth, and a fifth, but the beast was dead: not a cough or a splutter. Thinking I might have flooded the carburettor, I closed the choke and tried again, but nothing. I stood back to catch my breath and ponder the problem.

The choke was open which meant air was getting into the engine. The only other elements of a naturally aspirated combustion engine are fuel and ignition. I looked around the fuel tank for a shutoff valve. That's when it dawned on me. Was there any fuel in the tank?

I unscrewed the cap and peered inside. I grabbed the two Chopper-style handlebars and rocked the machine from side to side: empty. That was easily remedied. I filled it up and tried again.

Open choke, grab the starter cord, and pull.

This time a plume of blue smoke erupted into the cold morning air and oily fumes filled my lungs. The beast was ready for action. I moved the choke to the half-open position and squeezed the throttle lever. As I did the contraption lurched forwards and raced off down the garden like a bucking bronco. I stumbled after it, hanging on for dear life. Seven horse power might not sound a lot but they certainly had the measure of me.

Despite its galloping pace and uncontrollable power, the tines hardly scratched the surface. Something was wrong. I released the throttle lever and it shuddered to a halt. I stood back while the seven mares took a break. That's when I spotted the oversight.

In my enthusiasm to take up the reins I'd forgotten to raise the transport wheel. I pulled it out of the way and prepared to do battle. The difference was immediate. The tines cut into the ground and ejected lumps of grassy sods out of the back. Keeping it moving in a straight line was difficult but turning it around was an altogether different challenge. As I reached the limits of the plot the unruly stallions morphed into Dr Dolittle's Pushmi-Pullyu. I didn't know whether I was coming or going.

Eventually, I managed to get it facing in the opposite direction and headed back down the plot. Without warning, the tines stopped rotating and the engine screamed its disapproval. I hadn't covered two lengths and the chuffing thing had given up the ghost.

'I knew it,' I said, as I stormed into the kitchen.

'You knew what darling?'

'I knew this would happen. I just knew it.'

'What's happened?'

'The chuffing thing has stopped working.'

'You haven't broken it, have you?'

'I haven't done anything. It broke all on its own.'

'You'd better give Roy a call and see what he has to say.'

I picked up the phone and dialled.

'What did he say?' asked Melanie.

'He's coming to take a look and bringing Maria with him. She wants to see how Jazz is doing.'

While Melanie and Maria fussed over Jazz, Roy followed me into the garden.

'It's this bolt, it's come loose,' he said.

His instant diagnosis suggested a recurring problem and eased my liability concerns.

'Have you got a spanner?' he asked.

I fetched the required tool and within minutes the problem was sorted and the beast was raring to go.

By the end of the first day the area was looking much better. There was more work to do but I was pretty pleased with my efforts. My body, on the other hand, had taken quite a pounding. Anything with a joint or a muscle ached like hell. I couldn't complain though. One look at Jazz put my pains into perspective.

The following morning, I picked up where I'd left off. By lunchtime I was ready for a break. The tilling had unearthed an inordinate number of stones which would have to be removed before we planted the grapevines.

'Can you give me a hand to measure up after lunch?' I asked.

'Measure up, what for?'

'So we can work out how many vines we'll need.'

'What variety are we going to get?'

'I thought we'd plant Mencía.'

Mencía is the grape of Galicia. It's an ancient hybrid of two Portuguese varieties that produces a full-bodied, inky red wine.

Lunch in the garden is a real bonus at this time of year. We moved the table into the sun and nibbled our sandwiches: my favourite, egg mayo.

The plot measured sixteen metres wide by twelve and a half deep with a sweeping curve in the far corner. After careful consideration and a few unconventional calculations, I came up with an area of 176 square metres.

'How many vines are we going to need?' asked Melanie.

That was a very good question and one I didn't have the answer to. The two determining factors were the number of rows and the distance between each vine.

'How wide do you think the space between each row should be?' I asked.

'I don't know, it's your vineyard.'

It was my vineyard now but it would be ours when we started drinking its fruits.

'If each row was three metres apart that would give us four rows.'

Melanie looked puzzled.

'Hang on a minute, four times three is twelve,' she said.

'So?'

'So, how are you going to walk down the outside of the outer two rows?'

Melanie's tone had a certain smugness to it.

'Four rows of vines with three three-metre spaces in between makes nine metres. That will give us one and a half metres on each side on the outside, making twelve altogether.'

That wiped the smirk off her face.

'Just testing.'

Just testing indeed.

'How far apart do you think we should plant each vine?' I asked.

'I don't know. About that far I suppose.'

Melanie held her hands apart to indicate the distance.

'So, about a metre?'

'If that's what you think.'

'All we need to decide now is how long each row should be.'

'We're just using up a bit of spare land, not mapping out the whole of Galicia,' remarked Melanie.

Her sarcasm fell on deaf ears. Left to her, the new vineyard would end up looking like a jungle. I ignored her comment and continued.

'I think twelve metres for the three long rows and six for the short one. That will give us two spare metres top and bottom.'

The short row was a result of the curve in the far corner.

'Why so much spare space at the end of each row?' asked Melanie.

I'd hoped to get away without answering that question but Melanie had the measure of me.

'Just in case.'

'Just in case of what?'

Sometimes she's like a dog with a bone.

'In case I decide to buy a rotavator. Two metres will give me enough room to turn around at the end of each row.'

Melanie's glare spoke louder than words. What had started out as an inexpensive repurposing exercise had the potential to become a costly agricultural enterprise.

'OK, let's go,' I said, heading back towards the house.

'So, how many vines do we need?'

'Fifty should do it.'

Our horticultural shop of choice is a place called Otecoa on Avenida de Galicia in Monforte de Lemos.

'I don't have any in stock at the moment but I can order some for you,' said the shopkeeper.

'How much are they?' I asked.

'Two euros ten cents each.'

The price seemed very reasonable.

'How soon will you have them?'

'The day after tomorrow, Wednesday.'

'OK. Will you order fifty for us?'

'No problem. If you call in Wednesday afternoon, we should have them for you.'

'OK, *hasta miércoles* (See you on Wednesday).'

Jazz woke us three times during the night to go to the loo. By daybreak we were both shattered but at least she seemed to be improving. Her wayward stumbling had become more purposeful with each call of nature.

The glorious spring weather continued and the chilly morning made the arduous work more tolerable. While I struggled to tame the unpredictable roll and pitch of the rotavator, Melanie began raking the ground. Piles of stones were loaded into the wheelbarrow and tipped at the edge of the plot. Hour after hour we toiled on the land. Lunchtime came and went and before we knew it the sun was on the wane.

'It must be time for a Teatime Taster by now,' said Melanie.

We'd both had enough for one day. I glanced at my watch. The time was approaching 5:00 pm. It had taken all day but finally the tilling was finished and Melanie was making good progress removing the stones. There was more work to do before we could plant the vines but it felt as though we were getting there. Not long now and our would-be vineyard would actually be a vineyard.

'I think we've earned it,' I replied.

By 5:30 pm we'd showered, changed, and were sitting in the garden catching the last rays of spring sunshine.

Pop!

I'd chosen a chilled bottle of Ribeiro white: young, fruity, and refreshingly cool.

'Cheers,' I said as we chinked glasses.

The perfect way to end a busy day.

That night Jazz woke only once but in the morning her gait seemed to have taken a backwards step. I calmed Melanie's fears.

'I'm sure she'll have good days and bad,' I said.

I shared Melanie's concerns but Jazz wasn't yet halfway through her two weeks of convalescence. For the time being, both us and Jazz had to be patient.

'What have you got planned for today?' asked Melanie as we sipped our morning coffee.

'I want to finish the raking and take the rotavator back to Roy.'

'Will you need me to wheel the barrow?'

'If you wouldn't mind. Have you got any idea where we can buy some posts from?'

Melanie is used to such random questions. Once my brain is on a mission all manner of thoughts spring to mind.

'What kind of posts?'

'Wooden ones. The kind used in vineyards to secure the training wires.'

There are a number of different ways to support the growth of grapevines ranging from a single stake to complex trestles. Many of the older vineyards in the area expect the vines to support themselves. I wanted to create an orderly vineyard with neat rows of vines growing along training wires supported by wooden posts.

'They might sell them at the *ferretería* (hardware shop) in Sober,' suggested Melanie.

'I'll call on my way back from Roy's and see what they've got.'

I decided to spend the morning raking just in case I needed to run the rotavator over the plot one last time. As it turned out I didn't and by noon the ground was ready for planting.

'I'm going to take the rotavator back and call at the *ferretería.*'

'Do you want me to come?'

'No, but will you help me load the rotavator into the trailer?'

Melanie's eyes widened. If the worst came to the worst, she could always pick me up off the floor. Loading the beast proved equally as fraught as unloading it. Eventually we found a way and despite checking and rechecking my knots, I kept one eye on the load all the way to Roy's.

On the way back I stopped at the *ferretería.*

'*Buenos días,*' I announced as I entered.

In a scene typical of Galician hardware shops, two old men were disagreeing over what size screws a third man should buy. My interruption gave the first chap the chance to decide for himself.

While I waited to be served, I noticed some galvanised steel posts leant up against the far wall. What caught my eye was their design. Cut into the top half of each post were equally spaced teeth specifically created to support training wires. They were exactly what I was looking for. After much discussion, the two blokes in front made their purchases and left.

'How much are these?' I asked, pointing at the posts.

'Two euros sixty.'

That seemed very reasonable. I thought they'd be much more expensive.

'How many have you got?'

A soon as I'd asked, I knew what the answer would be.

'How many do you want?'

I hadn't a clue.

'How far apart do they need to be?' I asked.

'That's up to you,' replied the shopkeeper.

Where were the two wise men when I needed them?

The shopkeeper waited patiently while I mulled it over. From a purely aesthetic perspective, four equally spaced posts down a twelve-metre row would be ideal. The shorter row would have to suffice with three.

'Fifteen,' I blurted.

He counted them out and leant them against the sales counter.

'Anything else?' he asked.

'Wire.'

'What thickness?'

Nothing in a *ferretería* is ever straightforward. How many different thicknesses of wire could there be?

'It's for grapevines,' I replied.

He looked at me as if to say "So what?"

'What's a normal thickness?' I asked.

'That's up to you, some prefer thick, others thin.'

'Is there one in between?'

He walked around to my side of the counter and lifted a coil of wire off the floor.

'What about this?'

I went to take a look and he lifted up another.

'Or this?'

Offering two was one too many. In the end I chose the thinner of the two. Even I know that wire is sold by the kilo. The thinner the wire the more I'd get for my money, but had I made the right choice? His facial expression gave nothing away.

'How much do you want?' he asked.

Keep calm and work it out, I told myself.

There would be four rows of grapevines. Each row would have four training wires. Three rows were twelve metres long and the fourth was six metres. I had no idea that planting a vineyard would be so complicated. I paused for a moment, totting it up in my head. If my mental arithmetic was correct, I needed 168 metres. To be on the safe side I asked for 180.

'Anything else?' he asked.

'No, I think that's everything.'

At least I hoped it was.

'Have you got anchors?'

This was one of those questions asked by someone in the know of someone who hadn't a clue.

'Anchors?'

He walked slowly to the far end of the sales counter, bent down and picked up a steel rod with a DVD-sized steel plate on one end. Whatever it was, I certainly didn't have any. He passed it to me for a closer inspection.

'What's it for?' I asked.

Through a series of hand gestures and a few choice words he explained.

The anchors are used to secure each end post on every row. When the training wires are tensioned, they prevent the row from collapsing inwards. People say that a little bit of knowledge is a dangerous thing. That might be true but it's not half as dangerous as blind ignorance.

'Eight, I'll take eight,' I said.

'Have you got a tool?'

This was becoming embarrassing. Every answer led to another question.

'A tool?'

'To screw the anchors into the ground,' he replied.

He dipped below the counter and popped up holding a metre-long T-shaped spanner.

'This goes in here and that screws into the ground.'

The T-shaped spanner was actually a hollow metal tube. The shopkeeper slipped the anchor inside. Only then did I notice the disc on the end was slightly tapered which, when used in conjunction with the spanner, allowed the user to screw the anchor into the ground: simple but ingenious.

'No, I haven't got one of them,' I admitted.

'They're very expensive,' said the shopkeeper.

Here we go. It looked like all this knowledge was going to come at a price.

'Borrow this one if you like,' he added, laying it on the counter.

Galicia and its people never fail to amaze. The one thing he could have made a bit of money on and he was going to lend it to me.

'Thank you.'

'Just bring it back when you're finished. There's no rush.'

I settled the bill, loaded the car, and drove home.

'Did you get some posts?' asked Melanie, as I stepped inside.

'Did I? What a performance.'

I told her the tale which she found particularly amusing.

'And he said you could borrow the spanner?'

'I know, can you believe it?'

At 6:00 pm we drove into town to collect our fifty grapevines. The plants are created by grafting a bud of the donor plant onto hardy root stock. The graft is then dipped in paraffin wax to protect the buds from disease. The end result is a fifty-centimetre-long cane with a mass of straggly roots on one end and a globule of bright red wax on the other.

'Plant them in the ground up to here,' said the shopkeeper, pointing at the vine.

He indicated that ten centimetres should be above ground. That meant digging fifty holes half a metre deep. Crikey, is nothing easy?

'Put a handful of compost in the bottom of each hole. Have you got some compost?' he asked.

Here we go, more expense.

'No.'

'Fifty litres should be enough,' he said, pointing at a stack of bags in the corner. 'Trim the roots to roughly half their current length and splay them out at the bottom of the hole. Fill it in and give them a good watering.'

The vines were banded in tens. He brought five lots from the stockroom and wrapped the roots in old newspaper.

'Make sure you water them twice a day for the first week or so.'

We thanked him for his advice, paid the bill and left. I couldn't wait to get started.

20

Becher's Brook

Whispers in the darkness alerted me to Melanie's movement. Jazz needed another break. I rolled over and tapped the alarm clock. The digital display read 4:07. A draught of cold air swept into the bedroom when Melanie opened the door. Better that than a mop and bucket. By 8:30 am the three of us were wide awake. A light frost had formed on the car but a cloudless sky promised another fabulous spring day.

'I've been thinking,' said Melanie, as we sipped our morning coffee.

Wasn't that my line?

'Oh yes, what about?'

'Do you think we ought to tell Nemesio about the vineyard?'

Nemesio is our nearest neighbour and the owner of the field adjacent to the house. He lives in the village with his wife Rosa and his brother Felipe.

'It's a bit late now, don't you think?'

'I suppose so but it wouldn't harm to mention it.'

'What if he's not keen on the idea?'

'Don't be silly, he won't mind.'

Melanie was right. It would be better to get his blessing than incur his wrath. If living in Spain has taught us anything it's that courtesy costs nothing. Say the right thing to the right person and anything is possible.

'OK, we'll have a word with him later today. By the way, can you remember if I took the sledgehammer to *Campo Verde*?'

My first random question of the day and we hadn't yet got out of bed. Melanie looked aghast.

'Is that a joke?'

'No.'

'What on earth are you going to do with a sledgehammer in bed?'

'It's not for now. I'll need it later.'

'Well, I've no idea where it is.'

One of the many drawbacks of owning two properties is that whenever you need something it's always at the wrong house. If it was here, the only place it could be was in the shed.

The bedroom tiles felt icy cold as we readied ourselves. A ten-minute search in the shed drew a blank.

'It must be at *Campo Verde*,' I said, as I stepped back inside.

'What do you want it for?'

'To hammer in the posts.'

'Where have you looked?'

'Everywhere.'

'Well then, it must be at *Campo Verde*.'

'In that case, I'm going to nip up to Vilatán. Are you coming?'

'No, I've plenty to be getting on with here.'

Forty minutes later I was back home, sledgehammer in hand.

'You found it then?'

'Yes.'

'What time do you want to go and speak to Nemesio?'

I glanced at the clock: 12:15 pm. If we went now, they probably wouldn't keep us talking. Woe betide anyone who comes between a Galician and his lunch.

'Let's go now.'

'Good idea.'

Great minds think alike.

'Come in, come in,' said Rosa, gesturing us to enter.

Their downstairs kitchen occupies the whole of the ground floor and is absolutely enormous. Nemesio was sitting at a large dining table which, despite its size, looked lost in the cavernous space.

'How can we help you?' asked Rosa.

'Would you have any objection to us planting a vineyard in the land at the back of our house?'

'Come in, sit down,' she said, gesturing us towards the table.

Hopes of a speedy getaway were quickly dashed. We took a seat opposite Nemesio.

'What can I get you to drink?'

Galician hospitality often starts with refreshments.

'Thank you but not for me.'

'Do you like *licor café*?'

It seemed that no was the wrong answer.

'Yes,' I replied.

Licor café is made from *aguardiente*, a harsh spirit distilled using the remnants of the winemaking process.

'In that case, you must try ours. It's homemade.'

Nemesio, who hadn't uttered a word so far, stood up and walked across to a large oak dresser on the far wall. He took out a bottle and two shot glasses and placed them on the table in front of us. Gently, he pulled the cork and filled each glass to within a whisker of overflowing.

'Taste it,' he said.

It never fails to amaze me that guests are encouraged to drink while hosts rarely do. We took a small sip. The taste was delightful: strong, sweet coffee with hints of cinnamon and citrus fruits.

'What do you think?' he asked.

'Mmm, it's delicious,' we said in unison.

It couldn't harm to extol the virtues of his homemade liqueur, although on this occasion it was true. Nemesio beamed with pride.

'Now, how can I help you?' he asked.

'We're thinking of planting some grapevines on the land at the back of our garden where the *huerta* used to be. Would you mind if we did?'

'What about the *huerta*?'

Nemesio was clearly shocked. Abandoning a *huerta* in favour of a vineyard is as alien to Galicians as finding ET hiding under the bed.

'We don't need many vegetables. There's only the two of us.'

Melanie's quick thinking never fails to amaze me.

'Why don't you get some pigs?'

To many people, that comment would seem as random as asking for a sledgehammer with your morning coffee, but here in Galicia rearing pigs comes a close second to growing your own vegetables. How else can one get rid of all that leftover veg?

Melanie and I let out a nervous laugh, knowing full well Nemesio was quite serious.

'They don't want a pig. There's only the two of them,' Rosa said, coming to our defence.

Nemesio mulled it over.

'I suppose you're right but if you ever want a lettuce, don't hesitate to ask,' he replied.

Melanie and I smiled like two village idiots.

'So, you don't mind if we plant some grapevines?'

The conversation had finally come full circle.

'Not at all, you do what you want with that land.'

That was a relief.

'What variety of grapes are you going to plant?'

'Mencía,' I replied.

'Ah Mencía, that's what I grow.'

'Nemesio has a vineyard in the Amandi,' said Rosa. 'Do you know the Amandi?'

The Amandi is the most prestigious winegrowing area in the Ribeira Sacra. The vineyards are planted on narrow terraces cut into the steep valley of the river Sil. The growers are referred to as *viniculturas heroicas* (heroic winemakers) due to the difficulty of harvesting the grapes. It seemed inconceivable that anyone living in Canabal, or the surrounding area, would not know about the Amandi.

'Yes. The wines from the Amandi are the best,' I replied.

They're a little dry for my palate but I wasn't about to cut short our blossoming friendship.

'Yes, they're the best,' repeated Rosa.

'Where are you going to plant them?' asked Nemesio.

Sometimes, communicating with the neighbours is a bit like getting stuck in a time loop. Conversations are nothing if not repetitive. I used to question whether people had actually understood me, but confirming, reconfirming, and starting again form the beginning is part and parcel of chatting with the neighbours.

'On the land at the back of the garden,' I replied.

'Show me,' he said.

Nemesio stood up. Melanie and I followed suit.

'Would you like a bottle of *licor café*?' he asked, as we prepared to leave.

It would have been rude not to accept.

'That would be lovely,' replied Melanie.

Nemesio wandered back to the dresser and returned carrying two bottles.

'Here, take this as well. It's a bottle of my wine,' he said, handing them both to Melanie.

'It's lovely wine,' added Rosa.

Our neighbourly consideration had been rewarded with two bottles of homebrew and a generous measure of embarrassment.

Booty in hand, the three of us marched off home. Melanie took the bottles into the kitchen and Nemesio and I strolled to the end of the garden.

'It's going to end over there,' I said, illustrating the boundary with a sweeping arm movement.

'You can take more land if you like,' he replied.

A tempting offer but creating a vineyard was meant to ease the burden of maintenance, not increase it.

'Thank you but this will be big enough for us,' I replied.

Just then Melanie appeared.

'What's that?' she asked.

'Nemesio was saying that we could take more land if we wanted but I told him we had enough.'

'How many vines will you be planting?' he asked.

'About fifty.'

'Fifty?'

Nemesio's response gave me the distinct impression I'd miscalculated. While he was here, I might as well seek his advice.

'We were planning on having four rows three metres apart.'

'They don't want to be three metres apart. One and half is more than enough.'

Nemesio's insight threw our plans into disarray. If the gap between the rows was only one and a half metres, we had enough space for seven rows of vines.

'And how far apart should we plant each vine?' I asked.

'A metre twenty will be enough.'

Talk about a cock-up. Melanie's suggestion to involve the neighbours had proved useful in more ways than one. I thanked Nemesio for his advice and he headed home for lunch.

Using the new parameters, I worked out we'd need another twenty-one vines, taking the total to seventy-one. As for the posts, another ten would do the trick. Extra wire and additional anchors added to the expense. The costs of creating our little vineyard were starting to mount up.

That afternoon I put my bruised pride to one side and purchased the additional supplies. By the time we'd finished, another day had slipped by.

The next morning I woke with renewed purpose. The three of us had enjoyed a peaceful night's sleep for the first time since Jazz's accident. Dare we hope that the dark tunnel of recovery was becoming a shade lighter?

'I've been thinking,' I said, over morning coffee.

'Oh yes.'

'Yes.'

'And what exactly have you been thinking?'

'I've been thinking about the boundary.'

'What boundary?'

'The boundary of the vineyard. What do you think to the idea of a leylandii hedge?'

'Leylandii, are you sure?'

Melanie's tone reflected this evergreen's fearsome reputation for rampant growth and neighbourly disputes.

'Something like Dad used to have except not quite as tall,' I added, in an effort to reassure her.

'Not Becher's Brook?' remarked Melanie.

Dad had had a leylandii hedge at the bottom of his garden. He used to call it Becher's Brook after the famous fence in the Grand National horse race.

'Similar to that but not as high.'

Melanie looked less than enthusiastic.

'It'll provide a bit of colour in the garden during the winter months when the vines have lost their leaves,' I added.

'Actually, that might look really nice.'

She seemed to be warming to the idea.

'OK then, Becher's Brook it is.'

Melanie glowered at me.

'Except smaller,' I added.

Having finished our coffee, we pulled on our work clothes and made sure Jazz was comfortable before heading outside. We began by marking out the first row using a ball of string and a tape measure.

Digging the holes for the vines was far more difficult than I'd expected. The rotavator had tilled the top ten centimetres but below that the earth was littered with pebbles, some the size of a Galia melon. The first ten holes took over two hours to dig. When planted, the vines looked like little toy soldiers standing to attention in their bright red uniforms.

'Right then, let's hammer in the posts before we move on to the next row,' I said.

A change is as good as a rest and I certainly needed a break from digging.

'You hold it and I'll hit it,' I joked.

'Why is it always me who has to hold whatever you're hitting?'

'Here you go then. Knock yourself out,' I replied, offering her the sledgehammer.

I knew full well she could barely lift it, never mind wield it.

'I can't use that. Just make sure you don't miss.'

'Trust me.'

A wry smile did little to allay her fears.

Having hammered in the posts we turned our attention to the anchors. Try as I might, screwing them into the ground proved impossible; there were far too many stones. In the end I had to bury them in exactly the same way as we'd planted the vines.

It took us three days to finish the planting and erect the supports, but we were delighted with the result.

'It looks just like a proper vineyard,' remarked Melanie. Cheeky sod.

'That's because it is a proper vineyard.'

Completing the work coincided with Jazz finishing her prescribed course of Valium. With the exception of toilet breaks she'd been as still as a statue throughout. At times, her sad expression had pulled on our heartstrings but we knew it was for her own good. That evening we celebrated both events by popping the cork on a fine bottle of Spanish cava. Jazz joined us outside for our Teatime Taster and the three of us relaxed in the late afternoon sunshine.

Two weeks after attempting to break the land speed record we returned to the vets' at a more leisurely pace for a pre-arranged check-up. No sooner had we entered than Honario, the practice owner, came to see us. Both Jacie and Honario's wife, María Jesús, had brought him up to speed with Jazz's condition and he seemed delighted with her progress.

'It's not quite as easy to keep her still since she finished the Valium,' admitted Melanie.

'That's OK. You need to start giving her some light exercise to build up her muscles. Short walks but no running or jumping,' he said.

'What are her long-term prospects?' I asked.

'Her movement will improve but from now on she needs to take things much easier.'

Honario prescribed painkillers which we could reduce to half a tablet after the first three days and stop altogether after a fortnight.

That afternoon we took her out for a short walk. She waddled down the lane into the village and took her time on the way back. For us, it was a relief to see her out and about again.

The following morning we were woken by the sound of her coughing and retching. Melanie jumped out of bed, pulled on her dressing gown, and rushed her outside.

'It's as if she wants to be sick but can't,' she said on her return.

'Perhaps the new medication doesn't agree with her. What time do the vets' open?'

'Nine-thirty.'

'We ought to take her back and see what they think.'

Melanie agreed.

It wasn't until I picked her up to put her into the back of the car that I noticed a small lump on her back.

'She's got a tick,' I said, prising it off with my fingernails.

By the time we'd driven to the vets' she'd stopped coughing. Jacie conducted a thorough examination and prescribed some antibiotics to counter a high temperature.

No sooner had we returned home than the threatened vomit finally raised its ugly head all over the lounge tiles. That night her symptoms worsened. We contacted the vet who suggested pausing the antibiotics. From that moment on her condition improved. The road to recovery would be long and challenging but we were determined she would reach her destination, albeit one step at a time.

The weather in March had been fabulous: crisp mornings and bright sunny days. With Jazz on the mend, we entered April with a renewed sense of optimism.

'Someone's left a message on the phone,' said Melanie.

'Who?'

'It's a Spanish bloke called Mariano.'

The only two Marianos I knew were the contractor who'd installed the swimming pool and the husband of Isa, a couple who live in Madrid but spend their summers in Canabal. I couldn't imagine why either would be contacting me.

'Mariano who?' I asked.

'He wants to rent *Campo Verde*.'

'When?'

'Saturday.'

'Which Saturday?'

'This Saturday.'

Before the appropriate expletive passed my lips, it dawned on me what day it was.

'Ha ha, very funny. And April Fool to you too.'

'I'm not joking.'

Melanie's face didn't slip. I had to give it to her, she was playing a blinder.

'You'd better ring him back,' she added, handing me the phone.

'Are you serious?'

'Deadly serious.'

How she was keeping a straight face was a mystery to me. Oh well, it couldn't harm to play along.

'Hello, could I speak to Mariano please?'

'Speaking.'

'Oh hello, my name is Craig Briggs. My wife tells me you'd like to book our rental property for a week from this coming weekend.'

As soon as he replied I knew it wasn't a prank. This chap really did want to book. I turned to Melanie in disbelief.

'Told you,' she whispered.

My complete shock created an uncomfortably long pause in the conversation.

'Hello. Are you there?'

Mariano's interruption jolted me into action.

'Err yes. I'm still here. If you give me your email address I'll send you all the information.'

Doing it that way would give me time to compose myself. I noted down his email, confirmed it, and ended the call. Like a pre-emptive nuclear strike, holiday rental had just got real.

'What did he say?' asked Melanie.

'They'll be here on Saturday.'

'How many?'

'Mariano, his wife, and two children. Oh, and they've got a twelve-year-old short-sighted spaniel.'

'I thought we weren't taking dogs?'

'Well we are now.'

We'd spent the last three and a half years working towards this moment. Now it was here, the excitement of welcoming our first guests to *Campo Verde* was tempered with an overwhelming sense of apprehension.

21

Faux Pas

My mind had been racing all night. We had two days to ready *Campo Verde* before the first guests arrived and the list of things to do seemed endless.

'Are you awake?' I whispered.

'I've been awake for ages.'

It seemed I wasn't the only one whose brain was working overtime.

'Let's have a coffee and get cracking.'

Melanie pulled on her fleecy dressing gown and wandered through into the kitchen. Jazz waddled after her. I slid to the foot of the bed and flung open the window shutters. Cold air drifted into the bedroom and goosebumps rippled up my arm. Moments later Melanie and Jazz returned.

'I'll just put another load in the washing machine before I have my coffee,' said Melanie, as she set her mug down on the bedside table.

Since we'd taken Mariano's booking the washing machine hadn't stopped.

'How many more loads will you have to do?' I asked on her return.

'Another two should do it.'

'Is there anything else you need to do?'

Such a short timeframe demanded precision organisation.

'Once it's dried, everything needs ironing.'

'Anything else?'

'It's not easy ironing all that linen, you know.'

'I'm not saying it is. I'm just trying to get organised.'

'There's still a few bits and pieces to buy for the kitchen and we'll need to get a coffee maker. What have you got to do?'

'I want to put a cordon around the lawn.'

I'd been intending to do that job ever since a delivery driver turned his van around on the grass. In doing so, he'd left tyre tracks four inches deep running the length of the lawn. At the time I could have killed him. On reflection it was probably a blessing in disguise. To make sure it didn't happen again I'd decided to enclose it with a rope cordon.

'What will you need for that?'

'Nine wooden posts and twenty-five metres of rope.'

'And what about the television?' asked Melanie.

'What about it?'

'The guests are Spanish.'

Melanie had a point. All our marketing was aimed at English-speaking nations. With that in mind we'd installed a satellite dish to pick up programmes from the UK.

'We'll have to give them some Spanish TV channels,' she added.

'OK, we'll call at Bazar Lago and ask them to install an aerial.'

Bazar Lago was the electrical retailer in Monforte who'd installed the satellite system.

'There's also the starter pack to buy but we can get that on Saturday morning before we do the final clean,' said Melanie.

'Is that everything?' I asked.

'What about the tour guide and restaurant reviews?'

'They'll have to wait. There isn't enough time to do them.'

'Right then, we'd better get cracking.'

We downed our coffee, washed, dressed, and readied ourselves for a busy day.

'I'll peg out the washing before we go and get another load in,' said Melanie.

While Melanie loaded the washing machine, I pulled the car out of the driveway. Minutes later we were speeding towards Monforte to Bazar Lago, our first stop of the day.

'Can you install a TV aerial for us before Saturday?' I asked.

'Imposible,' said the shopkeeper.

'¿Imposible?'

'Si, es imposible (Yes, it's impossible),' he replied, adding, 'I can't leave the shop because my colleague is away on holiday.'

'What are we going to do now?' asked Melanie.

As far as I could see we had two options: abandon the idea or install it ourselves.

'I'll have to do it,' I replied.

'There's no way I'm letting you clamber around on the roof. You'll end up breaking your neck.'

There's confidence for you.

'I have no intention of clambering around on the roof.'

'What then?'

'I'll put it in the loft. We should be able to pick up a signal from there.'

'Are you sure?'

I hadn't a clue but it couldn't harm to try.

'I don't see why not and at least there, it won't be an eyesore.'

The manager had wandered off to serve another customer. On his return we asked to see his stock of aerials. The choice was limited to two.

'How much are they?' I asked.

The cheapest was over seventy euros. I looked at Melanie. Her expression mirrored my thoughts.

'We'll think about it,' I said, before wandering off.

'We're not paying that,' said Melanie.

'Let's go to BricoKing and see what they've got.'

As luck would have it, they had exactly what we wanted and for the bargain price of twenty-four euros. They also stocked the rope I needed for the cordon, but not the posts.

'I know where we can get them,' I said.

'Where?'

'That agricultural shop down the road from Ramón Otero's.'

Having promoted myself to TV aerial installer, we would have to go home to collect some tools. The supplier in question was en route.

Their stock of fence posts were stacked on pallets in the carpark.

'These will be fine,' I said, lifting one off a pile to take a closer look.

'They're a bit long, aren't they?'

I sometimes wonder how Melanie's mind works. Did she really think I was going to cordon off the lawn with two-metre-tall posts?

'We can saw them to whatever length we want.'

'Oh, yes.'

A more pressing matter was how to get them into the back of the car.

'We'll have to come back with the trailer,' I said.

We raced home, conscious that time was slipping by. I loaded the toolbox into the car while Melanie took the dry washing off the line, emptied the washing machine, pegged out the damp laundry, and reloaded the washer.

'That's the last load,' she said, closing the laundry room door.

'Great. I've got everything I'll need.'

'What about lunch?'

'Let's take some sandwiches.'

'How does tuna mayonnaise sound?'

'Delicious.'

While Melanie made lunch, I hooked up the trailer. Ten minutes later we were speeding back to the agricultural shop.

'Aren't you going in?' asked Melanie.

I'd pulled up on the road outside the carpark.

'It'll be alright here.'

If truth be told, I still hadn't mastered the art of reversing the trailer. The last thing I wanted was to make a fool of myself.

Within minutes of arriving we'd bought the posts, tied them securely to the trailer, and settled the bill. Fifteen minutes after that we were pulling into the driveway at *Campo Verde*.

'Do you want lunch before we get started?' asked Melanie.

'Why not.'

We perched on the garden wall and ate our sandwiches in the warm sunshine. Since seeding the lawns, we'd been watering them every day for the past month and the results were spectacular. It would be a while before I could mow the grass, but the young green shoots looked vibrant and healthy.

'Are you ready?' I asked.

'Ready when you are.'

'We'll start with the cordon.'

'What do you want me to do?'

'Can you hold the posts?'

'OK, but watch what you're doing.'

The cordon would follow the same line as the water pipes for the sprinkler system. To avoid any mishaps, I dug out the first six inches of soil with a trowel.

'We'll put the first one here,' I said, placing the post into the hole.

Melanie grabbed it with both hands, closed her eyes, and dipped her head. I picked up the sledgehammer.

'Hold it straight,' I said.

Thwack, thwack, thwack. Each hit sank the post further into the ground.

'OK, that'll do.'

Melanie opened her eyes and let go. Within the hour all nine were equally spaced along the edge of the lawn at three-metre intervals.

'How tall do you think they should be?' I asked.

'I don't know. It's your fence.'

'Shin height should be enough. It's only to stop people driving on the grass.'

I pulled out the tape measure and set it to forty centimetres.

'What do you think?'

'That looks fine,' replied Melanie.

I measured, marked, and cut each post to length.

'How are you going to attach the rope?' she asked.

'I thought I'd drill a hole at the top of each one and feed it through.'

I'd had my doubts about erecting a cordon but if anything, it actually enhanced the garden's appearance. We could rightly be proud of our efforts.

'Right then, the aerial.'

'Will you need me?' asked Melanie.

Installing the aerial would involve crawling around in the loft where headroom was limited.

'I don't think so.'

'In that case I'll make a start on the cleaning.'

The house had been completely rewired during the renovation which had given us the opportunity to install lighting in the loft. At least I wouldn't be working in the dark.

I climbed the ladder and sat with my legs dangling through the hatch. The aerial was about a metre long. I switched on the light and searched for a suitable place to fix it. All the roof timbers were either too thick or inaccessible. I stared at the fixing bracket, looking for inspiration. That's when it came to me. The bracket would fit perfectly around a forty-millimetre-diameter polyethylene water pipe, offcuts of which I just happened to have in the *bodega*. If I cut the pipe to the correct length, I could wedge it into position between the floorboards and the roof joist. That would eliminate the need for a permanent fixing. I measured the gap and climbed down. Minutes later I'd cut the pipe to the correct length and climbed back into the loft.

With a little persuasion I wedged the pipe into position and bolted the aerial bracket around it. The next job was to fix the connectors to the coaxial cable and connect the cable to the TV. Once everything was wired up, I could adjust the direction of the aerial to find the strongest signal. I climbed back down to get a Stanley knife from the toolbox.

'Have you got my Stanley knife?' I called.

I waited for a reply but nothing. I tried again, a little louder this time.

'I said, have you got my …'

'I heard you the first time.'

Melanie had poked her head around the bedroom door.

'What would I want with your Stanley knife?'

'Well it's not here.'

'Well I haven't got it.'

'Bugger.'

If I couldn't find a knife, I'd have to drive all the way home to get one. Perhaps there was one in the *bodega*. I walked downstairs to take a look. Hidden amongst an assortment of old electrical fittings was an adjustable knife with a rusty old blade.

'You found it then?' asked Melanie, as I walked through the lounge.

'Not really but it'll have to do.'

The outer sleeve of coaxial cable was soft and rubbery. I ran the blade around the sleeve but it didn't even leave an impression. A little more pressure was called for. I pressed down harder and pulled the knife towards me. Before I knew what had happened the knife had slipped and I'd sliced through my finger. Fearing the worst, I dropped the blade and grabbed my bleeding digit.

'Melanie!' I called.

My tone sent her scampering to the hatch.

'What?' she asked, staring up at me.

'I've sliced through my finger.'

'How did you do that?'

'The knife slipped. Can you hold the ladder while I climb down?'

Melanie steadied the ladder. Without releasing my finger, I carefully climbed down.

'How bad is it?' she asked.

In my eagerness to stem the blood flow I hadn't dared look and I and wasn't going to let go until a medical professional was on hand.

'It's bad. You're going to have to drive me to A&E.'

'Hold it up above your heart,' she said, as we made our way to the car.

Melanie locked up and opened the car door for me. As we sped towards the hospital the inquest began.

'What were you doing?' she asked.

'I was trying to strip the coaxial cable but the knife was blunt. I pressed down really hard and the next thing I knew it had slipped and sliced through my finger.'

'They do say you're more likely to cut yourself with a blunt knife than a sharp one.'

Hark at her.

Melanie's words of wisdom weren't helping. Keeping my finger aloft was starting to hurt. My arms felt like lead weights.

Within fifteen minutes we were pulling into the hospital carpark. Melanie raced around to open the door for me.

'How are you feeling?' she asked.

'Like an idiot.'

'Well, at least it hasn't affected your sense of humour.'

We marched into the hospital and headed for A&E. Standing behind the reception desk was a young man in a green uniform. Melanie handed him my health card and I explained what I'd done.

'Take a seat. We'll be with you in a minute,' he said, gesturing us towards a row of chairs.

Moments later he returned.

'This way,' he said.

On the few occasions we've needed the Spanish National Health Service the standard of care has been excellent. I followed him down a corridor and into a treatment room. A young lady wearing a white coat greeted me.

'So, what have you been doing?' she asked.

I assumed from her body language that she was a junior doctor and the young man the nurse.

'I've cut my finger,' I said, holding it out.

I was convinced she'd take one look and insist on stitches.

'What with?' she asked.

'*Una cuchara*,' I replied.

The doctor smiled. I failed to see what was so funny.

'*¿Una cuchara?*' asked the nurse.

He too seemed to find my predicament amusing.

'*Si, una cuchara.*'

'*¿Fue una cuchara afilada?*' he asked.

His question triggered a murmur of giggles. The doctor quickly regained her composure, cleared her throat, and focused on the job in hand. If I hadn't have known better I would have said they were making fun of me. Perhaps I'd misunderstood something. I wracked my brain for an answer.

The verb *afilar* means to sharpen. The question *fue una cuchara afilada* translates to "Was it a sharp knife?" If that was supposed to be funny then the joke was lost on me. I resolved to answer his question.

'*No, la cuchara estaba desfilada,*' I replied.

My response tipped their self-control over the edge. Laughter filled the room and I was the butt of their joke. What on earth could be so funny?

'*¿Estás seguro que era una cuchara y no un cuchillo?*'

The nurse's question sent a rush of blood flooding into my cheeks as embarrassment replaced my annoyance. Finally, the penny had dropped. In my haste to explain the circumstances surrounding my accident, I'd confused *cuchara* (spoon) with *cuchillo* (knife). My insistence that I'd sliced open my finger with a blunt spoon only served to reinforce my error. Eventually the giggles subsided and the doctor continued her examination. If nothing else, it had put me at ease.

'I don't think it needs stitching,' said the doctor.

That was a relief.

'The nurse will clean and dress it and then you can go,' she added.

My fears were ill-founded.

'When did you last have a tetanus injection?' she asked.

I knew exactly when it was and it wasn't recent.

'Nineteen-ninety-two,' I replied.

Tetanus was one of a series of inoculations I'd had prior to visiting Kenya.

'Perhaps it's time you had a booster,' she said.

I didn't know what was worse, stitches or an injection. It's not that I'm afraid of needles but given the choice, I'd rather not be subjected to either. Worse than that, if I'd known this morning I'd end up in A&E I would definitely have worn underwear. If they thought cutting myself with a blunt spoon was funny, they hadn't seen anything yet.

'That was a booster,' I blurted.

My knee-jerk response initiated a period of silent reflection.

'In that case …' she paused.

In that case what?

'In that case …' she repeated.

The suspense was killing me.

'In that case, I don't think you need one.'

My heart skipped a beat as she pulled a plastic-coated ring binder off the shelf and thumbed through the pages searching for confirmation.

'Here it is,' she said, pointing at the relevant section. 'Once every thirty years is sufficient.'

'Thirty years?' questioned the nurse.

I felt like telling him to button it. If the book said thirty years, then thirty years it was.

'That's what it says. It looks like you don't need one after all.'

Modesty preserved, the nurse finished dressing the wound and sent me on my way.

'What was all that laughing about?' asked Melanie, as we headed back to the car.

'Laughing, what laughing?'

22

Letting Go

My self-inflicted injury couldn't have happened at a more inconvenient time. Over the last twenty-four hours our list of things to do had shortened by one and my ability to complete the rest was severely restricted. The clock was ticking. In less than thirty-three hours our first guests would be arriving. We had to finish installing the aerial, buy the missing kitchen utensils, and find a suitable coffee maker. Whatever it took, all those jobs had to be completed that day. That would leave Saturday morning to buy the grocery starter pack and finish cleaning the house.

'Are you ready?' I asked.

Talk about all fingers and thumbs. The dressing on my injured finger was enormous. It had taken me almost five minutes to tie my shoelaces and I was eager to get cracking.

'Ready when you are.'

We locked up and jumped into the car.

'Are you sure you're alright to drive?' asked Melanie.

'Don't worry, I'll be fine. I've been thinking.'

'Oh yes.'

'Yes. Perhaps Haley will have a coffee maker?'

Haley is Monforte's premier supermarket. It's not the biggest shop in the world but it does have a non-food section which includes kitchenalia.

'It can't harm to take a look.'

Coffee making in Spain has evolved into a ritual art form. Not for them a teaspoon of instant coffee and a kettle of boiling water. Preparing a brew in Spain takes time and effort and involves coffee grounds and a cafetière.

The most popular type of coffeepot is a stove top, induction model. Water percolates through the ground coffee from a reservoir beneath the pot. For those with a gas stove they're ideal, but we'd opted for a ceramic hob. The challenge was to find something suitable at an affordable price.

Given the size of the shop, Haley's range of coffee makers was surprisingly comprehensive. I picked one off the shelf to take a closer look.

'That's no good,' said Melanie.

I hadn't yet read the instructions and she'd already dismissed it.

'This one's not suitable for a ceramic hob,' I replied, having read the label.

'Told you.'

I reached across to pick another.

'What about …'

'No.'

That told me. I glanced at my watch. Time was ticking by.

'They haven't got one. I'll see if they've got everything else we need,' said Melanie, before marching off.

Giving up was not an option and I'm nothing if not persistent. One by one I lifted every model off the shelf and read the label. Each one had the same information:

"Not suitable for use on a ceramic hob". I was just about to give up when I stumbled across a possible alternative. An induction coffeepot with its own heating element. It was a cross between a cafetière and an electric kettle. The only downside was the cost. All that ingenuity came at a price.

'I can't find a potato masher but other than that I've got everything.'

Melanie had crept up behind me.

'What do you think to this?' I asked.

'What is it?'

'It's a cafetière that plugs in.'

She took the box off me and gave it the once-over.

'It looks expensive.'

That was her way of saying "Well done".

'It's not cheap but beggars can't be choosers and the guests are Spanish,' I replied.

'OK, let's get it.'

Finally, we could get down to some real work.

Within ten minutes of leaving the supermarket we were trundling through the narrow lanes of Vilatán. My first job was to complete the installation of the aerial.

'Do be careful,' said Melanie, as I climbed the ladder into the loft.

This time I'd come prepared with a sharp knife. The problem I'd had tying my laces paled into insignificance compared to stripping the coaxial cable. A job that should have taken a few minutes took over an hour.

'Can you switch on the telly and tell me what we've got?' I shouted.

'Just a minute.'

I sat at the opening to the loft with my legs dangling through the hatch waiting for a reply.

'It's not a very good picture,' she called.

'Wait there and I'll move the aerial. Shout stop when it's clear.'

Rather than loosen the bracket and risk losing the picture altogether, I twisted the pipe.

'Stop,' shouted Melanie from the lounge.

'Try every channel,' I called.

'How many should there be?'

We'd lived in Spain for the best part of seven years and in all that time we hadn't had a telly. How on earth was I supposed to know how many channels there should be?

'How many have you got?'

'Four.'

'That'll do.'

I switched the light off, closed the hatch, and climbed down.

'What time is it?' asked Melanie.

'Half past two.'

'No wonder my stomach is rumbling.'

A subtle hint that she'd had enough for the day.

'What's left to do?' I asked.

'There's just the beds to make up and the lobby and staircase to clean. What about you?'

'I've got to sweep the terraces and put out the garden furniture.'

'Let's finish off tomorrow.'

She wouldn't hear any complaints from me. We'd had a good day and everything was back on track.

Saturday morning began with an unwelcome alarm call. After a quick cuppa we drove into town to get the starter pack. For the miserly sum of ten euros we bought: a bottle of red wine, a litre of beer, a one and a half litre bottle of water, half a dozen eggs, boiled ham, cheese slices, a litre carton of orange juice, a wholemeal loaf, a packet of chocolate wafer biscuits, two tomatoes and an onion, individual sachets of tea, coffee and sugar, and two single-serve packs of butter and jam for each guest.

'Do you think we should get the kids an Easter egg?' asked Melanie.

'That would be a nice touch, and perhaps a chocolate to put on the pillow for the adults.'

For many people, an annual vacation is an opportunity to forget their mundane lives and dream of something better. As far as I'm concerned, woe betide anyone who messes with other people's dreams. We were determined to deliver exactly what we'd advertised and ensure a stay at *Campo Verde* surpassed everyone's expectations.

Having bought the starter pack, we headed off to Vilatán. Two and a half hours after arriving, the place looked spotless, and the gardens were immaculate. Under normal circumstances we would have locked up and left the keys in a pre-arranged hiding place. After a long and tiring journey, we figured the last thing people would want to see was our smiling faces. But this booking was different. Due to the short timeframe I'd asked Mariano to bring the payment with him. This meant we would have to meet them on arrival. We decided to nip home and have a bite to eat before showering, changing, and heading back to greet them.

'What time do they arrive?' asked Melanie, on the drive home.

'Five-thirty.'

Before we knew it, we were driving back to *Campo Verde*.

'You turn the lights on and I'll open the gates,' I said.

The interior lighting had been chosen specifically to create a welcoming mood. Low wattage bulbs illuminated the display cabinet above the breakfast bar and a picture light in the dining room cast a warming glow over the exposed stonework. In the downstairs lobby a coach-style lamp gave it a warm and cosy feel and subdued lighting in the staircase softened the white walls.

As I walked down the driveway a car pulled up outside. We couldn't have timed our arrival any better. I opened the gates and Mariano drove in. The whole family loved the place and their visually impaired spaniel made himself at home. The Easter eggs went down a treat and his wife fell in love with the master bedroom.

'This is beautiful,' said Mariano, with an American twang.

'Where did you learn your English?' I asked.

'We lived in the US for five years. I work for IBM,' he explained. 'That's where I got into rugby.'

'Rugby, in the US?'

'It's a long story, but yes. I've got the whole Six Nations Championship on a hard drive. I can't wait to watch it. That looks nasty,' he added, nodding at my bandaged finger.

'Yes, another long story but I won't bore you with the details.'

Would you believe it. I'd almost amputated my finger in an effort to ensure they had some Spanish channels to watch and not only was their English as good as mine, but they'd even brought their own entertainment.

Hard drive indeed, whatever next?

'Well, we'll leave you to it. You shouldn't have any problems but if there's anything at all, our contact details are in the Guest Information book,' I said, handing him the keys.

Walking away felt like abandoning an only child. We'd put so much of ourselves into creating this beautiful home. On the drive back to *El Sueño* we hardly spoke a word.

'Teatime Taster?' I asked, as we stepped into the house.

'I think we deserve one.'

We spent the rest of the weekend relaxing at home. The last few days had been manic. Jazz's mobility continued to improve, albeit at a steady pace. Short walks at frequent intervals were the order of the day. By Monday morning, Melanie and I were raring to go.

'Let's make a start on the tourist guide,' I suggested over breakfast.

'OK, where to?'

'I thought we might go to Taboada.'

'Taboada?'

Melanie's surprise was understandable. We knew very little about the town but its proximity to Vilatán merited a visit.

'Why not? According to that map the area is littered with *pazos*.'

'What map?'

'That map on the placemat.'

I'd acquired the map from a local restaurant, *menú del día* not Michelin star. After taking our order the waitress had returned with cutlery, napkins, and paper placemats. Printed on the mat was a map of the surrounding area showing places of interest. These included castles and *pazos* (Galician manor houses). The town of Taboada, situated twenty-four kilometres north of Vilatán, seemed to be blessed with more than its fair share.

'Oh, that map.'

Melanie's lukewarm response queried the wisdom of my suggestion. Nevertheless, within the hour we were heading towards the town of Chantada and from there on towards Taboada. On the outskirts of the town I pulled over.

'Let's have another look at the map,' I said.

Melanie handed me the folded placemat. On closer inspection the illustration was more abstract than practical.

'It looks like we need to drive through the town and turn right before we rejoin the main carriageway. We're about here,' I said, pointing at the paper.

'And?'

Her sharp reply and single word response spoke volumes. When it comes to map reading, I'm on my own.

'I'm just saying,' I replied, handing it back to her.

Melanie took it and feigned interest. If I knew what was good for me, I'd leave it at that. I engaged first gear and continued on. The main high street was quiet as we drove through the town centre and out the other side.

'The turn should be around here,' I said.

Melanie said nothing.

Before I knew it, we'd rejoined the main carriageway, only now we were travelling in the wrong direction.

'I'm going to have to turn around.'

Still no reply.

I pulled over to the side and prepared to make a U-turn.

'Are we clear in front?' I asked.

'You're not supposed to turn here. It's a solid white line.'

From silent treatment to sarcasm. Was she having fun yet?

'I know, darling. Are we clear in front?'

'Wait … Wait … Clear now.'

The traffic was light and the carriageway wide. I completed the turn in one sweeping manoeuvre.

'What now?' she asked.

'I'll drive back into town and see if we can find someone to ask.'

Within minutes we were trundling back down the high street but there wasn't a soul in sight.

'Perhaps someone in there can help us?' I said, pulling up outside the Casa de Cultura.

Melanie hopped out and walked into the building. A few minutes later she reappeared accompanied by another woman. A conversation ensued and sweeping arm movements articulated the route.

'All sorted?' I asked, as she slipped into the passenger seat.

'That was the librarian. She was the only person in there.'

'What did she say?'

'She thinks there's a signpost. Go back to the main carriageway and it should be on the right.'

Melanie didn't sound convinced and I couldn't remember seeing one. Perhaps we'd missed it or maybe we hadn't driven far enough. With nothing but the good intentions of the town's librarian to rely on, we set off again and joined the main carriageway. As we approached the first exit, I checked my rear-view mirror and slowed to a crawl. There was a signpost but no mention of a *pazo*.

'It must be the next exit,' said Melanie, more in hope than expectation.

We fared no better at the next turn-off.

'This can't be right. Let's go back and see where that first road takes us.'

I completed another U-turn and headed back towards town.

'It's coming up on the left,' said Melanie.

I indicated and turned into a narrow country lane.

'Keep an eye out for someone to ask,' I said.

Two hundred metres further along we entered a small hamlet.

'There's someone,' said Melanie.

She'd spotted an old man working in his garden. I pulled alongside and lowered the window.

'*Buenos días*,' I called.

The man looked up.

'*Buenos días*,' he replied.

I could tell from his expression that encountering sightseers wasn't an everyday occurrence.

'Do you know where the Pazo de San Pedro is?' I asked.

'Where?'

'The Pazo de San Pedro.'

The old man tipped his head and stroked his stubble.

'San Pedro you say?'

'That's right, the Pazo de San Pedro.'

We were finally getting somewhere.

'Hmm.'

Or were we? I waited patiently for an answer.

'No, I don't know that one,' he replied.

Hopes crushed, I thanked him and prepared to move off.

'My brother might know,' he added.

Melanie and I watched as he wandered up the driveway and disappeared into the house.

'Do you think he's coming back?' whispered Melanie.

I was just about to answer when the door opened and he stepped out accompanied by another elderly man.

'My brother tells me you're looking for the Pazo de San Pedro.'

'That's right.'

I couldn't help thinking that he too was about to let us down.

'I know where it is.'

Shock turned to euphoria. At last we'd found a would-be guide.

The brother's directions were nothing if not comprehensive. After each new instruction he asked if we'd understood. I kept nodding and Melanie chipped in with a sporadic *sí*. We thanked him for his help and continued on.

'Did he say left at the next crossroad?' I asked.

'No, it's straight ahead and then turn left.'

It seemed prudent to follow Melanie's instructions.

'It's definitely next right though, isn't it?'

My hesitant question unsettled Melanie.

'I thought he said two left turns and then a right.'

We hadn't travelled two kilometres and we were already lost.

'It can't be far away,' I said in frustration. 'Can you see anything?'

'All I can see are drystone walls.'

It seemed inconceivable that we weren't within touching distance.

'There,' said Melanie.

I slammed on the brakes and the car shuddered to a halt.

'That's not it.'

'Not the house, the man.'

Melanie had spotted someone else to ask. I pulled up next to him and Melanie lowered her window.

'Go to the end of here and turn right. There's an information board at the end of a long driveway.'

'Thank you.'

At last we'd found our prize, but our moment of elation was short-lived. The information board confirmed the property's name as Pazo de San Pedro, but a sign on the gate read "Private Property – Keep Out". All this effort and for what?

'Well, that was a waste of time,' said Melanie, on the drive home.

Perhaps so, but better we waste our time than guests waste theirs. The last thing we wanted was people returning home with tales of a land oblivious to the needs of international tourists.

Our first foray into the world of writing a tour guide had been an unmitigated disaster. We needed to brush ourselves down, regroup, and come back fighting. Galicia, and the Ribeira Sacra, are places of outstanding natural beauty with stunning scenery and remarkable architecture. All we had to do was show our guests where to find it.

23

Dam Scary

With the benefit of hindsight, relying on a placemat to uncover hidden tourist attractions was a ridiculous idea. A more pragmatic approach was called for. In the past we'd spent hours ferrying family and friends around the area. It was time to draw on those experiences and produce a self-drive tour guide guests would truly appreciate.

'I know where we can go,' I said.

'Where?'

'Let's take a trip around the river Miño. We can drive downstream to Os Peares, cross the river, and come back up the other side.'

'That's a brilliant idea. The scenery is stunning and there's lots of things to do en route. We can stop for lunch at that restaurant in Os Peares.'

'Acea de Bubal?'

'That's the one.'

What a contrast to yesterday's indifferent response. Starting on such a positive note could only bode well for the day ahead.

'You'll need a pen and paper,' I said.

'What for?'

'To write down the directions.'

Melanie picked up a notepad and pen, I checked my wallet, and off we went. First stop, Vilatán. Before entering the village, I pulled over. The tour could now begin.

'OK, are you ready?' I asked.

'Ready when you are.'

'Right then, the first direction is, turn right along the LU-617 heading towards Chantada.'

'Right?'

'That's right, right.'

'But it's straight ahead.'

'I know it's straight ahead, but it wouldn't be if we were coming from *Campo Verde*.'

'Oh yes.'

Melanie wrote down the instruction and I pulled away.

'After 3.2 kilometres turn right, signposted Vilelos.'

'Where are you going?'

'I thought we'd take a look at that *torre*.'

'What *torre*?'

'The one marked on the map.'

'What map?'

'The placemat.'

'You're joking! After what happened yesterday?'

Melanie rolled her eyes.

It couldn't harm to try and find it. We were practically driving past.

'I think it's up here.'

'What's the distance?'

'Hang on a minute.'

I stopped to get my bearings.

'Yes, it must be up here.'

'OK, but what's the distance?'

'Erm … 1.4 kilometres and the signpost reads: A Bugalla, Bexe, and Pacios.'

'How are you spelling those?'

'Didn't you see the sign?'

'How fast do you think I can write?'

'Hang on a minute.'

I checked the mirror, slipped the car into reverse, and rolled back down the lane. Melanie scribbled down the names.

'Got 'em,' she said.

After three hundred metres we came to a fork in the road.

'Where now?' she asked.

The right-hand fork rose sharply up a steep incline. A signpost on the left read "A Bugalla" and "A Candaira". I turned left. Six hundred metres further along the Torre de A Candaira came into view.

'Well, I didn't expect to see that,' said Melanie.

I knew what she meant, even though it was marked on the map. Who would have thought it, a 12th century *torre* less than four kilometres from *Campo Verde*? I pulled off the road and we went to take a closer look.

The *torre*, like the *pazo* in Taboada, is privately owned, but unlike the *pazo* it's possible to get up close and personal to this curious monument. The tower is roughly ten metres square and eleven metres high. As a defensive structure, it would have sucked. The entrance is on the ground floor and its proximity to the hill behind would have meant would-be attackers could literally lob projectiles onto the roof.

'Where next?' asked Melanie.

As fascinating as the Torre de A Candaira is, it was time to move on.

'I thought we'd take a look at the church of Santo Estevo.'

'The one with the rose window?'

'That's it.'

We buckled up and continued on.

'Bear left after three hundred metres,' I said, as we came to a fork in the road.

Melanie scribbled it down. One hundred and fifty metres further along we turned left and then right onto the CG2.1. A road sign pointed to the church of Santo Estevo de Ribas de Miño.

This 12th century Romanesque-style church is perched high on the valley of the river Miño. It's one of the best examples of its type in the Ribeira Sacra and was declared a national monument in 1931. Its most outstanding features are the rose window above the main entrance and its location. Standing on the front terrace we stared out across the valley to the vineyards on the south facing slopes. Narrow terraces rise from the river's edge, climbing hundreds of metres to the summit.

Historic architecture is all well and good but Melanie was becoming restless. Once you've seen one gargoyle you've seen them all.

'Come on then, let's move on,' I suggested.

From there we followed a more familiar route. We rejoined the main road heading towards Chantada. A long road bridge, spanning the valley of the river Miño, marked the point at which we turned left. We descended to the river's edge through an ancient forest and onwards to a medieval bridge. It's here the route crosses paths with the Ruta Invierno (Winter Route) of the Camino de Santiago. A kilometre further along we entered the picturesque village of Belesar where reflections of brightly painted village houses shimmered in the dark water.

After exiting Belesar the road narrows and hugs the contours of the river as it meanders through vineyards and pine forests. Travellers are treated to outstanding river views. Seven kilometres downstream we reached the river beach at A Cova and began our ascent up the valley. The steep incline snakes its way up a precipitous slope.

'Would you like to stop for a coffee?' I asked, as we neared the restaurant Mesón Parrillada A Cova.

'Yes please.'

Talk about a room with a view. The restaurant is part of the Adega San Martiño winery and is perched high on the side of the valley. It rewards its patrons with outstanding views of the river. The coffee isn't expensive but the views are priceless.

'*Hola, buenos días. Dos cafés con leche* (Two coffees with milk).'

The waiter took our order. A stainless steel coffee maker burped and hissed as he filled the cups.

'Where next?' asked Melanie, as we sipped our morning coffees.

'I thought we could take a look at the Ecomuseo.'

'OK.'

The Ecomuseo de Arxeriz (Ecomuseum) is housed in a restored *pazo*. Its exhibits detail the history of the Ribeira Sacra, the river Miño, and the area's winemaking traditions. It's one of the few attractions with a dedicated English-speaking guide. The house and grounds give visitors an insight into the daily lives of the 17th century aristocrats who lived there.

We finished our coffees, settled the bill, and continued on up the valley.

'What about adding the viewing point to the tour?' suggested Melanie.

We'd just passed a roadside sign marked O Mirador (Viewing point).

'That's a great idea. Let's take a look.'

I pulled off the road and we strolled down a forest track to the viewing platform. This is the spot where professional photographers capture iconic images of the river Miño that magazine editors crave. I couldn't resist taking a few snaps, but don't expect to see them on the cover of *National Geographic* anytime soon.

Next stop the museum. The tour was interesting and informative and the exhibits were fascinating. By the time we'd finished, the clock had ticked around to 1:00 pm.

'Is it lunchtime yet?' asked Melanie.

'I don't see why not.'

We left the museum and joined the LU-P-4102 heading towards Ferreira de Pantón. After 3.5 kilometres we turned right following signs to Ourense before joining the N-120.

'Let's stop at the viewing point on the way down,' I suggested.

We'd joined the N-120 at the top of the Miño valley. From there, silky-smooth tarmac twists and turns as it tumbles down the valley. It's a real driver's road that's as much fun to zoom up as it is to career down. After 2.4 kilometres we pulled into a layby and strolled to another viewing platform.

The vastness of the wilderness was quite overwhelming. We stood in silence, lost in this landscape of deep river valleys, towering mountains, terraced vineyards, and flourishing forests. Then a grumbling stomach shattered our daydreams.

'Come on, let's get something to eat,' I said.

Infinite landscapes are one thing, but a man has to eat.

At the bottom of the descent we exited right following the sign for Os Peares. The confluence of the rivers Miño and Sil has split the village into three. The majority of the dwellings, including the restaurant, are on the far side of the river facing south. The quickest route across is via the railway bridge. The walk is not as dangerous as it sounds. Running parallel to the track is a designated footpath. Mind you, if you're halfway across when an express train thunders past it's quite unnerving.

The restaurant takes its name from the river Bubal which runs down one side of the building. This former chocolate factory has been sympathetically restored and combines contemporary fittings with many original features. At the rear of the property there's an old spillway that once powered a waterwheel. Leant up against a lamppost on the lane outside was a chalkboard with the words "*Menú del día*, 8 euros" scribbled on it.

I approached the owner who was working behind the bar.

'*¿Se puede comer* (Is it possible to eat)?' I asked.

'*¿Cuanto* (For how many)?'

'Just the two of us.'

'No problem. Follow me.'

The owner circled the bar and led us up a flight of stairs into a light and airy dining room. During the summer months patrons have the option to dine alfresco on a narrow terrace above the babbling stream. We took a seat inside and our host brought a basket of crusty bread.

'*¿Para beber* (What would you like to drink)?' he asked.

I looked at Melanie.

'White wine?'

'Yes please.'

'*Una botella de vino blanco*.'

The menu was delivered orally. Melanie opted for *entremeses* (an assortment of cured meats) for her starter and *lomo a la plancha* (grilled pork loin) for her main course. I chose *espaguetis* (spaghetti) and *merluza* (fried hake).

Service was swift and the host's wife soon returned with our starters.

'*Que aproveche* (Bon appétit),' she said, before returning to the kitchen.

Melanie's platter of *entremeses* looked delicious and the aromas of paprika and wood smoke smelt gorgeous. The selection included thinly sliced rounds of homemade chorizo, *salchichón* (a pork, salami-style sausage), *lomo* (cured pork loin), *jamón* (dry-cured ham), and triangles of *queso curado* (cured cheese). My bowl of spaghetti was enormous and cooked to perfection: plump, soft pasta with a Bolognese à la Español sauce of rich tomatoes, chopped peppers, and cubed meat.

The two main courses were equally delicious. The pan-fried hake was virgin white with a hint of garlic and flakes of fresh parsley and Melanie's pork was beautifully moist without being oily.

'Careful,' said Melanie, drawing air in through her rounded lips, 'the chips are hot.'

Which is quite a rare occurrence in these parts.

'This can be our first restaurant review,' I said.

Starters and mains whetted our appetite for dessert.

'Did you enjoy that?' asked the owner.

Clean plates spoke volumes.

'Delicious,' said Melanie.

'¿*Postre* (Pudding)?' she asked.

'¿*Qué hay* (What is there)?'

From the pocket of her apron she pulled out a notepad. The list of desserts seemed endless. When she stopped to draw breath, I jumped in.

'*Tarta de castañas para mi* (Chestnut tart for me).'

Melanie chose the *flan de huevos*, a type of set custard smothered in caramel sauce. Mine was delicious. Melanie was a little disappointed that hers wasn't homemade but enjoyed it nonetheless. While she polished off the wine, I ordered a *café solo* (espresso). A fabulous finale to a fine meal and all for the princely sum of sixteen euros.

'Right then, let's see what the other side of the valley has to offer,' I said.

Crossing the railway bridge on foot was a walk in the park compared to what followed. The only way to cross the river by car was along the top of the Os Peares dam.

'Where are you going?' asked Melanie.

The anxiety in her voice was understandable.

'Across the dam.'

'Are you sure you're allowed to do that?'

'How else are we supposed to cross?'

Cautiously, I turned into the narrow entrance and crept slowly along the single track. Halfway across I stopped.

'What are you doing?'

Anxiety had turned to fear.

'There seems to be something wrong with the car.'

'Stop messing around and get us off this chuffing dam.'

I'd had my fun. It was time to continue on.

I turned right at the end heading towards Chantada. The road on that side of the valley was deserted, which given the width of the carriageway was just as well. The recently laid road surface hugged the contours of the valley meandering in and out and up and down. The one constant was the river.

'Look at that,' said Melanie, who was clearly none the worse for her terrifying experience.

We'd travelled eleven kilometres since crossing the dam. Directly in front was a spectacular waterfall cascading down the valley before disappearing underneath the road. I pulled over to take a few snaps. Two kilometres further along another photo opportunity appeared: a small island in the middle of the river. It wasn't until we reached the twenty-eight kilometre mark that we passed the first sign for Belesar. We'd almost come full circle. The road had been climbing steadily for some time and the drop into Belesar was breathtaking, spectacular, and terrifying in equal measures. Hairpin bends weave their way through acres of terraced vineyards as the road descends steeply to the riverbank.

'You're too close to the edge,' said Melanie.

'I hope we don't meet anything coming up.'

'Don't even joke about it.'

Halfway down we passed a sign for the Adega do Viega winery. I couldn't resist pulling into their driveway.

'This looks as good a place as any to stop for a Teatime Taster,' I said.

Melanie agreed. If the truth be known, I think she was just happy to be off the road. We sat outside under a steel-framed gazebo. Grapevines had been trained to creep across the top to provide visitors with shade. We took a seat and waited.

'*Buenos tardes*, what can I get you?' asked a young waiter.

'Two glasses of red.'

'*¿Barrica o joven* (Oak aged or young)?' he asked.

'Which is the best?'

'*Barrica.*'

'Then *barrica* it is.'

There was something very special about sipping wine produced from the vines that surrounded us. The perfect way to end a fabulous day. We'd travelled eighty kilometres through the Ribeira Sacra and it hadn't disappointed. We'd seen some wonderful sights and enjoyed a fabulous meal. If anyone found fault with this tour, they'd chosen the wrong holiday destination.

All I had to do now was convert Melanie's spidery shorthand into legible driving instructions, do some research on the places we'd visited, write something interesting about each one, and choose which photos to use. One down and seven to go.

Completing the self-drive tour guide became our top priority. The day after our excursion along the river Miño we circumnavigated the area's other great waterway, the river Sil.

Two days after that we visited the Santuario de Nuestra Señora de las Ermidas, a 17th century monastery nestled at the foot of a deep valley. At first sight you think you're dreaming. The monastery appears as if by magic, but the most amazing thing about that trip was lunch.

Having left the monastery, we headed for the town of Viana do Bolo. The restaurant A Nosa Casa was offering a three-course *menú del día* including bread, wine, and coffee for ten euros per head. Within minutes of placing our order the waitress returned.

'I'm sorry, sir, but the last serving of pork fillet has just left the kitchen.'

My immediate thought was of Elvis Presley wearing a white jumpsuit. I shook the image from my mind.

'However, I can offer you *solomillo*, if you'd like,' she added.

Perhaps I'd misheard. Did she just offer me fillet steak? My delay prompted a response.

'Or something else if you'd prefer.'

'No, no, *solomillo* will be perfect.'

When the steak arrived, it had been cooked to perfection. To this day, it's one of the best fillet steaks I've ever eaten. Who would have thought that a three-course meal including wine, coffee, and fillet steak could be had for ten euros?

Over the next few days our portfolio of self-drive tours increased at the rate of one per day. They included a trip to the weekly open-air market in Valença, Portugal, a day out to the historic city of Tui, and a day at the coastal resort of Baiona.

'Does that take us up to six?' asked Melanie, on the drive home.

'Yes, two more should do it.'

On the 18th of the month I opened my inbox and found two more bookings: one week in July and nine days in September. I could hardly contain my excitement.

'We've done it,' I announced, as I raced into the kitchen.

'What have you done, darling?'

'Not me, us. We've smashed our ten-week target.'

'What ten-week target?'

'Reservations for *Campo Verde*.'

'I thought we'd done that with Mariano's booking.'

'We had, but that one was off the books.'
'So how many official weeks do we have?'
'Eleven.'
'That's brilliant.'

Five days later, on the 23rd of April, I braved the swimming pool for the first time that year.
'What's it like?' asked Melanie.
'It's chuffing freezing.'
The water was so cold my arms and legs went into spasm and my privates felt like two frozen peas and a chipolata. I managed two lengths before hauling myself out.
'Is that it?' asked Melanie.
Cold is one thing, but this was ridiculous. The afternoon sun quickly defrosted my frozen peas and before long I felt toasty warm. Lengthening spring days nudged our Teatime Taster ever later. I glanced at my watch: 8:00 pm.
'Drink?' I asked.
'Why not?'
I pulled the cork on a fruity white and we relaxed at the far end of the garden.
'I checked the weather forecast this morning,' I said, as we caught the last rays of sunshine.
'Oh yes. What did it say?'
'The ten-day forecast looks great.'
'That's good.'
'Yes. Perhaps it's time to take that break we promised ourselves.'
'What break?'
'To *Campo Verde*. To make sure everything works.'
'But we've already had some guests.'
'I know, but we said we would.'
Ignorance breeds paranoia and I wanted to be absolutely certain that everything worked exactly as it should.

'OK, when do you want to go?'

'What about this Saturday?'

'That sounds perfect.'

'And what about inviting friends over for a meal or something?'

'What for?'

'To let them have a snoop around. They're always asking how things are going and you never know, they might even recommend it to their friends.'

'It can't do any harm I suppose.'

'We can do the last two tours while we're there as well.'

'Where are you thinking of going?'

'I thought we could check out the Templar castle in Ponferrada and go to the monastery in Samos.'

'Those sound ideal. And what about the restaurant reviews?'

'I'm sure we'll be eating out during our holiday.'

'Holiday, I thought we were conducting research?'

'Yes of course, research.'

Melanie's remark brought a smile to our faces.

24

Career Move

I couldn't quite believe it, bag after bag and they just kept coming. I'd squeezed more into the car for a ten-day break to *Campo Verde* than I had for a month-long stay in the Costa del Sol. Luggage aside, I was really looking forward to our working holiday.

'That's it,' I said, walking into the dining room. 'Everything is packed and I'm ready for off.'

'OK. Come on Jazz.'

'Oh.'

'Oh what?'

'Erm … I'm not sure there's room for the dog.'

Melanie looked dumbfounded.

'How could you forget Jazz?'

'I didn't forget, I just didn't quite remember. Don't worry, I'll pop back for her.'

'I know you will.'

The drive to *Campo Verde* took fifteen minutes. By the time we'd unpacked and I'd gone back for Jazz, two hours had passed.

Melanie was busy making the bed when we returned. My priority was establishing an internet connection. I booted up the laptop and ran the setup wizard. The message "Failed to connect" didn't bode well. I lifted the phone receiver but the line was dead.

'What have you done to the phone?' I called.

'I haven't done anything to the phone.'

'Well it's not working.'

'Don't blame me, I haven't touched it.'

For many rural homes telecommunications is a privilege, not a right. We'd been lucky to secure a landline but decided against a dedicated modem. Guests would have to make do with a dial-up connection. Not ideal but beggars can't be choosers.

'We'll have to ring Telefónica and get someone to take a look at it,' I said.

As usual I was referring to the "royal we".

'When?'

'There's no time like the present. Would you mind?'

Melanie rifled through her handbag and pulled out her phone.

'There's no signal,' she said, wandering around the house.

'Try leaning out of the window, but do be careful.'

'I've got one bar.'

'You'll have to go into the garden.'

Melanie marched off outside and a thumbs-up confirmed a signal.

'Best they can do is Monday,' she shouted.

Forty-eight hours without the internet. Could I survive?

That evening I lit the open fire and we snuggled up in front of the telly.

Even with the curtains closed the bedroom seemed light and airy. Melanie made a cuppa and we sat up in bed sipping coffee and staring out of the French windows. Tiny finches were chattering in the garden and bright sunlight illuminated the chestnut trees at the end of the driveway.

'Let's go into Escairón this morning and find out what's open,' I suggested.

'When?'

'After breakfast.'

We were here to enjoy ourselves but mindful of our responsibilities. Sunday shopping in Galicia is unheard of. Discovering what guests could expect to find on their first day in a foreign land was important; how else could we advise them?

The side terrace was the perfect place to enjoy breakfast in the sun. By the time we were ready for off, the clock had ticked around to noon. With the exception of the Repsol filling station and a few bars and cafés, everywhere was closed.

'This is no good,' I said, as we drove slowly through the quiet streets.

'Let's try Chantada,' suggested Melanie.

The town of Chantada is bigger than Escairón and only sixteen kilometres from Vilatán. Once again, our search proved fruitless. Fortunately, we had a backup plan. The village of Ferreira de Pantón is home to two small supermarkets on opposite sides of the main street. In a rare display of commercial rivalry, both are open on Sunday mornings. The drive across country isn't the best, but at least guests could get what they needed to tide them over.

That evening we'd asked friends to join us for dinner. We were confident they'd like what we'd done to the place, but were a little apprehensive.

'Is there anything you want me to do?' I asked.

'I don't think so. Chuffing hell!'

'What's the matter?'

'This oven is useless.'

She pulled a smouldering meringue from the oven and placed it on the kitchen worktop. Her remarks had a certain familiarity. It wasn't that long ago she'd said exactly the same about the oven at *Casa de Elo* and again when we moved into *El Sueño*.

'Bang goes the strawberry pavlova,' she added, tossing the charred remains into the kitchen bin.

'Never mind. No one will know.'

'I'll know,' she snapped.

That told me.

In situations like this I've learnt to make a discreet exit. The sound of the electric whisk signalled her intention to try again. Thirty minutes later, an outburst of expletives announced the result. This called for a cautious approach. Slowly, I crept into the kitchen.

'It's done it again,' she said.

The difference between fan-assisted and convection ovens had caught her out for a second time.

'And that ring is not working properly either,' she added, making a vague gesture towards the hob.

'What's wrong with it?' I asked quietly.

'It doesn't get hot enough.'

The hob and oven were separate appliances, but this wasn't the time to split hairs. I made a mental note and added the hob to our list of things to sort out.

Our dinner guests were full of praise for the work we'd done on the house and a dessert of strawberries and cream went down a treat. As for the meringues, can you keep a secret?

'What have we got planned for today?' asked Melanie as she pulled up a garden chair.

The side terrace had become our favourite outside space.

'We need to sort out the hob,' I said.

'I think it's still under guarantee.'

'If it is, I know exactly where it'll be.'

A trip home was called for.

'What if Telefónica turn up?'

'They've got your mobile number. They'll have to ring.'

'OK.'

The narrow lanes of Vilatán require caution and compromise. It's rare to meet another vehicle but when we do, someone has to give way. Today it was my turn; a white van had precedence. I checked the rear-view mirror and reversed into a driveway. When it reached us the driver stopped.

'What's he playing at?' I moaned.

'It's Ramón,' said Melanie.

I looked again as the driver lowered his window.

'*Hola, buenos días,*' called Ramón, in a deep husky voice.

'*Hola. ¿Qué tal?*'

'Working,' he replied, shrugging his shoulders. 'I hear you have a problem.'

'Yes, the phone's not working. You carry on to the house and I'll turn around.'

We first met Ramón six years ago when he installed the phone line at *El Sueño*. He's something of a local celebrity. His light-hearted manner and predilection for practical jokes belies his technical ability and relentless hard work.

Back at the house he wasted no time and climbed into the loft to test the incoming line.

'No problem there, I'll check the village exchange. Wait here until I get back,' he said.

Ten minutes later he returned.

'All done. *Firma aquí* (Sign here),' he said, handing me a work docket.

I signed it and off he went.

'Right then, let's see if we can find that guarantee,' I said.

We hopped back into the car and headed home. The warranty was exactly where I thought it would be.

'There's no purchase date on it,' I said.

Melanie remembered that José Kitchen had told us not to register the guarantee until he gave the go-ahead. That was over a year ago and we hadn't heard from him since.

'What do you think we should do?' asked Melanie.

'I'm not sure. Give him a call and see what he suggests.'

'Register the guarantee today. Wait a few days and then call out an engineer,' he said.

I had my suspicions, but who were we to argue?

Road testing the house continued apace. Peter and Veronica were our next dinner guests followed by Penelope the day after for a lunchtime barbecue. Both events went off without a hitch and everybody loved what we'd done to the place. On Thursday we turned our attention to the penultimate self-drive tour.

'Let's go to Samos today,' I suggested.

'OK.'

For some people, walking the Camino de Santiago is a checkbox exercise rather than a spiritual pilgrimage, but even that comes at a price. To qualify for a certificate of completion or Compostela, pilgrims have to walk a minimum of one hundred kilometres. At a distance of 122 kilometres from Santiago de Compostela, the village of Samos has become one of the most popular starting places. However, there's more to Samos than a convenient jump-off point.

Records show there's been a monastery in Samos since the 6th century. The original structure has long since disappeared but the current building boasts the largest cloister in Spain and is a must-see excursion for anyone visiting the area.

It took us a little over half an hour to drive the fifty-four kilometres from Vilatán to Samos. We parked the car close to the monastery and strolled along the riverbank to the visitors' centre where a small group of tourists were waiting to enter the monastery.

'The tour starts at 11:30,' said Melanie, pointing at a notice pinned on the door.

I looked at my watch: 11:10.

'It's a bit expensive,' I quipped.

'Tsk!'

Three euros wouldn't break the bank. I purchased two tickets and we waited with the others. A steady stream of tourists swelled the numbers to twenty or so. The expectant murmur fell silent as a key turned in the lock and the ring gate latch clanked upwards. The door opened slowly and a strange figure appeared in the doorway wearing a black ankle-length robe. My first thought was Yoda but his ears weren't big enough. He was in fact a resident Benedictine monk.

The monk led us through into the grounds and on into the impressive two-storey cloister. Architectural treasures lay around every corner. The ground floor was impressive but there was more to come. We climbed a wide stone staircase to a covered walkway on the first floor. Adorning the walls on three sides of this upper level are colourful murals depicting biblical scenes and charting the history of the Benedictine order. The paintings were exquisite. From there we moved through into the church. It's neoclassical in design and features a lofty domed ceiling. Through accident or design the dome's windows flooded the chapel with daylight, illuminating its golden artefacts. The tour finished with a stroll around the gardens and out through the visitors' centre.

'What did you think?' I asked.

'It was amazing. Those murals are unbelievable and the church is really different.'

'I know what you mean. Whoever designed that dome knew what they were doing.'

As a rule, I'm not a fan of ambling around religious temples but the monastery at Samos left a lasting impression.

That evening Melanie set out on foot to discover exactly how long it would take to walk from *Campo Verde* to the nearest restaurant, Casa Pepe. I gave her a twenty-minute head start and followed in the car; someone had to drive home. Our timing couldn't have been better. Melanie was less than a hundred metres away when I pulled into a parking space.

'Perfect timing,' she said.

She slipped out of her trainers and changed into more appropriate footwear. Casa Pepe specialises in cooking *churrasco* which means barbecue in galego. According to the locals it's the best in the area. We'd been meaning to give it a go for years but never got around to it.

'I've chosen the wrong shoes,' said Melanie, as we stepped inside.

I smiled.

What Casa Pepe lacked in elegance it made up for in popularity.

'Have you booked?' asked a smiling waitress.

'No,' I replied.

'Is there just the two of you?'

'Yes.'

'OK, follow me.'

She led us to a table close to the window. A stiff vinyl tablecloth rubbed my legs as I nudged the seat forwards. My eyes were drawn to an enormous indoor barbecue clad in stainless steel. Logs hissed and crackled as flames lapped around them. To the right of the fire was a long grill, laden with meat sizzling above the glowing embers. The chef, who was none other than Pepe, used a long rake to drag lumps of smouldering wood from the fire to the grill.

The waitress returned with two bundles of cutlery wrapped in white paper serviettes and a paper tablecloth. We lifted our arms and helped her straighten the ruffled sheet.

'What would you like?' she asked.

The lack of a written menu is not uncommon, but no menu at all was a new one on us. Our surprise prompted a response.

'Beef, pork or mixed?' she asked.

The choice was *churrasco* and the options were threefold. What could be simpler?

'Shall we try the mixed?' asked Melanie.

'Why not?'

'Would you like salad with it?' asked the waitress.

'Yes please.'

'And what would you like to drink?'

'Red wine.'

Moments later she returned with two tumblers and a stoppered bottle of unlabelled wine. I pulled the cork and poured.

'Cheers,' I said.

'Cheers.'

We chinked glasses and sipped. At its best, local table wine is as good as any; at its worst I wouldn't use it for salad dressing.

'We've had worse,' remarked Melanie.

The waitress returned with a mixed salad swimming in red wine vinegar and olive oil, and a basket of freshly cut, crusty bread. Melanie couldn't resist. Crusty splinters scattered across the tablecloth as she tore into a piece and dipped it in the dressing.

I was mesmerised by Pepe's energy and enthusiasm. The two-metre-wide grill was loaded with steaks, chops, and sausages. Oozing droplets of fat burst into flames as they dribbled onto the flaming embers, sending clouds of smoke filtering through the meat. Working in such conditions would be difficult at any age, but Pepe was old enough to be collecting his pension.

'Here you go,' said the waitress, placing two stainless steel platters on the table.

The portions were enormous. On the first platter were four pork chops, four beef steaks, strips of crispy belly pork, and two pork sausages. On the second were enough chips to feed an army. Melanie and I stared at each other, speechless.

'Where's mine?' I joked.

The food was delicious and everything was cooked to perfection. The pork chops were moist and salty, the beef steak tender, and the spicy pork sausages were to die for.

'These *criollos* (pork sausages) are gorgeous,' said Melanie.

'Is everything OK?' asked the waitress.

'*Muy rico* (Delicious),' we replied.

'Would you like some more?'

'No thank you.'

'Are you sure you won't try another sausage?'

Our host was nothing if not persistent.

'Go on then,' said Melanie.

I couldn't believe it.

'Are you sure you don't want one?' she repeated to me.

'No thanks, I couldn't eat another thing,' I replied.

The waitress returned with Melanie's sausage and presented it to her as if she'd won a prize.

Throughout the evening customers had been stopping at the bar to settle their bill. When we were ready to leave, we did the same.

'Will you take a *chupito* (shot of liqueur) on the house?' asked Pepe, as I handed over the cash.

'Certainly.'

Locals would have you believe that *licor con hierbas* aids digestion. For the life of me I can't imagine why. Its colour is more reminiscent of liquids leaving the body than something you might want to drink. As for the taste, I'd rather swallow diesel, but to refuse would have been impolite. Down in one seemed like the best option.

'Another?' he asked.

'No thanks, I have to drive,' I chimed.

Melanie was struggling to drink the first one.

The restaurant Casa Pepe is one of those must-try dining experiences. I had no doubt that some guests would love it and others not so much. As for me, I couldn't wait to return.

Our stay at Campo Verde was drawing to a close. One more excursion would complete our compendium of self-drive tours.

'What's on the agenda for today?' asked Melanie, as we nibbled toast and jam in the morning sunshine.

'Today, me hearties, we go in search of gold.'

My impersonation of Hector Barbossa fell well short of a starring role in *Pirates of the Caribbean*.

'Really?'

'I thought we could visit Las Medulas and then drive on to Ponferrada.'

In the 1st century, Las Medulas was the most important gold mine in the Roman Empire and the castle at Ponferrada was once a stronghold of the Knights Templar. Both destinations are across the border in Castile and León.

We began our trip by heading towards Monforte de Lemos and joining the N-120 in the direction of Ponferrada. Outside the town of Quiroga we made our first stop of the day at the Castillo de Torrenovaes. This 10th century castle and adjacent palace occupy a prominent position overlooking the river Sil. The garrison was home to knights of the Order of the Hospital of Saint John of Jerusalem, and provided a refuge for pilgrims walking the Camino de Santiago.

'Wow, look at that,' I said, peering through the ramparts at the river below.

Melanie was catching her breath after the steep ascent.

'Lovely. Where next?'

She'd seen enough. Ruined castles aren't really her thing.

'Montefurado.'

We returned to the car and continued east, following the course of the river. Two thousand years ago the area surrounding the village of Montefurado was rich in gold deposits, many of which lay hidden on the riverbed. This presented a conundrum for any would-be prospector: how to collect the gold from a fast-flowing river. When it came to problem solving the Romans were nothing if not ingenious. Their solution was to divert the course of the river by excavating a four-hundred-metre-long tunnel through solid rock. The result was a dry riverbed and easy pickings.

I parked on rough ground close to the river and we made our way along a forest footpath towards the tunnel.

'Do be careful,' said Melanie, as I edged closer to the water.

The riverbank was littered with boulders, most of which were covered in a luminous green slime. Gingerly, I slipped from one rock to the next until I could see straight through the tunnel. I took out the camera and snapped a few frames.

'That'll do,' I said.

One wrong move and I'd end up covered in green slime or worse still with a broken leg. I put the camera into my pocket and used both arms to steady myself. Thankfully, I made it back to terra firma with only my hands to clean. Leafy foliage rustled in the breeze and bright sunlight dappled the pathway as we made our way back to the car.

'Shall we stop for a cuppa at Pazo do Castro?' I asked.

'Why not?'

Pazo do Castro is a restored 17th century manor house reincarnated as a luxury hotel. We often stop for afternoon tea when we're out that way. The façade of the property features grand stone arches which support the upper floor.

This design has created a covered terrace where hotel guests can take refreshments and enjoy outstanding views over the valley. This is the Valdeorras wine region but our favourite tipple is a pot of Earl Grey served with a plate of biscuits. Having finished our morning tea break, I settled the bill and we headed off to our next destination, Las Medulas.

From Pazo do Castro we drove through the town of O Barco and joined the N-536 before crossing the river Sil into slate country. Who would have thought that 90% of all roof slates produced in the EU are mined in Galicia? Fifteen kilometres further east we crossed the border into Castile and León. As you'd expect, the UNESCO World Heritage Site of Las Medulas is well signposted. In the village of Carucedo we turned right and headed into the wilderness.

'Next left,' said Melanie, pointing at a sign for the Orellán Mirador.

The road climbed steadily, narrowing as it went.

'Are you sure this is the way?' I asked.

The road had become so narrow it seemed inconceivable that tourists would be directed that way.

'That's what the sign said.'

Four and a half kilometres after making the turn we arrived at our destination.

'It's busy,' quipped Melanie.

One other vehicle had made the trek.

The walk from the carpark to the viewing point is a near vertical, six-hundred-metre hike.

'I hope it's worth it,' said Melanie, gasping for air.

So did I.

When we reached the top, we could hardly believe our eyes. We'd never seen anything like it. The Romans used a method called *ruina montium* or hydraulic mining to unearth the gold. It relied on high-pressure water jets to literally dissolve the mountain. What remains is a unique landscape of exposed red hillocks and steep-sided pillars, knitted together with a sea of green foliage.

'At least the walk back should be a little easier,' said Melanie.

I wasn't too sure. By the time we got back to the car my knees and calves were screaming for mercy.

'I think I saw a restaurant in that village we passed through. Shall we give it a go?' I asked.

'What time is it?'

'Half past one.'

'Why not?'

The Mesón El Lagar, in the village of Orellán, proved worthy of inclusion in our book of restaurant reviews. The homemade puddings were particularly noteworthy. We started with a platter of locally produced *entremeses*. For our main courses Melanie chose pork and I opted for a beef steak, but the star of the show was dessert: a delicious homemade *tarta de castañas*.

Fed and watered, we drove back to the main road and headed into Ponferrada to visit El Castillo de los Templarios (The Castle of the Templars). In the 12th century King Fernando II struck a deal with the knights. In exchange for being granted permission to build the castle the Templars agreed to protect pilgrims travelling the Camino de Santiago. The castle's recent facelift has given this magnificent medieval structure a new lease of life.

We clambered over the ramparts for an hour or so before heading home. By the time we got back to Vilatán we'd covered over 280 kilometres.

Spending time at *Campo Verde* had been a real privilege. We'd completed the self-drive tour guide, fixed a few teething problems, written reviews of local restaurants, and enjoyed the company of friends. The website was up and running and the advertising sites were generating a steady flow of enquiries. *Campo Verde* was ready to welcome paying guests. Our time as property developers was at an end and our career in property management was about to begin. Only time would tell if we'd made a wise investment. Wish us luck.

HASTA LA PROXIMA

Continue the Journey

**The following is an excerpt
from book seven in
The Journey series**

A Season
To
Remember

Finding the right balance
without tipping the scales

1

What a Charmer

When Benjamin Disraeli coined the phrase, "Hope for the best but prepare for the worst", I doubt he had a Spanish holiday rental in mind. We'd worked tirelessly to ready the house for the start of the letting season, but doubts remained. Had we done enough? It's not the problems you envisage that catch you out, it's the ones you don't. Years of hard work and planning would soon be put to the test. Our financial future was hanging in the balance. Thumbs up, and we'd live to fight another day; thumbs down, and the consequences could be catastrophic.

We'd spent the last three years managing a rental property for our friends Bob and Janet. During that time, we'd perfected our Meet and Greet (the slogan we'd adopted for our official welcome). Now we were owners, and I for one was feeling a little nervous. We'd left home and driven the twenty-four kilometres to the sleepy village of Vilatán, location of *Campo Verde*, our holiday rental property. I'd pulled up outside and Melanie was about to jump out and open the gate.

'Are you ready?' I asked.

'As ready as I'll ever be.'

'Just remember, happy smiling faces and nothing is too much trouble.'

Melanie grinned at me like a Cheshire cat.

The guests presiding over our fate were Dr Gerald Cann and his wife Elizabeth, from Strathclyde. They'd arrived yesterday. We'd left a key in a secret location and a contact phone number just in case. The fact that they hadn't rung was a positive sign.

Melanie hopped out, pressed the doorbell mounted on the gatepost and opened the gate. I drove through and she closed it behind me. By the time I'd crept slowly to the end of the driveway, a woman, who I presumed was Mrs Cann, had opened the front door and stepped outside. The palms of my hands felt sweaty as I fumbled for the door handle. I glanced in the mirror; Melanie was almost alongside. I stepped out, beaming like the proverbial village idiot.

'Good morning, I'm Craig, and this is my wife Melanie,' I said, offering my hand.

Melanie stepped forwards, smiling in such a way it looked like she was trying to hold in a fart. I couldn't believe how nervous we were.

'I'm Elizabeth, please come in to your lovely home.'

A sweeping arm gestured us inside.

'It's your home for the next two weeks,' said Melanie.

Elizabeth smiled.

Without further ado we climbed the staircase to the first floor where Dr Gerald Cann was awaiting our arrival.

'I'm Gerald,' he said.

Their friendly nature melted our anxiety. They loved the house and thought we'd done a great job. Compliments rained down and their interest in us and our endeavours seemed genuine and comprehensive. Time flew by and before we knew it, an hour had passed.

'Anyway, we must let you good people get on with your holiday. If there's anything at all, don't hesitate to give us a call,' said Melanie.

'We'll be back at the same time on Saturday to change the linen and mow the lawns. Don't worry if you're going out, we can let ourselves in,' I added.

We shook hands one final time and left.

'That seemed to go well,' I said, as we drove through the village.

'They were a lovely couple.'

'Definitely not a Gerry though.'

My remark brought a smile to Melanie's face. When Gerald had made the reservation, we had wondered if he'd be a Gerald Cann or a jerrycan.

If their reaction was anything to go by, our decision to pitch the house at the upper end of the market had been justified. We drove home with a renewed sense of confidence. Today we could relax in the knowledge that our best efforts had been good enough.

Swapping the six-and-a-half-tog duvet for the four-tog confirmed the arrival of summer. Even the weather gods were playing their part in the success of our new venture.

'We've got another,' I announced, as I stepped outside.

Melanie was pegging out the washing and I'd been checking the inbox.

'Another what, darling?'

'Another booking.'

'That's good.'

We'd set ourselves a target of ten weeks and had passed that by mid-April. Since then, enquiries had dried up which led me to believe the booking season was over. This reservation threw cold water on that theory, much to my surprise and delight.

'How long is it for?' she asked.

'One week, from the 11th until the 18th of July.'

'It's your birthday that week.'

'It doesn't matter.'

'How many people is it for?'

'Just two.'

'Good.'

We preferred small parties; it meant less work for the same money.

We spent the rest of the day lounging in the sunshine and dipping in and out of the pool to keep cool. In the evening I fired up the barbecue and we dined alfresco.

'What's that?' said Melanie.

Something had startled her. She jumped to her feet and dashed towards the pool. I wasn't hanging about to find out and scampered after her.

'What's what?' I asked.

'Over there, something is moving,' said Melanie, pointing in the general direction of the kitchen door.

The dog couldn't wait to see what all the fuss was about and wandered over for a closer look. That's when I saw it.

'Jazz, come here,' I called.

The urgency in my voice did the trick and she retreated immediately. Hiding in the shadows was a small grass snake. It had slithered unnoticed into the garden and seemed intent on finding out what lay beyond the flyscreen guarding the kitchen doorway.

'What is it?' stammered Melanie.

'It's only a grass snake.'

'It's going in the house. Get rid of it.'

From holiday rep to snake charmer in less than twenty-four hours. Are there no limits to this boy's talents?

'Wait here,' I said.

'Where are you going? Don't leave me on my own.'

'I'm going to get the net.'

'What net?'

'The net for the swimming pool.'

'It's a snake, not a dead fly.'

'Do you have a better idea?'

That silenced her.

The pool net is attached to a three-metre-long pole. A reassuring length when faced with a slippery serpent. My plan was simple: scoop the snake into the net and throw it over the garden wall.

'Do be careful,' cautioned Melanie.

I knew from experience how fast these little critters can move. Any sign of resistance and I was out of there. Cautiously I approached my quarry.

'Come on then, fella.'

Speaking nicely to it was unlikely to assist its capture, but it helped relieve my tension. The creature hadn't moved a muscle since I'd first clapped eyes on it. I had the distinct impression it was weighing up its options: fight or flight? I was hoping for neither. Slowly, I edged the net towards it.

'Here we go.'

My heart was racing as I eased the net under its stomach.

In the blink of an eye, it flicked its body and made a beeline for the kitchen.

'Stop it!' screamed Melanie.

What did she think I was trying to do?

'Oh no you don't.'

My reactions were equal to the task. I darted forwards and crashed the net down between it, and the open doorway. It didn't stand a chance. With that route blocked, it had no other option but to bypass the door and head towards the corner of the house.

'Now I've got you.'

It was out in the open. I had to move quickly. I slid the net across the tiled terrace and was just about to catch our uninvited guest when it darted between the wall and the drainpipe and disappeared.

'Where's it gone?' asked Melanie, fear reverberating in her voice.

I couldn't believe it. Like a magician's illusion, Hissing Sid had transformed into Harry Houdini and done a vanishing act.

'It must be hiding behind the drainpipe,' I replied.

'Well, take a look.'

That was easy for her to say; she was standing on the other side of the terrace.

Nervously I edged forwards, straining my eyes in the darkness to see where it'd gone.

'I can't see a thing.'

'Get closer.'

I had visions of it coiled up behind the drainpipe waiting to launch itself at the first idiot stupid enough to get within range, and sink its fangs into their eyeballs.

AVAILABLE NOW FROM AMAZON

About the Author

Craig began writing a weekly column for an online magazine in 2004. Over the last few years he has written a number of articles for the Trinity Mirror Group and online publications such as CNN, My Destination, and Insiders Abroad.

In 2013 he published his bestselling travel memoir, *Journey To A Dream*. It told the story of a turbulent first twelve months in Galicia. Since then he has added *Beyond Imagination*, *Endless Possibilities*, *Opportunities Ahead*, *Driving Ambition*, *The Discerning Traveller*, and *A Season To Remember* to The Journey series.

As well as writing, Craig is an enthusiastic winemaker and owns a small vineyard.

Printed in Great Britain
by Amazon

67431411R00194